The Birth of the Grand Old Party

The Birth of the Grand Old Party

The Republicans' First Generation

Edited by ROBERT F. ENGS
and RANDALL M. MILLER

Afterword by James M. McPherson

Published in Cooperation with The Library Company of Philadelphia

PENN

UNIVERSITY OF PENNSYLVANIA PRESS

Philadelphia

Copyright © 2002 University of Pennsylvania Press
All rights reserved
Printed in the United States of America on acid-free paper

10 9 8 7 6 5 4 3 2 1

Published by
University of Pennsylvania Press
Philadelphia, Pennsylvania 19104-4011

Library of Congress Cataloging-in-Publication Data

The birth of the Grand Old Party : the Republicans' first generation / edited by Robert F. Engs
and Randall M. Miller ; afterword by James M. McPherson.
  p. cm.
  ISBN 0-8122-3674-2 (cloth : alk. paper).—ISBN 0-8122-1820-5 (pbk. : alk. paper)
  "Published in cooperation with the Library Company of Philadelphia."
  Includes bibliographical references (p.) and index.
  1. Republican Party (U.S. : 1854–)—History—19th century. I. Engs, Robert Francis. II.
Miller, Randall M. III. Library Company of Philadelphia.
JK2356 .B52 2002
324.2734—dc21   2002020335

Contents

Preface

This collection of original essays examines the origins and evolution of the Republican party over the course of its first generation. The essays consider the party in terms of its identity, interests, ideology, images, and individuals, always with an eye to the ways the Republican party reflected and affected mid-nineteenth-century American concerns over national character, political power, race, and civil rights. Collectively, the authors extend their inquiries roughly from the 1850s through the 1870s to understand the processes whereby the "second American party system" broke down, a new party emerged, the Civil War came, and a new political order developed. They especially consider the ways the belief in "free soil, free labor, free speech, and free men"—the glue holding together the nascent Republican party's disparate supporters in the 1850s—congealed during war and Reconstruction to produce both a call for expanded political and civil rights for the freedmen, and sometimes others, and a concern over expanded federal involvement in the protection of those rights, while at the same time leading the Republican party to push legislation that opened the West to further settlement and development, advanced commerce, and protected manufacturing. In so doing, the party of many parts—"anti-Nebraska" Democrats, former Whigs, Free Soilers, temperance advocates, nativists and anti-nativists, and others who came together to oppose the extension of slavery in the 1850s and to save the Union in the 1860s—increasingly bore the likeness of a new Whig party. The essays also point to the importance of "decisive moments" and significant individuals that shaped the party's identity during its formative period.

By observing the transmutation of a sectional party born in the 1850s into the "Grand Old Party" of the 1870s, the authors show, in the end, how the war and its aftermath recast political categories and shifted national power to northern interests, where it largely stayed well into the twentieth century. Although Republican Reconstruction failed in the 1860s and 1870s, and although the party began to divide over issues of continued support for Republican governments in the South, corruption in the Grant regime, patronage, foreign policy, and economic issues, the party still triumphed in other ways in the new national political order of the postwar era. By the 1870s, however, much of the first generation of Republicans had passed from the scene, having retired from office, been defeated for reelection, or died. New men and new interests came to rule the "Grand Old Party."

The essays in this book try to seize the historiographical moment of renewed interest in political history and new thinking on the place and meaning of the Civil War in American life by getting hold of a subject more often implied than explained. For all the historical attention devoted to the Republican party and the Civil War, the birth and growth of the party have received surprisingly little sustained inquiry. Previous works on the early Republican party have focused on particular events and individuals and rarely have tracked the history of the "charter" generation of Republicans and the formative ideas of Republicanism over their political life span. General treatments of the party too often cast its history in terms of the political identities and fortunes of a few figures and slight the interplay of principle, partisanship, and politics that defined the party and the age. This collection offers various perspectives on party formation and growth and modern syntheses and assessments of the best, recent scholarship on the party and the period. In it, the authors not only see the party in terms of its architecture of belief and interests, but also observe its organic qualities of men, and women, struggling to translate belief and interest into policy. And they recognize, too, that such struggles sometimes pushed the party in directions its original structure and composition did not intend. By bringing together leading historians on the genesis of Republicanism, this book, we hope, opens up the conversation on the meaning of party and politics and of the Republican party experiment and experience.

*   *   *

This book, like the early Republican party, is a product of many hands. While historians dispute the site of the "first Republican party" meeting, there is no doubt about the origins of this book. It rests squarely and comfortably at 1314 Locust Street, Philadelphia, at the Library Company with Librarian John C. Van Horne, Phillip Lapsansky, Chief of Reference and Curator of its Afro-American Collection, and the rest of the staff of the Library Company. They first recognized the need to raise the issue of the genesis of Republicanism, and then mounted an exhibition and symposium to draw scholarly attention to the subject. The result was "The Genesis of Republicanism: The Birth and Growth of the Grand Old Party, 1854–1872," held in October 2000, which provided the inspiration for this book. The efficiency and good humor of the staff in preparing the exhibition and assembling materials for the book kept the project on pace and in order. This is their book as much as anyone's.

All the illustrations in this book come from the Library Company of Philadelphia collections, and virtually all were represented in the exhibition, which included hundreds more documents and materials, from broadsides, campaign literature and paraphernalia, playing cards, songsters, and voters' tickets, to book-length biographies, published speeches, and pamphlets and booklets from hosts of organizations and individuals arguing about people, politics, and principles. The book also includes an illustrated overview of the "Genesis of Republicanism" drawn directly from the exhibition. The illustrations, though, only hint at the rich collection of print and illustrative resources the Library Company has acquired on mid-nineteenth-century politics and public life. In that regard, this book comes not only as an invitation to explore further the issues of party politics and process during the Civil War era, but also to use the Library Company collections in doing so.

Generous support for the exhibition and symposium came from the Louise Lux-Sions Exhibition Endowment Fund, the Pennsylvania Humanities Council, the Pennsylvania Historical & Museum Commission, The Pew Charitable Trusts, the Philadelphia Cultural Fund, and the Quaker Chemical Foundation.

Moving this book from conception to realization was Robert Lockhart, our editor at the University of Pennsylvania Press. He immediately understood the foundation and framework of the project and supported it with encouragement and wisdom, while steadily nudging it along as it matured from idea to book. All historians should have an editor as sensible and sensitive as Bob Lockhart and a press so willing to support its editor and authors.

Librarians and staff at several institutions helped us in gathering information, checking references, and more. The Library Company of Philadelphia led the way, with its vast and deep collections providing not only the texts for the exhibition but also context in presenting the exhibition and organizing the book. The librarians at the Historical Society of Pennsylvania helped in research queries relating to the exhibit and the book. The editors also profited from materials at or received through the good offices of the libraries at the Civil War Library and Museum in Philadelphia, the Free Library of Philadelphia, Haverford College, Saint Joseph's University, and the University of Pennsylvania. At Saint Joseph's University, Maureen Carothers did bibliographical searches and other tasks with intelligence and energy. Michael Birkner, Paul A. Cimbala, Daniel Crofts, and John David Smith provided useful suggestions to improve the content and character of the book.

To all who provided support, assistance, and guidance, we give our thanks. We hope that this book will repay their encouragement in the free exchange of ideas.

Introduction

The historical period discussed in these essays is the most transformative era of American history. There was one nation, called the "United States of America," in 1850 and another very different nation, using the same name and occupying the same space, in 1876. The primary instrument and chief beneficiary of this transformation was the Republican party. All the major issues that had divided the early Republic and led to civil war were settled for at least the next century by 1876. And all of them had been decided in ways that empowered the region and classes represented by the Republican party.

By the end of this era, the issue of state versus central government power had been settled; the federal government was indisputably superior, however much states' rights resurfaced periodically thereafter as a shibboleth of the white South. The question of the regional locus of power also had been resolved in favor of the Northeast over the South and West. The right of the Northeast to settle the West and to spread its institutions westward was now uncontested. And the distribution of national wealth had been realigned. Henceforth, the great agricultural bounty of the South would profit New York financiers more than it would southern farmers.

During these same years an agricultural nation became an industrial one. The triumph of "free" over "slave" labor was assured, as was the supremacy of capital over labor. The dominance of white upper-class males over other Americans who were women, poor, or nonwhite was established for at least the rest of the century, though this dominance remained contested, sometimes violently so.

Most dramatically, the great shame of the nation—slavery—had been exorcized. But emancipation was at best a limited success. The Constitution had been rewritten to abolish slavery, provide national citizenship, and guarantee equal protection under the law, but African

Americans remained repressed and despised in all regions of the nation, brutalized and exploited most harshly in their own southern homelands. For these triumphs and this enduring tragedy, the Republican party also bore a primary responsibility. The dilemma of racial slavery created the climate of crisis in which the Republican party was born. More than fifty years ago the great scholar of the sectional crisis, Allan Nevins, completed his multivolume study of Civil War causation. After nearly 2,000 pages of intricate argument, and in tortuously opaque language designed to give least offense to either side, Nevins offered his conclusion about the coming of the Civil War:

> The main root of the conflict (and there were minor roots) was the problem of slavery *with its complementary problem of race-adjustment*; the main source of the tragedy was the refusal of either section to face these cojoined problems squarely and pay the heavy costs of a peaceful settlement. Had it not been for the difference in race, the slavery issue would have presented no great difficulties. But as the racial gulf existed, the South inarticulately but clearly perceived that the elimination of this issue would still leave it the terrible problem of the Negro.[1]

In the years before the war, northern politicians had to tread delicately among their constituents' intertwined and often contradictory passions: hatred of slavery, hostility toward the white South, and antipathy toward black people—wherever they might reside in the nation. Most northerners, in their Negrophobia, were prepared to let blacks continue to suffer in southern bondage, but also were determined that the new territories of the West would be reserved for free white men and their families. As our essayists note, it was the threat of expansion of slavery, specifically, the Kansas-Nebraska Act of 1854, that brought the Republican party into being. The new party was an amalgam of many northern elements: Free Soilers, who were antislavery but also frequently antiblack; supporters of the "American" or Know-Nothing party, which was anti-immigrant and anti-Catholic; some remnants of the old Whigs; along with abolitionists, women's rights advocates, and friends of temperance and other reform groups. They all agreed only that the South and slavery "must be contained."

The Republican party capitalized especially on northern resentments of southern bullyrag and abuses of power, whether by southerners in Congress blocking legislation to promote internal improvements, raise tariffs, or open western lands that would benefit northern interests, or by southerners demanding that northerners do their bidding in chasing fugitive slaves under the Fugitive Slave Act of 1850 and silencing antislavery voices in the North. The image of "the Slave Power" looming over the map, threatening to force slavery everywhere in the "free territories" and secure slaveholders' interests everywhere in the nation, increasingly defined "the South" in the northern mind. Republicans understood this because their existence and reason-for-being derived from it. And Republicans used every means of politicking to awaken voters to the dangers of an expanding "Slave Power" and to the virtues of the new party's positions on "free soil, free labor, free speech, and free men." Through torchlight parades and other public processions, speeches, newspapers, and all manner of publications, the new party brought its case to the people. In an age when politics was a form of outdoor entertainment, and when politicking went on almost all the time, Republicans traded on popular imagery to mobilize many new voters and to galvanize supporters to support a cause. In doing so, the party staked out its claim to legitimacy. It also masked policy differences in a party of many parts.

But there was no assurance Republicans would survive as a party. Republicans were not the only new party or the only voice for "freedom." And by defining itself principally in terms of protecting a northern sectional interest, the Republican party had few prospects anywhere in the South or among Unionists worried that the constant drumbeat of sectionalism in politics would cause disunion. As Michael Holt argues, the Republicans' overtly anti-South, regional stance left in doubt whether they could become the chief alternative to the divided and vulnerable Democratic party. At a time when old party structures were realigning or coming apart and new parties were emerging, no one was sure where or to what extent to invest political loyalties. The sectional crises of the 1850s revealed the fragility and impermanence of parties that made party organizers overly conscious of the need to court voters vigorously and build party infrastructure rapidly. Achieving party unity became as important as espousing party principles. To achieve its all-important national victory in 1860, the new Republican party had to modulate its anti-South, antislavery stance. It would not be the last compromise of principle in exchange for power committed by the Republican party as it consolidated its position during war and Reconstruction.

Control of the national government ensured the survival of the young Republican party. While conducting a war and presiding over an enormously expanded central government, the party also saw to many of the agenda items desired by its variegated constituency. It responded to its white, middle-class, free soiler base with the Homestead Act, which parceled out millions of acres to native and immigrant white families during and after the war. Congress also passed the Morrill Land Grant Act, creating the system of agricultural and mechanical colleges that became a mainstay of American higher education in the postbellum years.

At the same time, the party was able to satisfy its "Whiggish" element even more generously. The higher protective tariff, the Pacific Railroad Act, and currency and banking reforms passed by Republican majorities in Congress were all longstanding planks in the Whig platform. More important, as Phillip Shaw Paludan demonstrates, party officials created partnerships with business and industry that would survive and expand long after the war. The needs of capital overwhelmed the needs of labor, and the mantra of wartime patriotism was often used to enforce labor's submission.

And in the course of the war the party helped institutionalize a form of civic religion that celebrated the national state in terms that were assertively northern and Protestant. Thus the regional and sectarian biases of Republicanism were well established by war's end and lasted well into the following century. The three major American Protestant denominations (Baptists, Methodists, and Presbyterians), which had divided over slavery and theological issues, retained separate northern and southern branches throughout a similar period.

One element crucial to the prewar formation of the Republicanism and its well-being during the conflict was largely ignored by the party leaders. As Jean Baker explains, women and advocates for the expansion of their rights were relegated to the fringes of the party as soon as victory was won. Even Frederick Douglass, longtime supporter of women's rights, believed—inaccurately as would soon be apparent—that the postbellum era was, in abolitionist Wendell Phillips's words, "the Negro's hour."

On all these issues save the last, the leaders of the Republican party managed to situate themselves on the side of both virtue *and* power. But on the two elements of Nevins's conundrum—slavery and race—the new party was forced into near schizophrenia. To placate its more conservative elements, the Republicans adopted a platform in 1860 that was notably less strident on slavery than that of 1856. Indeed, in pursuit of a Lincoln victory, Republicans promised in their 1860 platform that they would respect the Constitution and protect slavery where it existed. In an attempt to reassure the South of that position, Lincoln even signed and conveyed to the states a version of the Thirteenth Amendment passed by Congress during the secession crisis and earlier endorsed by outgoing President James Buchanan that would have forbidden congressional interference with slavery in the states forever. But Republicans in 1860 and early 1861 walked a tightrope, not wanting to alienate conservative "Union" supporters by threatening slavery directly but needing also to satisfy their primary constituency, which expected them not to capitulate to southern threats or relax efforts to check slavery's advance into the territories.

Secession and war changed the politics of slavery. Saving the Union soon demanded attacking slavery. Republicans in Congress and the president both took steps that would undermine slavery in the first two years of the war. The Confiscation Acts and Lincoln's preliminary emancipation proclamation in 1862 provoked a northern backlash that cost the party several congressional seats in the 1862 elections and hurt Republicans in several state contests in 1863. Chastened by the backlash and criticism of Lincoln's conduct of the war, the party emphasized Union, not emancipation, in the 1864 elections, even while the North grew increasingly dependent on black soldiers to win the war.

Union victory presented the Republican party with a number of dilemmas as well as opportunities. Not least among these was the status of the former slaves. The freedpeople immediately and fully embraced the antebellum Republican equation of land ownership and freedom. Unhappily for them, as well as for poor farmers and industrial workers nationally, the reconfigured Republican party of the Reconstruction era had little interest in remaking the South into a yeoman society by distributing land to former slaves or anyone else. The governing assumption about what freedom meant, for Republicans, was that people should be free to do for themselves, to make their own way without government assistance. The postwar party *did* reshape the Constitution and, for a brief period and for a variety of motives, sought to incorporate ex-slaves and white southerners into a new constitutional understanding of citizenship and the equal protection of the laws. The effort was a failure for that generation of Republicans and newly free blacks. By the 1870s,

African Americans were increasingly disempowered and disenfranchised, along with many of their poor white neighbors.

Race, of course, proved to be the central element of the debate and of Reconstruction's failure. The freedpeople had hoped, at a minimum, for land and suffrage in recognition of previous years of servitude and their vital part in saving the Union. They would be disappointed in both, though the chimera of voting lasted late into the nineteenth century. Still, there was a moment during early Reconstruction, at the height of Congress's battle with Andrew Johnson, when the Republican party treated African Americans as no other group of white Americans would do for another century. Republicans approached newly enfranchised African Americans neither as dangerous proto-barbarians, as did their ex-masters, nor as benighted innocents in need of guidance and charity, as did some northern philanthropists. Rather, the party leadership saw them as much desired potential *voters*. The hotly contested 1868 presidential contest and the crucial role of the black vote in Grant's victory proved the sagacity of the Republican approach.

*   *   *

Unhappily, another indispensable element of the party—northern working-class and middle-class whites—retained their preexisting prejudices. Once it became apparent that the freedpeople would not inundate the North, northern white concern about security of blacks in the South diminished despite escalating violence against them. The white South mounted a campaign of terror against its black citizens and was permitted to seize control of Republican governments illicitly, an outcome that would never have been tolerated had the victims been white. As in the antebellum sectional crisis, race trumped reason—and the newly strengthened Constitution as well. The Republican party, in desperate trouble after 1872, and losing control of the House in the 1874 elections for the first time since 1861, chose survival over affirmation of principle. A few diehards from the first generation of Republicans struggled to realize the promise of freedom and equality before the law with a Civil Rights Act of 1875 prohibiting segregation, but most Republicans now catered to northern voters and interests and followed the chant of disengaging from "the Negro problem."

Bereft of its radical wing, the no-longer-young Republican party of

1876 embraced an arrangement, the so-called Compromise of 1877, accepting the defeat of its Reconstruction policy while permitting it to retain the presidency. The agreement by white North and white South allowing the racism of both regions to continue with little change cemented the "reconciliation" between the two. The post-Civil War Republican party seemingly had abandoned its antebellum heritage; in truth, it was in a continued process of evolution and redefinition, now as a major party with a history of electoral success and government policies and legions of supporters demanding attention to their interests. The party's elasticity and adaptability to new circumstances gave it strength to prosper at the polls, in a new day with new men. From its formation the party had been a composite of many elements. During the early years of the war, the reformers had been able to institute much of their agenda, including land for white homesteaders, educational reform, and, most important of all, emancipation. But the measures necessary to save the Union and protect those reforms left the new party beholden to the forces of commerce and industry that had also always been a part of it. By Reconstruction's end, this conservative element had full control of the national party structure. It would dominate both the party and the presidency, even through the Progressive era interlude, at least until the New Deal.

Just as it learned to do in its formative years during the sectional crisis, war, and Reconstruction, the Republican party in the twenty-first century continues to transform itself, its constituency, and its proclaimed values as necessary to maintain a predominant role in national politics. And still the threads of race and irresolution are intertwined in the party's evolution.

Despite the failure of emancipation in terms of equality and incorporation into the larger society, it was on the issues of race and the expansion of the promise of liberty that the early Republican party actually transcended its original vision and the prejudices of its constituency. As these essays remind us, these are accomplishments that no modern party, even the one that claims descent from Lincoln, has surpassed.

CHAPTER ONE

The Ideology of the Republican Party

Eric Foner

In August 2000, the Republican party gathered in Philadelphia for its national convention, and nominated George W. Bush for president. Few delegates realized that the party's first national nominating convention, in 1856, also took place in the City of Brotherly Love. But that party was a far different institution from its counterpart today. The sight of a Republican presidential candidate from Texas and a Republican leader of the Senate from Mississippi would certainly have surprised the party's founders. So too would the sight of the party that saved the Union and emancipated the slaves embracing the Old South's doctrine of state sovereignty and expressing deep hostility to civil rights enforcement, to affirmative action—indeed, to any measures that seek to redress the enduring consequences of slavery and segregation. Nonetheless, in some ways we still live in a world shaped by the achievements of the early Republican party—the destruction of slavery, preservation of the Union, and establishment of a national principle of equal rights for all Americans.

In my first book, I argued that the key unifying principle of the Republican party before the Civil War was opposition to the expansion of slavery.[1] Few Republicans, to be sure, should be classified as abolitionists—critics of slavery who called for immediate emancipation and equal rights for black Americans. The abolitionists never commanded more than a small fraction of the northern public. But they helped create a public opinion hostile to slavery and especially to its further expansion.

When Congress in 1854 approved the Kansas-Nebraska Act, repealing the Missouri Compromise and opening a vast new area in the nation's heartland to slavery, party lines shattered and a new organization, the

Republican party, rose to prominence on a platform of stopping slavery's expansion once and for all. In the new party, belief in the superiority of the "free labor" system of the North and the incompatibility of "free society" and "slave society" coalesced into a comprehensive world view or ideology. The distinctive quality of northern society, Republicans insisted, was the opportunity it offered wage earners to rise to property-owning independence. Slavery, by contrast, was an obstacle to progress, opportunity, and democracy. No one expressed this vision more eloquently than Abraham Lincoln. Having served a number of terms in the Illinois legislature and two years in Congress in the 1840s, Lincoln had retired from active political involvement in 1849. He was swept back into politics by the Kansas-Nebraska Act.

Lincoln once remarked that he "hated slavery, I think as much as any abolitionist." Yet he was not an advocate of immediate emancipation. He revered the Union and the Constitution and was willing to compromise with the South, including the much-despised Fugitive Slave Act of 1850, to preserve them. Moreover, he shared many of the era's racial prejudices, affirming in 1858 that he did not favor blacks' voting or holding office in Illinois, and frequently speaking of colonizing African Americans outside the country. In this he represented the mainstream of white northern opinion, by now convinced that slavery posed a threat to "free society," but still convinced of the inherent inferiority of African Americans. But Lincoln also believed that the nation could not survive forever "half slave and half free," and he insisted that the founders had intended to place the peculiar institution on the road to "ultimate extinction." Like the abolitionists, Lincoln maintained that slavery violated the essential premises of American life—personal liberty, political democracy, and the opportunity to rise in the social scale. "I want every man to have the chance," he proclaimed, "and I believe a black man is entitled to it, in which he *can* better his condition." And, like the abolitionists, Lincoln insisted that America's professed creed was broad enough to encompass all mankind. When his opponent in the celebrated 1858 Illinois Senate race, Stephen A. Douglas, proclaimed that the United States government was created "by white men for the benefit of white men and their posterity for ever," Lincoln responded that the rights enumerated in the Declaration of Independence applied to "all men, in all lands, everywhere," not merely Europeans and their descendants. Blacks, he added, might not be equal to whites in all respects, but in their "natural right" to the fruits of their labor, they were "my equal and the equal of all others."[2] It ought not to be surprising that when Lincoln won election as president in 1860, seven southern states concluded that slavery would not be safe under his administration.

The Civil War reinforced many elements of the Republicans' prewar ideology, while subtly transforming others. Despite his antislavery convictions, Lincoln's aim in the first year of the war was to retain the loyalty of the border slave states, secure the largest base of support in the North, and attract wavering white southerners to the Union cause. All these goals would, he felt, be compromised by making the destruction of slavery a war aim. But many factors, beginning with the actions of the slaves themselves in abandoning plantations as soon as the Union army made its appearance, converged to make the initial policy untenable. From the outset of the war, many northerners, especially abolitionists and Radical Republicans in Congress, insisted that, as the "cornerstone" of the Confederacy (the oft-cited phrase employed by the South's vice president, Alexander H. Stephens), slavery must become a military target. In 1862, as the disintegration of slavery continued, the danger of losing the border states receded, the manpower needs of the Union military continued to grow, and success on the battlefield continued to elude Lincoln's armies, pressure for emancipation mounted. In March 1862, Congress prohibited the army from returning fugitive slaves. Then came abolition in the District of Columbia and the territories, followed by the Second Confiscation Act, which liberated slaves of disloyal owners in Union-occupied territory. On January 1, 1863, Lincoln issued the Emancipation Proclamation. It did not liberate all the slaves. With the exception of the South Carolina Sea Islands, occupied by the Union navy in November 1861, it applied only to areas under Confederate control. Excluded from its purview were nearly half a million slaves in the border states, and more than 300,000 in Tennessee and parts of Virginia and Louisiana. But the vast majority of the nation's slave population, more than three million men, women, and children, declared the Proclamation, "are and henceforth shall be free."[3]

The old image of Lincoln singlehandedly abolishing slavery with the stroke of his pen has long been abandoned, for too many other Americans—politicians, reformers, soldiers, and slaves—contributed to the coming of emancipation. Yet the Emancipation Proclamation profoundly altered the nature of the war, the future course of American history, and the Republican party's ideology. The Proclamation transformed a war of armies into a conflict of societies, and ensured that Union victory would produce a social revolution within the South and a redefinition of the place of blacks in American life. There could now be no going back to the prewar Union. A new system of labor, politics, and race relations would have to replace the shattered institution of slavery, and a new status for the former slaves would have to be worked out. Emancipation, in other words, made a revolution in southern life and an era of Reconstruction inevitable.

The Emancipation Proclamation represented a turning point in Lincoln's own thinking. It contained no reference to compensation to slaveholders or colonization of the freedpeople—issues he had promoted before 1863. And for the first time it announced that black men would be enrolled into military service. In the end, black soldiers played a crucial role not only in winning the Civil War but also in defining the war's consequences. More than any other single development, military service, as Frederick Douglass had anticipated, placed the question of black citizenship on the national agenda. The inevitable consequence of enrolling black men in the army, one U.S. senator observed in 1864, was that "the black man is henceforth to assume a new status among us." The service of black soldiers affected the outlook of Lincoln himself. He insisted that they must be treated the same as whites when captured by the Confederacy (the southern government had declared that black soldiers would be deemed rebellious slaves, not prisoners of war, and sold into bondage). When the Confederacy refused to include captured blacks in prisoner-of-war exchanges, Lincoln suspended the entire program rather than admit a racial distinction among the men who fought and died for the Union. In 1864 Lincoln, who before the war had never supported suffrage for African Americans, urged the governor of Unionist Louisiana to work for the partial enfranchisement of blacks, singling out former soldiers as especially deserving. At some future time, he observed, they might again be called on to "keep the *jewel of Liberty* in the family of freedom."[4]

Racism was hardly eradicated from national life. During the New York City draft riots in 1863, black men, women, and children were hunted by mobs and lynched on the streets of the nation's commercial metropolis. Yet by the war's end many Republicans had come to embrace the old abolitionist view that the abolition of slavery must bring not only an end to bondage but a national citizenship whose members enjoyed

Figure 1.1. *Freedom to the Slave*, colored lithograph (n.p., 1863?). The reverse of this depiction of black soldiers fighting for freedom is a recruiting poster for black troops: "All Slaves were made Freemen. By Abraham Lincoln, President of the United States, January 1st, 1863. Come, then, able-bodied Colored Men, to the nearest United States Camp, and fight for the Stars and Stripes."

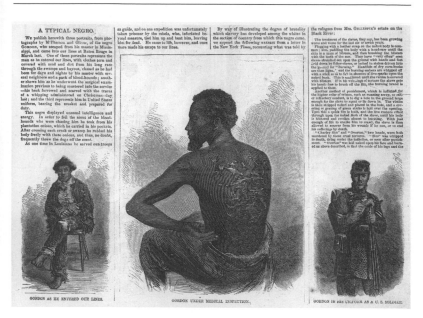

Figure 1.2. "Typical Negro," *Harper's Weekly*, July 4, 1863. Much of the northern press was transfixed by a new American drama wherein the southern slave was transformed into a freedman, soldier, and citizen, as in the case of the Mississippi slave Gordon, shown here in his ragged clothes, displaying his whip-scarred back, and finally dressed in the Union uniform.

the equal protection of the laws regardless of race. Indeed, one of the first acts of the federal government to recognize the principle of equality before the law was the decision, as the war drew to a close, to grant black soldiers retroactive equal pay with their white counterparts.

Ironically, both sides fought the Civil War in the name of freedom. "We all declare for liberty," Lincoln observed in 1864, "but in using the same *word* we do not all mean the same *thing*." To the North, freedom meant for "each man" to enjoy "the product of his labor"; to southern whites, it conveyed mastership—the power to do "as they please with other men, and the product of other men's labor."[5] The Union's triumph consolidated the northern understanding of freedom, with free labor at its center, as the national norm. In the process, the meaning of freedom and the identity of those entitled to enjoy its blessings were themselves transformed.

But more than redrawing the boundaries of citizenship, the Civil War linked the progress of freedom directly to the power of the national state. "It is war," declared the nineteenth-century German historian Heinrich von Treitschke, "which turns a people into a nation." Begun to preserve the old Union, the Civil War brought into being a new American nation-state. The mobilization of the Union's resources for modern war created what one Republican leader called "a new government," with greatly expanded powers and responsibilities. Equally important, the war forged a new national self-consciousness. "Liberty, . . . true liberty," Francis Lieber proclaimed, "requires a country." This was the moral of one of the era's most popular works of fiction, Edward Everett Hale's short story "The Man Without a Country," published in 1863. Hale's protagonist, Philip Nolan, in a fit of anger curses the land of his birth. As punishment, he is condemned to live on a ship, never to set foot on American soil or hear the name "the United States" spoken. He learns that to be deprived of national identity is to lose one's sense of self.[6]

The attack on Fort Sumter crystalized in northern minds the direct conflict between freedom and slavery that abolitionists had insisted on for decades. Before the war, many Americans, North and South, could speak with no sense of irony of their slaveholding republic as an empire of liberty. But the war, as Frederick Douglass recognized as early as 1862, merged "the cause of the slaves and the cause of the country." To be sure, a generation of northern schoolchildren had learned to recite Daniel Webster's impassioned words spoken on the Senate floor in 1830: "Liberty *and* Union, now and forever, one and inseparable." But Webster was condemning the doctrine of states' rights, not the South's "peculiar institution." When Douglass proclaimed that "Liberty and Union have become identical," his target was chattel slavery—not simply a moral abomination, but an affront to national power. The master's undiluted sovereignty over his slaves, insisted Charles Sumner, the antislavery senator from Massachusetts, was incompatible with the "paramount rights of the national Government."[7] And the destruction of slavery—by presidential proclamation, legislation, and constitutional amendment—was a key act in the nation-building process. It announced the appearance of a new kind of national state, one powerful enough to eradicate the central institution of southern society and the country's largest concentration of wealth.

The scale of the Union's triumph and the sheer drama of emancipation fused nationalism, morality, and the language of freedom in an entirely new combination. Proponents of America's millennial mission interpreted the Civil War as a divine chastisement for this paramount national sin (a vocabulary the nonchurchgoing Lincoln himself adopted in his Second Inaugural Address). But with emancipation the war also offered an opportunity for national regeneration, as well as providing incontrovertible proof of the progressive nature and global significance of the country's historical development. A "new nation" emerged from the war, declared Illinois representative Isaac N. Arnold, new because it was "wholly free." Central to this vision was the antebellum principle of free labor, now further strengthened as a definition of the good society by the North's triumph. In the free-labor vision of a reconstructed South, emancipated blacks, enjoying the same opportunities for advancement as northern workers and motivated by the same quest for self-improvement, would labor more productively than slaves. Meanwhile, northern capital and migrants would energize the economy. Eventually the South would come to resemble the "free society" of the North, with public schools, small towns, and independent producers. Unified on the basis of free labor, proclaimed Carl Schurz, a refugee from the failed German revolution of 1848 who rose to become a leader of the Republican party, America would become "a republic, greater, more populous, freer, more prosperous, and more powerful, than any state" in history.[8]

The concrete reality of emancipation raised in the most direct possible form the question of the relationship between property rights and personal rights, between personal, political, and economic liberty. "What is freedom?" asked Representative James A. Garfield in 1865. "Is it the bare privilege of not being chained? If this is all, then freedom is a bitter mockery, a cruel delusion."[9] Did freedom mean simply the absence of slavery, or did it imply other rights for the emancipated slaves, and if so, which ones: civil equality, the suffrage, ownership of property? Here were the issues on which the turbulent politics of Reconstruction turned. And the political crisis that followed the Civil War compelled Republicans to define and extend the ideology they had brought out of the Civil War.

Most white southerners insisted that blacks must remain a dependent plantation work force in a laboring situation not very different from slavery. During Presidential Reconstruction—the period from 1865 to 1867 when Lincoln's successor, Andrew Johnson, gave the white South a free hand in determining the contours of Reconstruction—southern state

Figure 1.3. *Emancipation*, lithograph (Philadelphia: John L. Magee, 1865). Both the black slave and the southern poor white are elevated by emancipation in this Republican vision of a free labor America.

governments enforced this view of black freedom by enacting the noto-
rious Black Codes, which denied blacks equality before the law and political rights and imposed on them mandatory year-long labor contracts,
coercive apprenticeship regulations, and criminal penalties for breach
of contract. Through these laws the South's white leadership sought to
ensure that plantation agriculture and black subordination survived
emancipation.[10]

Thus the death of slavery did not automatically mean the birth of
freedom. But the Black Codes so flagrantly violated free-labor principles
that they invoked the wrath of the Republican North. Southern reluctance to accept the reality of emancipation resulted in a monumental
struggle between President Andrew Johnson and the Republican Congress over the legacy of the Civil War. The result was the enactment of
laws and constitutional amendments that redrew the boundaries of citizenship and expanded the definition of freedom for all Americans.

Johnson, a Unionist Democrat from Tennessee who had been added
to the Republican ticket in 1864 to symbolize the party's desire to extend
its reach into the South, was not only an accidental president but in many
ways wholly unfit for that exalted office. An inveterate racist and believer
in states' rights, he could not envision any federal action to protect the
rights of the former slaves. At the other end of the political spectrum
from Johnson stood the Radical Republicans, representatives within politics of the antislavery impulse that had grown so markedly in the wartime North. Although they differed on many issues, such as tariff and
fiscal policy, Radicals shared the conviction that slavery and the rights
of black Americans were the preeminent questions facing nineteenth-
century America. The Civil War, they believed, was caused by the aggressions of the "Slave Power," and its outcome offered the nation a golden
opportunity to recast itself in accordance with the principle of equal rights
for all regardless of race. For decades, Radical leaders like Thaddeus
Stevens, representative from Pennsylvania, and Charles Sumner, senator
from Massachusetts, had defended the unpopular cause of black suffrage
and equality before the law for black Americans. Now they insisted
that the enfranchisement of blacks was the sine qua non of a successful Reconstruction. More than other Republicans, as well, the Radicals
embraced the expanded powers of the federal government born of the
Civil War. Traditions of federalism and states' rights, they insisted, must
not obstruct a sweeping national effort to protect the equal rights of all

citizens. "The same national authority," declared Sumner, "that destroyed slavery must see that this other pretension [racial inequality] is not permitted to survive."[11]

Occupying the political terrain between the Radicals and Johnson were the moderate majority of the Republican party, led in Congress by senators like Lyman Trumbull of Illinois and John Sherman of Ohio. Unenthusiastic about black suffrage—which they viewed as a political liability in the North and an experiment whose outcome could not be predicted in the South—moderates were nonetheless fully committed to ensuring "loyal" governments in the former Confederate states and protecting the basic rights of the former slaves in a free-labor economy. They tended to view Reconstruction as a set of practical problems, not, as many Radicals believed, an invitation to a social revolution. In the moderates' view, the states of the old Confederacy were neither conquered territory, as Stevens insisted, nor states retaining all their rights, as Johnson held. In 1865 the moderates sincerely hoped to work with Johnson to devise a just and lasting plan of Reconstruction. But Johnson's policies and the actions of the state governments created under his supervision eventually drove them into the Radicals' arms, uniting the Republican party against the president.

By 1866 a consensus had emerged within the Republican party that civil equality was an essential attribute of freedom. The Civil War had elevated "equality" to a status in the vocabulary of freedom it had not enjoyed since the Revolution. At Gettysburg, Lincoln spoke of a nation "conceived in Liberty, and dedicated to the proposition that all men are created equal"—an invocation of the Declaration of Independence and a recognition of the inner logic of emancipation. Now the Republican Congress sought to identify and protect the equal rights of all Americans. The first statutory definition of American citizenship, the Civil Rights Act of 1866, declared all persons born in the United States (except Indians) national citizens and spelled out rights they were to enjoy equally without regard to race. Equality before the law was central to the measure, as were free-labor values: no state could deprive any citizen of the right to make contracts, bring lawsuits, or enjoy equal protection of the security of person and property.

But it was the Fourteenth Amendment, approved by Congress in 1866 and ratified two years later, that for the first time enshrined in the Constitution the ideas of birthright citizenship and equal rights for all

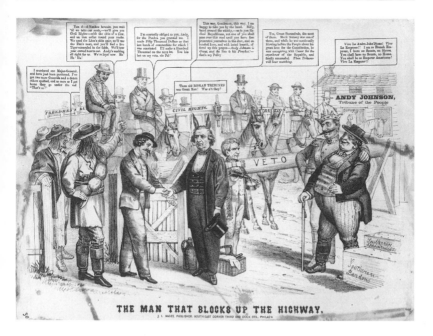

Figure 1.4. *The Man That Blocks Up the Highway*, lithograph (Philadelphia: John L. Magee, 1866). "Andy Johnson is Great, and the Veto is his Prophet" describes Johnson as he welcomes southern rebels back into the Union while vetoing such Republican measures as the Civil Rights Bill and the Freedmen's Bureau Bill.

Americans. The Amendment prohibited states from abridging the "privileges and immunities of citizens" or denying them the "equal protection of the laws." This broad language opened the door for future Congresses and federal courts to breathe meaning into the guarantee of legal equality, a process that occupied the courts for much of the twentieth century. Although most immediately intended to raise the former slaves to the status of equal citizens, the Amendment's language did not apply only to blacks. The principle of equality before the law affected all Americans, including, as one representative noted, "the millions of people of foreign birth who will flock to our shores . . . to find here a land of liberty." The Amendment was a moderate measure, not a creation of the Radicals. It did not grant black men the right to vote. Rather than forging a "perfect republic" by purging American institutions of "inequality of rights,"

Stevens told the House on the eve of the Amendment's passage, "I find we shall be obliged to be content with patching up the worst portions of the ancient edifice, and leaving it, in many of its parts, to be swept through by the storms of despotism." Nonetheless, Stevens voted for passage. Why? "Because I live among men and not among angels." Soon afterward, however, the Fifteenth Amendment, ratified in 1870, barred the states from making race a qualification for voting. Strictly speaking, suffrage remained a privilege rather than a right, subject to numerous regulations by the states. But by the time Reconstruction legislation had run its course, the federal government had redefined American citizenship to embody civil and political equality regardless of race.[12]

Stevens realized that, whatever their limitations, the Civil Rights Act of 1866 and Fourteenth Amendment embodied a profound change in the federal system and the nature of American citizenship. Less than a decade earlier the Supreme Court had decreed that no black person could be a citizen of the United States. Now the abolitionist dogma of equal citizenship as a birthright was written into the Constitution. The laws and amendments of Reconstruction reflected the intersection of two products of the Civil War era—a newly empowered national state and the idea of a national citizenry enjoying equality before the law. Rather than a threat to liberty, Charles Sumner declared, the federal government had become "the custodian of freedom." What Republican leader Carl Schurz called "the great Constitutional revolution" of Reconstruction transformed the federal system and with it the language of rights so central to American political culture.[13] Before the Civil War, disenfranchised groups were far more likely to draw inspiration from the Declaration of Independence than from the Constitution. (The only mention of equality in the original Constitution, after all, had occurred in the clause granting each state an equal number of senators.) But the rewriting of the Constitution during Reconstruction promoted a sense of the document's malleability and suggested that the rights of individual citizens were intimately connected to federal power.

The Bill of Rights had linked civil liberties and the autonomy of the states. Its language—"Congress shall pass no law"—reflected the belief that concentrated power was a threat to freedom. The Reconstruction amendments assumed that rights required political power to enforce them. They not only authorized the federal government to override state actions that deprived citizens of equality, but each ended with a clause empowering Congress to "enforce" the Amendment with "appropriate legislation." The Reconstruction amendments transformed the Constitution from a document primarily concerned with federal-state relations and the rights of property into a vehicle through which members of vulnerable minorities could stake a claim to substantive freedom and seek protection against misconduct by all levels of government.

That the United States was a "white man's government" had been a widely held article of political faith before the Civil War. Reconstruction Republicans rejected this premise, but their universalism, too, had its limits. In his remarkable "Composite Nation" speech of 1869, Frederick Douglass condemned prejudice against immigrants from China, insisting that America's destiny was to transcend race by serving as an asylum for people "gathered here from all corners of the globe by a common aspiration for national liberty." Any form of exclusion, he insisted, contradicted the essence of democracy. A year later Charles Sumner moved to strike the word "white" from naturalization requirements. Senators from the western states objected vociferously. They were willing to admit blacks to citizenship but not persons of Asian origin. At their insistence, the naturalization law was amended to add Africans to the "whites" already eligible to obtain citizenship when migrating from abroad. The ban on Asians remained intact; the racial boundaries of nationality had been redrawn, but not eliminated. The juxtaposition of the Fourteenth Amendment and 1870 naturalization law created a strange anomaly. Asian immigrants remained ineligible for citizenship, but their native-born children automatically became Americans.[14]

Advocates of women's rights likewise encountered the limits of Reconstruction egalitarianism. Given the era's intense focus on equality, the movement for women's suffrage, which had more or less suspended operations during the war to join in the fight for Union and abolition, saw Reconstruction as a golden opportunity to claim for women their own emancipation. The rewriting of the Constitution, declared suffrage leader Olympia Brown, offered the prospect of severing the blessings of freedom from race and sex—two "accidents of the body" that did not deserve legal recognition—and to "bury the black man and the woman in the citizen." Women should now enjoy not only the right to vote but the economic opportunities of free labor. The Civil War had propelled many women into the wage labor force and left many others without a male provider, adding increased urgency to the argument that the right to work outside the home was essential to women's freedom. Women, wrote Susan B. Anthony, desired an "honorable independence" no less fully than men, and working for wages was no more "degrading" to one sex than the other. Few in Congress, however, even among Radical Republicans, responded sympathetically to feminists' demands. Reconstruction, they insisted, was the "Negro's hour" (the hour, that is, of the black male). Even Charles Sumner, the Senate's most uncompromising egalitarian, feminist Frances Gage lamented, fell "far short of the great idea of liberty," so far as the rights of women were concerned.[15]

Despite its palpable limitations, Reconstruction wrote a remarkable chapter in American history. Most remarkable of all was the brief moment of Radical Reconstruction in the South (1867–77) during which black men, for the first time in American history, enjoyed the right to vote in significant numbers and held a genuine share of political power. The southern experiment in interracial democracy proved short-lived, succumbing during the 1870s to violent opposition by the Ku Klux Klan and the North's retreat from the ideal of equality. Even while it lasted, moreover, Radical Reconstruction revealed many of the tensions inherent in the free-labor ideology. Efforts to give the former slaves land failed to receive congressional approval. If emancipation, as Douglass had remarked, represented a convergence of the slaves' interests and those of the nation, eventually those interests, and their respective definitions of freedom, were destined to diverge. Only a minority of Republican policymakers, most notably Radical Representative Thaddeus Stevens, sought to resurrect the older view—the view put forward by the ex-slaves—that without ownership of productive property, genuine freedom was impossible. In this respect, the high hopes inspired by emancipation remained unfulfilled.

In retrospect, Reconstruction emerges as a decisive moment in the transformation of the free-labor ideology, fixing the dominant understanding of economic freedom as self-ownership and the right to compete in the labor market, rather than propertied independence. The policy of according black men a place in the political nation while denying them the benefits of land reform fortified the idea that the free citizen could be a dependent laborer. Thus Reconstruction helped solidify the separation of political and economic spheres, the juxtaposition of political equality and economic inequality, as the American way. Henceforth it would be left to dissenters—labor radicals, populists, socialists, and the like—to resurrect the older idea of economic autonomy as the essence of freedom.

Figure 1.5. *The Reconstruction Policy of Congress, As Illustrated in California*, lithograph (n.p., 1867). Unsuccessful gubernatorial candidate John Gorham advocated universal manhood suffrage for all races of Americans. In this cartoon, Brother Jonathan, an Uncle Sam type national figure, admonishes him that "this ballot box was dedicated to the white race alone—The load you are carrying will sink you to perdition, where you belong." Calls for universal manhood suffrage, regardless of race, met strong opposition throughout the North. Whites balked at enfranchising blacks or Chinese, and women reformers disliked any proposal to expand voting that did not include women.

Figure 1.6. Edward H. Dixon, *The Terrible Mysteries of the Ku-Klux-Klan, A Full Expose of the Forms, Objects, and "Dens" of the Secret Order; With a Complete Description of their Initiation, From the Confession of a Member* (New York, 1868). Violence was the South's most effective strategy for suppressing the black vote and unseating Republican governments, and the "Klan" was its most infamous and widespread terrorist organization. Republicans tried to discover the inner workings of the Klan through official investigations, while the popular press offered its own lurid details, as in this pamphlet, which purports to be the confessions of a "reformed" Klansman.

The end of Reconstruction is usually dated as 1877. But the Republican retreat from the broad definition of equality and national power of the immediate postwar years had begun well before then. The campaign of 1872 suggested that the Republican party was no longer united in support of Reconstruction. An influential group of party leaders—among them founders like Carl Schurz of Missouri and Lyman Trumbull of Illinois and prominent editors and journalists such as E. L. Godkin of *The Nation* and Samuel Bowles of the *Springfield Republican*—held their own convention and nominated Horace Greeley for president. The dissidents called themselves Liberal Republicans. Initially, their alienation from the Grant administration had little to do with Reconstruction. The liberals, or self-styled "best men," were alienated by the corruption that seemed pervasive in the Grant administration and by what they considered the degradation of a party increasingly under the control of local political machines and bosses. They were also alarmed by a rising tide of labor and farmer unrest in the North. These economically aggrieved groups called on the activist state spawned by the Civil War and Reconstruction to redress their own grievances. They sought to extend the Reconstruction principle of equality into economic relations within the North.

Although hardly as sweeping as the destruction of slavery, the North experienced an economic revolution of its own in the Civil War era, as manufacturing output expanded rapidly and the railroad knitted the country into a single giant market. The rapid expansion of agriculture, mining, and railroad construction exemplified the shift from Lincoln's America—the world of the small farm and artisan workshop—into a mature industrial society. Increasingly, the Republican party was taking on a new identity, developing close relations with business corporations and, through railroad land grants and other largesse, seeking to promote economic development. It was this combination of machine politics, political corruption, and new demands on government that spurred Liberal Republicans to action. Many were former Radical Republicans, committed to the Reconstruction agenda of equal rights for all. But now that the legal framework of equality had been achieved, they insisted, the government should step back and let the economy develop according to its own internal laws.[16]

Increasingly, the language in which the Liberals condemned northern politics echoed white complaints against the new governments in the South. The alleged corruption of carpetbaggers seemed to parallel the depredations of political bosses in the North. Black demands for land seemed analogous to northern labor's pressure for special favors. Complaints by the South's planters, merchants, and prewar politicians that the region's "natural leaders" had been excluded from power paralleled the reformers' sense that less than able men had pushed them to the side in the North. Violence and corruption in the South, reformers became convinced, arose from the fact that Reconstruction had not won the allegiance of "the part of the community that embodies the intelligence and the capital."[17]

Realizing that the Republicans' split offered them a golden opportunity to repair their political fortunes, Democrats endorsed Greeley as their candidate (a difficult decision, since Greeley had spent much of his political career denouncing the Democratic party). Many Democratic voters could not stomach their party's candidate, and Greeley went down to a devastating defeat. But his campaign placed on the northern agenda the one issue on which he, the reformers, and the Democrats could agree— a new policy toward the South.

In the mid-1870s the northern retreat from Reconstruction pioneered in the Liberal Republican campaign became irresistible. Many factors contributed to this development. In 1873 the United States fell into the most severe economic depression in its history to that point. In the wake of factory closings, business bankruptcies, and widespread unemployment, economic recovery replaced Reconstruction as the focus of political concern among northerners. The depression revitalized the Democratic party, which in 1874 won control of the House of Representatives for the first time since before the Civil War. White southern complaints about Reconstruction were winning a more and more sympathetic hearing in the North. In the 1870s racism increasingly reasserted its hold on northern thought. Influential journals like The Nation and widely read journalists like James S. Pike of the New York Tribune placed the blame for Reconstruction's problems squarely on the alleged incapacity of the region's black voters. Racism offered a convenient explanation for the alleged "failure" of Reconstruction.[18]

By 1876 it was clear that, whoever succeeded Grant as president, Reconstruction was doomed. The Democrats nominated Samuel J. Tilden, the governor of New York; Republicans chose Rutherford B. Hayes, the governor of Ohio. As fate would have it, the result centered on the three states where Republican government still survived in the South—South

Carolina, Louisiana, and Florida. After a suspenseful election night, it became clear that the presidential election hinged on the results from these three states, which both parties claimed to have carried. In the end, Congress appointed an Electoral Commission, composed of five representatives, five senators, and five members of the Supreme Court, to adjudicate the disputed returns. By a series of 8–7 votes, strictly following party lines, the commission awarded the three states to Hayes, certifying him as victor by one electoral vote.

Even as the commission deliberated, however, behind-the-scenes negotiations were underway between leaders of the two parties. Hayes's representatives agreed that if he became president, he would recognize Democratic control of the entire South and refrain from further intervention in southern affairs. He also pledged to place a southerner in the cabinet and to work for federal aid to the Texas and Pacific Railroad, a transcontinental line projected to follow a southern route. For their part, Democrats promised not to dispute Hayes's election and to respect the civil and political rights of blacks. Thus was concluded the Bargain or Compromise of 1877. Some of its parts were fulfilled—Hayes became president, Democrats took control of Florida, Louisiana, and South Carolina, and David M. Key of Tennessee was appointed postmaster general. Some were violated—the Texas and Pacific never got its land grant. More ominously, the triumphant southern Democrats would never truly recognize blacks as equal citizens.

Within two months of taking office, Hayes ordered federal troops to stop guarding the state houses in Louisiana and South Carolina, thus allowing Democratic claimants to seize the two remaining Republican governorships. (Florida had earlier declared a Democrat the victor in the 1876 election.) "The whole South—every State in the South," commented one former slave, "had got into the hands of the very men who held us as slaves." Contrary to legend, Hayes did not "remove" troops from the South—he simply ordered them to return to their barracks. But it was clear that a major change in national policy had occurred. No longer would the federal government intervene to protect the rights of the freedpeople. "Do you mean to make good to us the promises in your Constitution?" Frederick Douglass had asked the nation in a speech to the Republican National Convention of 1876. By 1877 the answer was clear—it would not.[19]

As a distinct era of national history, when Republicans controlled much or all of the South, blacks exercised significant political power, and the federal government accepted the responsibility for protecting the fundamental rights of all American citizens, Reconstruction had come to an end. Nonetheless, it left behind the first national civil rights laws and profoundly important constitutional amendments—sleeping giants that would be awakened, almost a century later, when the nation again attempted to confront the consequences of the emancipation of the slaves and the promise of equal citizenship—the enduring legacy of the early Republican party.

CHAPTER TWO

Making and Mobilizing the Republican Party, 1854–1860

Michael F. Holt

Most Americans were taught in high school that the early Republican party was the product of an escalating sectional conflict between the North and South over slavery extension that helped disrupt an earlier system of two-party competition, propel northern voters toward the Republican column, and elect a Republican president within six years of the new party's formation. This clear and straightforward account of the party's birth and infancy continues to possess much merit. In the last thirty years, however, historians have complicated it by demonstrating that the formation and rise to power of the Republican party were considerably more difficult achievements than they appear on their face. This chapter seeks to recapitulate this reinterpretation.

The Republican party first emerged in the summer of 1854 as a small part of a broad northern protest movement against the recent passage of the Kansas-Nebraska Act. That law repealed the ban on slavery north of the 36° 30′ line in the as yet unorganized portion of the Louisiana Territory and opened it to potential settlement by slaveholders. In July 1854, the Michigan Republican state platform, the first ever issued by the embryonic Republican party, cogently justified the mission and name of the new party. After denouncing the institution of African American slavery as a "relic of barbarism" and insisting that Congress stop slavery expansion to end the "unequal representation" of the South in Washington, it declared that the purpose of the Kansas-Nebraska Act was to "give the Slave States such a decided and practical preponderance in all measures of government as shall reduce the North . . . to the mere province of a few slaveholding oligarchs of the South—to a condition too shameful to be contemplated." It then proclaimed that "in view of the necessity of battling for the first principles of republican government and against the schemes of aristocracy the most revolting and oppressive with which the earth was ever cursed, or man debased, we will cooperate and be known as Republicans until the contest be terminated."[1]

Five years later, in 1859, New York's Edwin D. Morgan, chairman of the new Republican party's national committee, broadcast hundreds of thousands of copies of an important document. "The republican party had its origins in the obvious aggressions of the slave power," this circular began. Although some of the problems necessitating the party's initial organization had been resolved by 1859, it admitted, "the attitude of the slave power is persistently insolent and aggressive." Because the South was now demanding a reopening of the international slave trade and a federal slave code for western territories, "Upon no organization except the republican party can the country rely for successful resistance to these monstrous propositions and the correction of the gross abuses which have characterized the present administration."[2]

Seventeen years later still, in 1876, when Republicans were the "ins" rather than the "outs" as they had been in 1854 and 1859, their national platform explicitly announced that "the work of the Republican party is not yet finished." It then went on to list these unfinished tasks, most of which had to do with securing the achievements of the Civil War and Reconstruction. That platform closed with a remarkable plank warning voters that, should Democrats win the impending presidential election, the champions of treason and "unrepentant rebellion" would seize control of the national government, "sending Union soldiers to the rear, and promoting Confederate soldiers to the front."[3]

Although the last of these quotations falls outside the chronological boundaries of the years on which this essay focuses, together these three quotations tell us three very important things about the early Republican party. They also hint indirectly at a fourth factor that was indispensable to its emergence and subsequent growth.

First and most important is the repeated and quite self-conscious insistence that Americans needed the Republican party, that it served a vital purpose, that it was indispensable. Although that party remains alive and kicking today, its longevity was not in fact etched in stone from its founding in 1854. Instead, the party's very existence was repeatedly challenged—by diehard Whigs and Know-Nothings in the mid-1850s, by

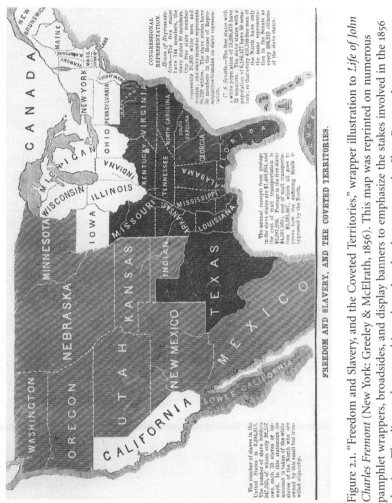

Figure 2.1. "Freedom and Slavery, and the Coveted Territories," wrapper illustration to *Life of John Charles Fremont* (New York: Greeley & McElrath, 1856). This map was reprinted on numerous pamphlet wrappers, broadsides, and display banners to emphasize the stakes involved in the 1856 election. The distorted geographic scale makes the slave states—the Slave Power—loom menacingly over the free states, threatening to consume the vast uncontested territories.

an attempt to start a new bisectional anti-Democratic party in 1858–59, by calls from the Upper South for a new, non-Republican Union party in the secession winter of 1860–61, by Andrew Johnson's attempt to displace the Republican party with a centrist Union party in 1865 and 1866, by the Liberal Republican movement in 1872, and by multifold economically oriented third parties in the off-year elections between 1872 and 1876. Hence the recurring need to rally disparate anti-Democratic voters under the Republican banner and to justify the party's existence in the three documents quoted above. Unless one recognizes the constant threat that rival anti-Democratic parties posed to the Republican party's survival, as well as the apparent plasticity of the electorate's allegiances from the mid-1850s to the mid-1870s that such attempts implied, one cannot fully understand the first twenty years of the party's history.

Second—and this is the implicit message of these quotations—the threat that other new parties posed to the Republican party helps, if only indirectly, to pinpoint a crucial factor in its own emergence as the dominant party in American politics after 1860. Like the other parties that constantly challenged it for twenty years, the Republican party began as a minor or third party.

Given the implosion of the Reform party during the 2000 presidential campaign and the fact that since the end of World War II almost all independent challenges to the major parties' domination of the electoral political system have consisted of Lone Ranger presidential candidacies, not full-fledged party challenges for offices at all levels of the federal system, one must ask how or why it was that new, third, or minor parties that *did* compete for offices at all levels of the federal system constantly gave established major parties such fits throughout the nineteenth century.

The reallocation of effective governmental power from local and state governments to the national government between the nineteenth and twentieth centuries largely accounts for the different orientation of challengers to the major parties in those two centuries.[4] But the greater frequency of significant third party challenges in the nineteenth century is primarily attributable to the different rules of the political game in that century. Simply put, those who were discontented with the existing major parties, for whatever reason, could launch new parties more easily than could dissidents in the twentieth century. Until the 1890s, when so-called reform laws gave state governments the responsibility for supplying state-printed ballots to voters and with that responsibility the power to restrict which parties or candidates appeared on those ballots, political parties themselves printed and distributed the ballots voters cast. This practice meant that dissident groups who objected to both major parties or ambitious politicos who sought to bypass them by starting a new party had a much greater access to the electorate than do their counterparts today. They did not have to jump through hoops to "get on the ballot." They could print and distribute their own ballots, which were just as legal as those distributed by the existing major parties. Without this ability, the Republican party, which sought to displace the Whigs and defeat the Democrats, might never have been launched in the mid-1850s. At the same time, however, the political system's openness to all competitors left Republicans vulnerable to yet other new party challengers for over twenty years. That vulnerability, in turn, made aggregating the various and fragmented opponents of the Democrats behind the Republican banner a central task of early Republican leaders.

Third, the quotations from 1854, 1859, and 1876 illustrate that the formation, rise to power, and retention of power by the Republican party were above all else products of specific events and of the northern public's reaction to those events. Virtually every historian who has written about the rise of the Republican party in the 1850s—Don E. Fehrenbacher, Richard H. Sewell, Eric Foner, and William E. Gienapp, to name just four—have noted the importance of events like the Kansas-Nebraska Act, the *Dred Scott* decision, or the Lecompton controversy in crystalizing support for the new party. Yet some of them have often credited those events with reinforcing northerners' commitment to basic principles such as moral antipathy toward the institution of slavery or celebration of the North's free-labor system. In my opinion, the three quotations point to a rather different conclusion. What united Republicans in the 1850s and for almost two decades after the start of the Civil War was what they were against, not what they were for. The party's adherents feared and loathed common enemies; certainly in the 1850s, when the party was still in the process of being formed, they did not share a mutual positive attachment to the Republican party as an organization. It was only in the later stages of Reconstruction that people began to think of the Republican party as the Grand Old Party.

Fourth, the common enemies that mattered most to early Republicans were the Democratic party and especially white southern slaveholders. In the prewar years, those southerners were labeled an insolent, aggressive, and tyrannical Slave Power, "the most revolting and oppressive [aristocracy] with which the earth was ever cursed." During and after the Civil War, they were denounced as Confederate traitors, rebels who sought to destroy the Union and then to win the postwar peace after their rebellion had failed. During the 1850s, in short, Republicans discovered that South-bashing was the easiest way to defeat Democrats in the North, and that knowledge shaped their electoral tactics for at least twenty years after Lincoln's election in 1860.

This assertion is controversial because it appears to minimize or marginalize the genuine commitment of some Republicans to abolition and racial justice. There can be no doubt, in fact, that some Republicans—and no historian has supplied or ever can supply a verifiable estimate of the size of that fraction—considered African American slavery as morally intolerable before the war, always insisted that abolition be a goal of the North during the war, and remained committed to equal civil and political rights for blacks after it. Nonetheless, the preponderance of evidence suggests that Republican politicians discovered very quickly in the 1850s that fanning and exploiting white northerners' fear and resentment of white southerners paid far greater political dividends in the North than professing sympathy for blacks' rights to freedom and equality. Thus the famous black abolitionist Frederick Douglass later recalled of Republicans in the 1850s that "the cry of Free Men was raised, not for the extension of liberty to the black man, but for the protection of the liberty of the white." Thus William Henry Seward, the Republicans' most prominent leader in the 1850s, declared in 1860 that "the motive of those who have protested against the extension of slavery [has] always been concern for the welfare of the white man, not an unnatural sympathy for the negro."[5]

This lowest common denominator of opposition to southern whites and their northern Democratic allies, whom Republicans always portrayed as lackeys of and surrogates for the Slave Power, best explains how Republicans built their polyglot coalition in the 1850s and rebuffed attempts during that decade to displace it with a differently organized and differently oriented anti-Democratic party. The antebellum Republicans ultimately succeeded in bringing together under a common partisan umbrella a theretofore unimaginable northern coalition of mutually suspicious Free Soilers, Whigs, Democrats, and Know-Nothings. Especially at the leadership level, all these disparate groups distrusted each other and had different programmatic priorities for the party, to say nothing of their rival ambitions for political office and political prefer-ment. For historians, therefore, the central questions about the early Republican party have been how Republicans managed to stitch this crazy-quilt coalition together, what proportion of the party each of these former enemies represented, and how, especially at the leadership level, former rivals interacted with each other.

The difficulty of combining these groups was apparent from the outset. Unsurprisingly, Free Soilers, who had abandoned the major par-ties in the 1840s and sought since then to build a broader northern anti-slavery coalition, were the first to seize on the provocation provided by the Kansas-Nebraska Act in order to do so. It was the few remaining Free Soilers in Congress whose famous "Appeal" in January 1854 defined the as-yet-unpassed Nebraska bill as proslavery aggression against freedom in the West. Then, on May 22, 1854, the very day the legislation finally passed the House of Representatives, the Free Soil newspaper in Wash-ington urged all northern representatives who had opposed it to call "upon the people to disregard obsolete issues, old prejudices, mere party names, and rally as one man for the reestablishment of liberty and the overthrow of the Slave Power."[6] This plea had been the unsuccessful mantra of Free Soilers since 1848, and in 1854 it once again failed to unite all anti-Nebraska representatives, let alone all northern voters seeking to punish the Democrats for enacting the law.

Republican parties emerged in 1854 in Wisconsin and Michigan, both still lightly populated states. Fusion anti-Nebraska "People's" coalitions also sprouted in Ohio, Indiana, and three Illinois congressional districts. Yet Ohio's coalition explicitly signaled that it was only a temporary, emer-gency popular front, not the foundation of a new party, while Indiana's was utterly dominated at the leadership level by Know-Nothings, who had a very different agenda from that of the Free Soilers, who wanted to build a new northern antislavery party.[7]

Elsewhere attempts at fusion sputtered or took place only under the aegis of the existing Whig party, not the new Republican party. In 1854, indeed, most northern Whigs, who had unanimously opposed the Nebraska Act both inside and outside Congress, were determined to retain, not jettison, the Whig party. Until the leaders and followers of that party consigned it to the scrapheap, the Republican party had no prayer of surviving its birth pangs, let alone growing to maturity. It is true that many northern Whig leaders announced that they would never again cooperate with southern Whigs, most of whom in the Senate and House had voted for the Nebraska bill. But these defiant avowals hardly meant that they were ready to abandon the Whig party in the North. Instead, northern Whigs, and many northern Democrats as well, believed that Whigs could sweep the North's 1854 state and congressional elections and then the White House in 1856 by lacerating Democratic responsibility for the Nebraska Act. Such men had no interest whatsoever in joining a new Republican party.

Abraham Lincoln exemplifies these northern Whig holdouts. In 1854 he renounced a position on a fledgling Republican state committee in Illinois that extreme antislavery men had tried to launch. He ran for the state legislature that year as a Whig and campaigned for other Whig candidates. And he passionately advocated the preservation of the Whig party. Precisely his devotion to the Whig party, in fact, explains why former Free Soilers and anti-Nebraska Democrats refused to allow his election to the United States Senate when the new legislature met in early 1855.[8]

But it was in New England and the Middle Atlantic states that Whigs' rejection of fusion behind a new Republican party proved most important. In the summer of 1854 a Whig state convention in Massachusetts emphatically spurned coalition with Free Soilers. Pennsylvania's Whigs insisted on running their own state and congressional tickets, despite efforts by Free Soilers to bring about fusion behind their party instead. By far the most significant Whig holdouts, however, were New York's Seward and his alter ego, Thurlow Weed, editor of the *Albany Evening Journal* and legendary boss of the state Whig organization. To the fury and consternation of Free Soilers, who begged Seward to lead the fusion movement, he instead insisted on preserving not just the northern wing of the Whig party but its alliance with southern Whigs as well. Weed sabotaged efforts by his erstwhile editorial ally Horace Greeley of New York City to form a New York Republican party in the summer of 1854. Simultaneously, he insisted in his editorial columns that only the Whig party had ever done anything effective to stop slavery's expansion and that therefore "it is best, now and ever, 'for the Whig party to stand by its colors.'"[9]

Far more worrisome to early Republican organizers than northern Whig holdouts during 1854 and 1855 was the astonishing spread of the rival anti-Catholic, anti-immigrant, and anti-party Know-Nothing movement. Most northern Know-Nothings undoubtedly shared other northerners' outrage at the Kansas-Nebraska Act and at the aggression against northerners' rights by an autocratic Slave Power, which that legislation seemed to prove. Nonetheless, to incipient Republicans' dismay, Know-Nothings clearly placed priority on smashing the political influence of Catholics and foreigners. In many northern communities, in fact, that influence seemed far more menacing and immediate to voters than did the threat of slavery's spread onto the distant plains of Kansas. Thus Know-Nothings gravely complicated the task of putting together an antislavery, anti-southern Republican coalition precisely because they appeared capable of defeating Democrats and capturing control of local, state, and congressional offices on a nativist, not an antislavery, platform. They scored stunning successes in New England and the Middle Atlantic states in 1854 and 1855, often stymieing attempts even to launch Republican parties in those states, and they were crucial components of the opposition parties in Ohio, Indiana, and Michigan as well.

However inevitable the rise of the Republican party and the centrality of the slavery issue may seem to the modern observer, Republican leaders in 1854 and 1855 knew all too well that many northern voters worried more about Catholics, immigrants, and booze than they did about slavery extension and that those priorities inhibited the growth of the Republican party. "This election has demonstrated that, by a majority, Roman Catholicism is feared more than American slavery," wrote a New Yorker in 1854. The following year a frustrated Republican in Massachusetts complained that "the election is most disastrous. . . . The people will not confront the issues at present. They want a Paddy hunt & on a Paddy hunt they will go."[10]

Ironically, however, the very strength of Know-Nothingism had one benefit for Republicans. Know-Nothings' victories in the North's 1854 elections destroyed most northern Whigs' hopes that their party could survive intact; those triumphs caused antislavery Whigs like Lincoln and Seward, who had shunned the Republican party in 1854, to join it during 1855 or early 1856. Nonetheless, because the mushrooming nativist party had electoral strength in the South that Republicans could not match, many people at the start of 1856 expected Know-Nothings, not Republicans, to win that year's presidential election and permanently succeed the Whigs as the Democrats' primary foe.

Instead, developments during 1856 doomed both the Know-Nothings and the Whigs to political oblivion and established the Republicans, at

Figure 2.2. *The true Holy Alliance*, lithograph (New York: G. Daelly, ca. 1855). To the nativists, Catholicism was the agent of European despotism in the struggle against democracy, as captured in this cartoon wherein the Pope and the Austrian Empire join hands over a fallen America. The Pope pledges: "I swear to employ all the arts of Catholicism in order to crush in this manner the liberties of the New World as I have done to those of the old." Such rabid anti-Catholic images were the stock in trade for nativist political imagery.

least temporarily, as the Democrats' main opponent. This achievement can be understood in part in terms of specific organizational mileposts the Republicans passed that year—the election of Nathaniel P. Banks, a recent Republican convert with Democratic and Know-Nothing lineage, as Speaker of the House of Representatives; the Republicans' first national organizing convention in Pittsburgh in February; and a successful presidential nominating convention in Philadelphia in June. But its primary causes were, first, a merger with the great majority of northern Know-Nothings; second, the development of a powerful appeal to the northern electorate; and third, a series of incidents that gave resonance to that appeal by increasing northerners' fear and resentment of the southern Slave Power.

Many northern Know-Nothings defected from the American party after it nominated Millard Fillmore for president in February on a platform that failed to call for repeal of the Kansas-Nebraska Act. Naming themselves North Americans, these bolters then vowed to nominate their own presidential candidate at a convention scheduled for New York City on June 12, five days before the Republicans were to gather in Philadelphia. Through some clever maneuvering, however, Republicans and their Know-Nothing sympathizers like Banks bamboozled the North Americans into adopting the Republican presidential candidate John C. Frémont as their standard bearer.

Historians agree that this merger with the majority of northern nativists was crucial to the ultimate success of the Republican party.[11] During the 1970s and 1980s, however, there was a lively debate among historians about whether Republicans made any concessions to Know-Nothings' anti-Catholic and anti-immigrant prejudices to forge it. This question no longer arouses much passion among erstwhile combatants, but the evidence seems clear that Republicans did consciously use anti-Catholic, and to a much lesser extent antiforeign, appeals in those states—Connecticut, Michigan, Indiana, Pennsylvania, New York, and Massachusetts—where they believed them necessary to bring Know-Nothings into the Republican camp in 1856 and thereafter.

That one-time Know-Nothings constituted a crucial part of the Republican electorate in 1856 and even in 1860, when Lincoln attracted 500,000 more votes than had Frémont, has been demonstrated beyond cavil by William E. Gienapp, who has conducted the most sophisticated statistical analyses of northern voting patterns in the 1850s. According to his estimates, former Know-Nothings constituted 67 percent of Frémont's vote in Connecticut, 54 percent in Massachusetts, 20 percent in New York, and 12 percent in Pennsylvania, where Frémont won less than a third of the popular vote primarily because most Know-Nothings instead supported Fillmore. Although it is impossible to estimate statistically the contribution of Know-Nothings to the Republican vote in Indiana because they had been part of the People's/Republican coalition since its formation in 1854, the dominance Know-Nothings exerted over the leadership of that coalition suggests it must have been substantial there as well. In the off-year state and congressional elections between 1856 and 1860, most Fillmore voters in the North joined the Republican camp, and by 1860 almost all former Know-Nothings in that section were in Lincoln's column.[12]

Yet if former Know-Nothings palpably contributed to the creation of a Republican electoral majority in the North, there is little evidence that they immediately identified themselves as Republican party loyalists. What is striking, instead, is how frequently the state and local coalitions that supported Frémont in 1856 and nominally "Republican" gubernatorial and congressional candidates in the late 1850s shunned the straight Republican label and instead ran on tickets that indicated the ad hoc alliance nature of those coalitions: Anti-Administration, Independent, Union, American-Republican, and, above all, People's tickets. As late as 1860, in fact, People's parties, not Republican parties, ran electoral slates for Lincoln in New Jersey and Pennsylvania, and after the election representatives of those state parties were quick to inform Lincoln that they would be doomed to defeat if they dared call themselves Republicans.[13] As late as 1860, in sum, the Republican party should be conceived of as a popular front, not a cohesive organization. Its members shared common enemies, not mutual attachments to each other or loyalty to the Republican party per se. Only Republicans' presidence over the North's conduct of the Civil War would create, and then only for part of the Republican constituency, that institutional allegiance.

Despite Republicans' use of anti-Catholic appeals to attract Know-Nothings in 1856 and thereafter, the common enemy that mattered most to this growing alliance was not Catholics and immigrants. Many Republican leaders and voters, in fact, had never been Know-Nothings. Instead, they had often contemptuously repudiated the nativists as intolerant bigots or lower-class thugs.

Ultimately, what was even more important in turning the tide toward the Republicans was the crafting of an appeal that engaged the interest and emotions of the northern electorate, an electorate that was often apathetic about the plight of enslaved blacks in the South and overtly hostile to free blacks in the North. In the words of an Indiana Republican in 1856, this appeal attempted to "convince the laboring class that [slavery] is at war with our republican institutions and opposed to their interests."[14]

The urgent necessity of stopping slavery expansion into the new western territories had ignited a powerful anti-Nebraska protest movement across the North and in two states—and only two states in 1854—precipitated the formation of the Republican "parties," although even designating those incipient coalitions as organized "parties" is to engage in

Figure 2.3. *The Great Republican Reform Party, Calling on their Candidates,*
lithograph (New York: Currier & Ives, 1856). The Republican party is shown
here as a group of cranks and fanatics. Welcomed by Frémont are an abolitionist
and a free black; a temperance supporter, a Socialist, and a suffragette; a Roman
Catholic priest (Frémont was charged with being a closet Catholic); and, in the
middle, a free love advocate—"We are all Fremounters." Democrats regularly
tarred Republicans as radicals and misfits, and Republicans responded in kind
with images of Democrats as besotted Irish immigrants and lords of the lash.

authorial largesse. And from the summer of that year until Lincoln's
election in 1860, Republicans insisted that free northern workers and
farmers could never coexist with the institution of African American
slavery should it gain a foothold in Kansas and Nebraska. Yet the results
of the 1854 and 1855 elections clearly demonstrated that protest against
slavery extension in the West was *not* enough to rally a majority of northerners behind the Republican banner. More was needed to persuade artisans, factory workers, farmers, and other northerners that an exclusively
northern and overtly anti-southern party was necessary to protect "their
interests."

Historians have disagreed about precisely what those "interests" were and how Republicans appealed to them in order to mobilize the northern electorate. Prior to 1960, a few historians insisted that Republicans sought outright abolition of slavery in the South or were at least direct ideological descendants of the abolitionist movement that emerged in the 1830s.[15] Since 1960, historians like Don E. Fehrenbacher, Richard H. Sewell, and David Potter have insisted that Republicans shared a deep conviction that slavery was morally intolerable and sought to restrict its spread in order to induce southerners themselves to end slavery once it was no longer economically sustainable. For them, Lincoln's famous words about stopping slavery's expansion in order to put slavery on the road to "ultimate extinction" encapsulated the core of Republicans' belief and message.

Still others, following the argument of Eric Foner's seminal book on Republican ideas in the 1850s, *Free Soil, Free Labor, and Free Men: The Ideology of the Republican Party Before the Civil War*, see northerners' "interests" essentially in economic and sociological rather than moral terms. From this perspective, Republicans cherished and celebrated the superiority of the North's free-labor-based society and economy, with its opportunities for upward social mobility, over the hierarchical, socially stagnant, and economically backward slave-based social system of the South. To protect that superior social and economic system and the opportunities it entailed for them, Republicans told northern voters, slavery extension must be stopped in order to preserve the West for the extension of the North's more vibrant and open social system. In short, it was northerners' concern about what happened to and in the West with regard to slavery that explains how Republicans appealed to northerners' "interests."

We can, of course, never completely capture the motives and intentions of people from that decade, whether in the North or the South. There can be no question that opposition to slavery expansion and an insistence that Congress prohibit it by statute was the programmatic principle on which the polyglot members of the early Republican coalition most agreed. Nonetheless, a number of historians, including this author, find the core of the Republican appeal elsewhere. We contend that it had less to do with what ultimately happened to the West than with the immediate threat of the so-called Slave Power to the rights and liberties of northerners, most of whom had no intention of decamping to Kansas or Nebraska. By this reading, Republicans attracted voting support because they presented themselves as defenders of the "republican institutions" mentioned in the quotation above and of the "republican principles" alluded to in the 1854 Michigan Republican platform. We insist that the part of the Republicans' appeal that had the greatest resonance with northern voters was not their denunciations of African American slavery's immorality or even their determination to stop the institution's westward expansion. Rather, it was white southerners' supposedly outrageous violation of the cherished tenets of republican self-government—self-government by consent of the governed; majority rule in the nation; and defense of individual and collective political freedom, at least white citizens' freedom, from tyrannical power—that appealed to northern sensibilities. By this reading, both the name of the new party, "Republican," and its identification of the enemy as the "Slave Power" had profound ideological ramifications with the electorate because Americans had believed since the era of the American Revolution that power in any form was the mortal enemy of republicanism.[16]

The defense of the widely understood principles of and institutions achieved by the generation of heroic Revolutionary "Fathers" or "Founders" also contributed to a certain ambiguity in the Republicans' message. At times they asserted that they were defending the nation's founding principles, not just the interests of the North. Democrats, not Republicans, they insisted, were the sectional party because the Democratic party by the 1850s was wholly controlled by and subservient to the southern Slave Power, whereas Republicans sought to restore the entire country, North and South, to its founding principles. Just as often, and more potently in my opinion, however, Republicans explicitly presented themselves as the paladin of the North against the aggressions of the South. That Republicans won virtually no support in slave states prior to 1860 was hardly accidental. Republicans went out of their way to present themselves as champions of the North and the northern majority of the national population against the pretensions and aggressions of the slaveholding elite, which, Republicans said, utterly dominated the minority South.

Republicans repeatedly and stridently complained that an insolent and aggressive minority of slaveholders, the so-called Slave Power, had seized control of the Democratic party, and through it of the national government. With that control, Republicans charged, white southern slaveholders contemptuously treated white northerners themselves like slaves. And it was an escape from *that* slavery, that subjugation to southern tyranny, that Republicans promised northerners. Vote for us, they trumpeted, and we will eject the Democratic party from power, restore self-government by the northern majority, and thereby save the liberty and rights of white northerners from enslavement to an overweening Slave Power. "A sectional and aristocratic oligarchy, trampling upon faith and encroaching on our rights, aspires to rule the American people," declared one Republican orator in 1856, and the Democratic party was characterized by "its abject subserviency to [that] slave power." Conversely, the purpose of the Republican party was "resistance to their aggression upon our rights," an insistence that "slave-masters . . . shall no longer monopolize the control of the nation, no longer use the Federal government to extend and support their sectional interest, no longer interfere as they are now interfering with the rights of free laborers."[17] Or as Seward put it in his famous "Irrepressible Conflict" speech in October 1858, "The designs of the slaveholders can and must be defeated," and there was only one way to do that. "The Democratic party must be permanently dislodged from the Government," for the Democratic party "is identical with the Slave Power."[18]

Endless variations on this theme of the Slave Power's threat to northerners' own liberties and self-government could be quoted from both the public statements and the private correspondence of Republicans between 1856 and 1860. The salience and credibility of these warnings, however, depended on evidence that southerners, or at least southern slaveholders, were in fact treating northerners like slaves. Here is where the importance of concrete chronological events came into play.

Between the summer of 1855 and Lincoln's election in November 1860, a succession of developments bolstered the Republicans' case that northerners needed a new party to ward off the threat of enslavement to the Slave Power. Again, this case was not always presented in exclusively sectional terms. Often Republicans spoke of saving the nation and its founding republican principles, and not just the North, from slaveholders' tyrannical designs. But even more often Republicans portrayed events as evidence of southern aggressions against northerners' rights in order to fan and exploit northerners' fear and resentment. By far the most important of the sectional shocks occurred in the spring of 1856. More than anything else—certainly far more than the poorly funded and poorly coordinated campaign that the Republican national committee ran that year—those incidents explain why Frémont outpolled Millard Fillmore by more than three to one among northern voters in November that year.[19]

Since the 1970s, historians have properly stressed the critical importance of the "sack" of Lawrence, Kansas, by Missouri Border Ruffians and the caning of Massachusetts Republican senator Charles Sumner by South Carolina's Democratic representative Preston S. Brooks, both of which occurred in May, in converting northern voters, especially northern Know-Nothings, to the Republican column. Because both incidents involved direct physical aggression by southern whites against northern whites, they were easily portrayed as concrete examples of brutal slavemasters treating northern whites like slaves. Most northerners considered laws passed by the proslavery territorial legislature of Kansas that deprived free-state settlers there of basic civil liberties as equally tyrannical. "Bleeding Kansas" and "Bleeding Sumner" thus provided invaluable ammunition for the Republicans' case that northerners themselves faced imminent enslavement.[20]

Few historians, however, have recognized the importance of a third incident, also occurring in May 1856, that provided further evidence of this charge.[21] Exactly one week to the day before Brooks caned Sumner, a Democratic representative from California named Philemon T. Herbert got into a brawl with an Irish waiter named Thomas Keating in a Washington hotel dining room and shot and killed him. At first, the Republican press simply criticized Herbert as an example of the brutally uncouth and uncivilized leaders Democrats elected. But then Republicans discovered that Herbert was originally from Alabama and from a slaveholding family to boot. Almost instantly Republicans raised the charge that Keating's murder proved that slaveholders contemptuously treated northern free laborers like slaves. In short, the Republican case against Brooks's bullying attack on Sumner was already in place before that incident occurred; they were already making it against Herbert. When the same Democratic judge, an appointee of the Pierce administration who spared Herbert from prosecution for the shooting, almost simultaneously refused to hear any charges against Brooks for his assault on Sumner, the connection between the two incidents was reinforced, as was the Slave Power's control of the Democratic party.

A speech by New York Republican John Jay in October 1856 illustrates how Republicans wove the Keating, Kansas, and Sumner affairs into a pattern of ominous Slave Power aggression. "A man is known by his friends," he intoned, "and Mr. Buchanan is the candidate not only of Pierce and Douglas, but of Herbert who shot the Irishman [and] of Brooks, who assaulted Sumner." The issues of the election were thus clear. "Shall peace and freedom shower their blessings over western territories? Or shall club-law rule in Washington? Shall honorable murderers stalk unpunished in the capital? Shall military despotism trample the life-blood of our territories, and an arrogant oligarchy of slave masters rule as with the plantation whip, twenty million of American citizens?"[22]

Keating's murder, however, had a special dimension, for, unlike the Harvard-educated and self-righteous patrician Sumner, he was a common laborer, a lowly table waiter. Here is how Republicans appealed directly to the "interests" of the "laboring class" in 1856. It was not just the potentially pernicious economic consequences of slavery's spread that were at stake, they insisted. It was slaveholders' obvious contempt for the rights, indeed the very lives, of northern workers. A portion of a campaign pamphlet issued by the Michigan State Republican Committee and entitled "The Murder of Keating Approved by the Democratic Party, in Congress and out, by a Pro-Slavery Court and Jury" illustrates this appeal. It was "not a crime for a locofoco member of Congress to murder an Irishman," the pamphlet huffed. By allowing Herbert to resume his seat in the House after he had resigned to stand trial, "The Slave Power has not only justified the infamous act, but has invited its repetition upon all Northern men." Therefore, it concluded, "The working man, the free man of the North, who in view of these facts casts a vote for the so-called 'Democratic' party, votes to declare that he himself should be made a slave."[23]

Despite such rhetoric, few unskilled laborers, and especially unskilled immigrant laborers, who had traditionally supported the Democratic party apparently defected to the Republicans in 1856. But skilled artisans in places as diverse as New Hampshire, Iowa, Chautauqua County, New York, Cincinnati, and Pittsburgh did gravitate to the new party.[24] Some of these men were former Democrats and, as Eric Foner has pointed out, Republicans consciously gave a disproportionate share of their first nominations for governors, congressmen, U.S. senators, and, in Frémont's case, president to erstwhile Democrats in order to attract Democratic voters to the new party.[25]

Republicans could never have carried former Democratic strongholds like Maine, New Hampshire, and Michigan without some Democratic converts. Nonetheless, William Gienapp's careful estimates, along with those of Lex Renda for New Hampshire, demonstrate that Whigs contributed the great majority of Frémont's supporters in 1856. Former Democrats supplied about one-fourth of his vote in Connecticut, Ohio, and Pennsylvania, one-fifth in Maine and New York, and less than 15 percent in Massachusetts and New Hampshire, while their contribution to his column in midwestern states like Illinois, Indiana, and Iowa was negligible. Almost all former Democrats who supported Frémont, moreover, had joined the anti-Democratic opposition in 1854 and 1855, often as Know-Nothings. The events and campaign rhetoric of 1856 apparently caused few new defections; if anything, a significant fraction of Democrats who had bolted to the Know-Nothing party earlier now returned to their traditional party home.[26]

The stubborn refusal of most northern Democrats to abandon James Buchanan and the stubborn insistence of many nativists and former Whigs to support Fillmore rather than Frémont allowed Buchanan to carry New Jersey, Pennsylvania, Indiana, Illinois, and California. Buchanan also captured every slave state except Maryland. Thus, even though Frémont captured 45.2 percent of the North's popular vote compared to Buchanan's 41.4 percent and Fillmore's pitiful 13.4 percent, and even though Frémont carried eleven of the sixteen free states, Buchanan won the election.

This result made it clear that the key to Republican success lay in carrying Illinois, Indiana, and Pennsylvania. To do that, Republicans had to attract Fillmore's supporters in those states, make deeper incursions into the Democratic rank-and-file, or mobilize the preponderant share of new voters who entered the potential electorate between 1856 and 1860.

This was a significant challenge. Men who voted for Fillmore or Buchanan in 1856 were clearly more conservative than those who had supported Frémont. It was not simply that they had been unswayed by the purported Slave Power aggressions of 1856 that propelled other northern voters into the Republican camp. Both the Fillmore and the Buchanan campaigns had loudly and repeatedly warned that a Republican victory would provoke southern secession, and we may infer that fear of disunion in part motivated the men who voted for them.[27] Republicans had somehow to assuage those fears without alienating their original supporters.

But the Republicans' challenge went beyond that necessity. Frémont

Figure 2.4. *The Republican Campaign Songster: A Collection of Lyrics, Original and Selected, Specially Prepared for the Friends of Freedom in the Campaign of Fifty-Six* (New York and Auburn: Miller, Orton & Mulligan, 1856). Songsters were a staple of nineteenth-century political campaigns, published in abundance for free distribution. Campaign songs fired the enthusiasm of rallies and mass meetings. The songs were usually poetic creations set to well-known tunes. The Frémont literature also often featured Frémont's attractive and adventurous wife, Jessie Benton Frémont, daughter of Missouri Senator Thomas Hart Benton and an important strategist in Frémont's campaign.

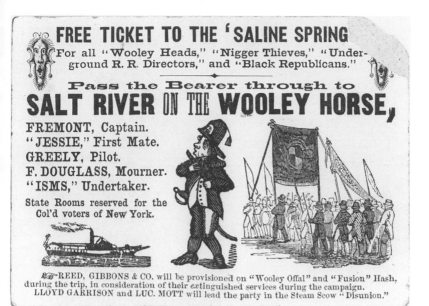

Figure 2.5. *Free Ticket to the 'Saline Springs,' For all "Wooley Heads," "Nigger Thieves," "Underground R.R. Directors," and "Black Republicans"* (Philadelphia, 1856). Triumphant Democrats distributed cards and handbills mocking Frémont's defeat in pro-southern and antiblack Philadelphia. Here the Republicans are being sent down to Salt River, or political oblivion. This cartoon typified the persistent and consistent denigration of Republicans as abolitionists. Note the references to Frederick Douglass, William Lloyd Garrison, and Philadelphia's Lucretia Mott.

had been as successful as he was largely because he won over a majority of northern Whigs and mobilized a significant share of men who could not or did not vote in 1852. Contemporary testimony strongly suggests that Republicans did so because they skillfully exploited a series of events that aroused fierce northern indignation against the South—the murder of Thomas Keating, the caning of Charles Sumner, and affairs in Kansas. Yet if sectional conflict waned during Buchanan's administration and memories of those events faded, it was not clear that the new Republican party could retain all its 1856 supporters, let alone convert the Fillmore men, especially if they were presented with a less threatening, nonsectional vehicle for opposing the Democrats. Despite Frémont's stunning vote in 1856, in short, it was by no means assured that anti-Democratic voters would rally behind the Republican banner in 1860. We now know that Republicans in fact surmounted this challenge. The great majority of Fillmore voters moved into the Republican column by 1860, and most had done so by the end of 1858. We also know from Gienapp's research that a preponderant majority of young men who became eligible to vote only after 1856 supported Lincoln in 1860, if they bothered to vote at all, especially in the crucial swing states of Illinois, Indiana, and Pennsylvania. Finally, Gienapp's statistical estimates also suggest that whereas very few 1856 Democratic voters later swung to the Republicans in midwestern states or New York, about one-ninth of them did in all-important Pennsylvania.[28] The question is how Republicans managed to achieve these gains.

Negative reactions by northerners to actions by and events during the Buchanan administration contributed mightily to this accomplishment. Its apparent complicity in and endorsement of the Supreme Court's *Dred Scott* decision and especially its unsuccessful attempt to push Kansas's proslavery Lecompton constitution through Congress, despite evidence that a clear majority of Kansas voters opposed it, split the Democratic party while reinforcing the belief that the administration was subservient to the Slave Power. The Lecompton question consumed Congress for the first half of 1858, and outrage over the administration's attempt to force Kansas's admission as a slave state helped drive former Fillmore voters into alliances with Republicans in the 1858 congressional elections, even when the name "Republican" itself was avoided. In that year, in fact, Republicans or Republican-leaning anti-Lecompton alliances achieved majorities in the statewide vote in all the northern states Frémont had lost except California and bolstered their majorities in other northern states. Yet sharp declines in the turnout rates of Democrats disillusioned by the administration's flouting of the Democratic formula of popular sovereignty contributed as much, if not more, to these proportionate gains by the Republicans, as did an increase in their absolute vote.[29]

Economic issues, moreover, clearly contributed to Republican (or People's party) gains in Pennsylvania and New Jersey. The outbreak of a financial panic in the fall of 1857 raised both an opportunity and a problem for Republicans. The problem was that former Whigs and former Democrats in the new party had long disagreed about federal economic policies. Thus, when Democrats tried to exploit the panic to divert attention from Kansas matters by resurrecting Jacksonian assaults on bankers and paper money, Republicans were unable to formulate a coherent party response. Many Republicans with Democratic antecedents denounced bankers just as stridently as did Democrats. Only the exigencies of the Civil War would force Republicans with Democratic antecedents to acquiesce in essentially Whiggish Republican banking and monetary policies.[30]

In most northern states ex-Democrats among Republicans were also at odds with new Whig allies over tariff policy, but not in Pennsylvania and New Jersey. As James L. Huston's study of this matter demonstrates, the ironmaking and coal-mining counties in those two states suffered severe unemployment throughout 1858. Opponents of Buchanan's administration immediately blamed hard times on Democrats' stubborn adherence to the low tariff of 1857 and called for higher rates to revive the economy and protect American workers from cheap European competition. This assault had two results. First, it turned many of the unemployed against the incumbent Democrats, if not yet converting them into Republicans. Most of the decline in Democratic turnout in the 1858 congressional elections, where Democrats lost ten seats in Pennsylvania, came in those counties most dependent on coal and iron production. Second, while statistical evidence strongly suggests that most of those disillusioned Democrats did *not* immediately defect to the opposition, pushing for a higher protective tariff *did* help facilitate a merger between former Whigs who had supported Fillmore in 1856 and Republicans in a new "People's party" coalition in both Pennsylvania and New Jersey.[31]

As we now know, these gains in 1858 by Republicans or People's coalitions affiliated with them would carry over into the 1860 presidential election. But Republican strategists in 1858 could not be sure of that, since their percentage gains had again depended on reaction to what might be evanescent events and on a lopsided plunge in Democratic turnout. What is more, they were *acutely* aware that the bruising fight among Democrats over the Lecompton constitution, with Stephen A. Douglas leading a substantial minority of northern Democratic representatives against the Buchanan administration, menaced their ability to paint northern Democrats like Douglas as lackeys of the Slave Power. Simultaneously, the emphatic decision by Kansas voters in a new referendum on the Lecompton constitution in August 1858 to spurn entry as a slave state effectively ended the possibility of the extension of slavery into any of the existing federal territories, thereby spiking one of the Republicans' biggest guns. Together with the resurrection of the tariff issue by hard times, the apparent cessation of sectional conflict over slavery extension raised a possibility that a different kind of anti-Democratic party could be created that would displace the Republicans. The exposure of systemic corruption in the Buchanan administration by anti-administration elements in Congress between 1858 and 1860, corruption that offended southerners as well as northerners, only increased the potential attractiveness of such a new party.

The leaders of this new party effort were two southern ex-Whigs in the Senate, John Bell of Tennessee and especially John J. Crittenden of Kentucky, both of whom had endorsed the Know-Nothings and supported Fillmore in 1856. In 1858 Crittenden delivered two powerful speeches in the Senate. One lambasted Buchanan for trying to force the Lecompton constitution through Congress and insisted that it be resubmitted to an honest vote by all eligible Kansas residents, even if that vote killed any chance that Kansas would become a slave state. The other mocked the inadequacy of the administration's response to hard times and demanded an increase in tariff rates to generate economic recovery and put the unemployed back to work.

Crittenden was immediately swamped with letters from both North and South praising him for providing the basis for a new opposition party that could supplant the exclusively northern and therefore dangerous Republicans and elect Crittenden president in 1860. This new party, gushed his enthusiastic correspondents, would combine all the 1856 Fillmore voters in the North and South, all former Whigs, regardless how they had voted in 1856, anti-Lecompton Democrats in the North, and northern Know-Nothings who had supported Frémont in 1856 because of their outrage at southern aggressions that year, but who now might join a bisectional opposition party since the slavery extension issue appeared to be resolved.[32]

Fending off this new party challenge was the most important, if least studied achievement of the Republican party between 1856 and 1860.[33] Its threat to Republicans in the short run was that it could attract the 1856 Fillmore supporters, anti-Buchanan Democrats, and moderate Whigs already in Republican ranks whom Republicans desperately needed to win in 1860. In the long run its threat was that it might replace the Republican party entirely. Its promise to men who wanted to oust the

Figure 2.6. "Prominent Candidates for the Republican Presidential Nomination at Chicago," *Harper's Weekly*, May 12, 1860. Going into the Republican convention, no one knew who would get the nod from the party of many parts. The prospect of victory and the lack of any one candidate controlling the party made the presidential nomination inviting to several factions and their favorites.

Democrats from office was that it could bring southern votes to the anti-Democratic cause, something the Republican party itself could never do beyond a handful of supporters in the border states. But this new opposition party could attract that southern support only by abandoning the anti-Slave Power, South-bashing themes that Republicans had thus far exploited to win office in the North.

Worried Republican leaders, unlike later historians, fully recognized how dangerous this threat was. A nervous Philadelphian wrote national chairman Morgan that "the object is to break down or override the Republican party & elevate John Bell or some other Old Line Tariff Whig to the Presidency or in other words the object is to reestablish the old Whig party under a new name & crush out all 'Slavery agitation.'" Similarly, Ohio Republicans complained to Salmon Chase that the political comeback of the extremely conservative ex-Whig Thomas Corwin as a Republican congressional candidate in 1858 was meant "to bring down our doctrines and position to the Fillmore level in order to make Corwin our leader and *Senator* and Crittenden our President in 1860."[34]

Republicans' responses to this new party challenge varied. In some places they sought to coopt northern conservatives who might be attracted to it. Thus they worked all the harder to bring Fillmore men into the party by pushing anti-immigrant laws Know-Nothings favored, nominating known conservatives like Corwin as Republican candidates, or, as in Pennsylvania and New Jersey, raising the cry for protective tariffs and downplaying the slavery issue in 1858. Primarily, however, Republicans insisted that, despite the settlement of the Kansas question, the southern Slave Power remained a vital threat to northerners' rights and interests and that neither anti-Lecompton Democrats like Douglas nor southern oppositionists like Bell and Crittenden could be trusted to resist it. Only the Republican party, they chanted, met northerners' needs.

Thus Lincoln raised the charge in his famous "House Divided" speech and subsequent debates with Douglas in 1858 that there was a Slave Power conspiracy abetted by Douglas and other Democrats to obtain a Supreme Court decision that would legalize slavery throughout the North. Thus Seward gave his equally famous "Irrepressible Conflict" speech in October 1858. Thus Morgan circulated the document, quoted at the beginning of this essay, that justified the continued necessity of the Republican party. Thus Republicans in a number of northern states resurrected attacks on the Fugitive Slave Act of 1850, an issue that had been eclipsed for four years by events in Kansas and Washington. And thus Republicans pooh-poohed the need or desirability of incorporating southern Whigs into the party—and thus watering down its anti-southern platform—in order to defeat the Democrats in 1860. "If the rotten democracy shall be beaten in 1860," Lincoln coldly rebuffed an advocate of the new party scheme in June 1859, "it has to be done by the North; no human intervention can deprive them of the South."[35]

For opponents of Democrats, indeed, the chief lure of the new party movement ignited by Crittenden's speeches was always that it could deliver southern electoral votes against the Democrats in 1860. Happily for Republicans, however, very few state and congressional elections were held in the South in 1858 that might demonstrate the strength of the anti-Democratic opposition. Nor had any been held by June of 1859, when Lincoln wrote his emphatic rejection of a bisectional anti-Democratic rather than anti-southern strategy. Later that year, however, the anti-Democratic opposition did very well in congressional elections in the Upper South, increasing their number of House seats from Kentucky, Tennessee, North Carolina, and Virginia from six to twenty-two. Nonetheless, the opposition secured statewide majorities in none of these states, let alone in the Deep South, where organized political opposition to the Democrats was nearly moribund. This failure of Buchanan's southern opponents to demonstrate their ability to carry electoral votes in the South greatly helped the Republicans who spurned cooperation with them.

Still, the presidential nomination of Crittenden's ally John Bell by the Constitutional Union party in 1860 raised once again the threat that Fillmorites who had joined in tenuous alliances with Republicans in 1858 and 1859 might yet be wooed away. That year Republicans responded in four ways. First, they consciously decided to offset any defections by recruiting and mobilizing young voters who had no prior loyalty to conservative Whiggery and seemed little inclined to warm to an "Old Fogy" Constitutional Union ticket of John Bell and Edward Everett. Thus Republicans organized the famous Wide Awake marching clubs, consisting almost entirely of young men and teenagers, in 1860. Given the preponderant support first-time voters gave Lincoln, that effort appears to have paid dividends.

Second, Republicans also made greater efforts than they had four years earlier to attract Protestant German support. Their 1860 platform contained a plank that explicitly opposed any attempts to lengthen the

Figure 2.7. "Grand Procession of Wide-Awakes at New York on the Evening of
October 3, 1860," *Harper's Weekly*, October 13, 1860. The Wide-Awakes were
local political clubs, originally organized by the Know-Nothing movement in
the mid-1850s but converted to the Republican party by 1860, that raised
campaign hoopla and enthusiasm through torchlight parades and mass
meetings. Such outdoor politics were especially pitched to young and new
voters. Wide-Awakes were well-organized in New York, several New England
cities, Chicago, and Philadelphia.

naturalization period for aliens and any state legislation that impaired
the political rights of naturalized citizens. There is little evidence that
these efforts increased the German vote for Republicans in Indiana or
Illinois, but they did produce significant gains in Pennsylvania as well as
in Iowa and New York.[36]

Third, while moving to offset Fillmorite defections, Republicans
simultaneously sought to cement the allegiance of the Fillmorites they
had won over in 1858 and 1859. Their national platform had a less stridently anti-southern tone than the 1856 version. It jettisoned the language
about slavery's being "a relic of barbarism," condemned John Brown's
raid on Harper's Ferry as "among the gravest of crimes," and announced
the party's "abhorrence of all schemes of disunion." Republicans also

added planks that demanded passage of a homestead act, federal subsidies for rivers and harbors improvements, which were in great demand in Great Lakes states like Illinois and Indiana, and a revision of tariff duties that "encourage[d] the development of the industrial interests of the whole country." However ambiguous this tariff plank was, it was clearly aimed at all-important Pennsylvania and New Jersey, and in fact James Huston's study indicates that the increase in Lincoln's vote over Frémont's total in the Keystone state occurred primarily in counties with substantial capital investment in manufacturing and mining.[37]

Significantly, as previously noted, the anti-Democratic coalitions in those two states still called themselves "People's Parties" because of the radical implications of the very name Republican, and Fillmore's 1856 supporters in Indiana and Illinois were perhaps even more worried by the radical antislavery and sectionalist tone of Republicans in 1856. Thus the Republicans' fourth response to the threat of Fillmorite defection in 1860, the nomination of Abraham Lincoln, was especially critical in explaining their capture of Illinois, Indiana, and Pennsylvania that year. Since Stephen A. Douglas, the northern Democratic nominee, was also a native son of Illinois, Republicans may not have eked out their narrow victory in that state with a different nominee.[38] More important, Lincoln's nomination meant that Seward was not the Republican candidate. Seward was anathema to both diehard nativists and the conservative Whigs who had supported Fillmore in 1856. With him as their candidate, Republicans may have lost Illinois and Indiana, and they most certainly would have lost Pennsylvania, the key to the election.

This, then, is how Republicans in the 1850s cobbled together a coalition—and only in the North, it should be emphasized—that was numerous enough to elect Abraham Lincoln president in 1860 with a majority of the electoral votes, despite garnering less than 40 percent of the nationwide popular vote.[39] No other new party in American history has achieved such instant success. And given the rules of the political game today that are intentionally designed to preclude the possibility of any powerful new party from ever arising, it seems unlikely that we shall ever see the likes of the early Republican party again.

However historic, the Republicans' achievement in the 1850s needs to be put in perspective. At the most pragmatic level, they had succeeded in electing a president because of the winner-take-all rules in the electoral college, but they had *not* elected a majority in either the House of

Representatives or the Senate. Only the secession of southern states in response to Lincoln's victory gave Republicans control of Congress. Yet the Republicans' calculated refusal to reach out to most of the southern opponents of Buchanan's administration, especially the slaveholding ex-Whigs who ended up supporting John Bell in 1860, had much to do with secession itself, for in the South they were correctly perceived as the overtly anti-southern party of the North. It is inconceivable that a victory in 1860 by a bisectional opposition party that ran John J. Crittenden or John Bell could have provided the excuse for fire-eating southern secessionists that Lincoln's victory did.

Nor did Lincoln's election assure harmony in the new Republican party. As noted, the polyglot elements in the Republican coalition had always agreed more on what they were against than what they were for. Ex-Whigs, ex-Free Soilers, ex-Democrats, and ex-Know-Nothings had largely finessed their disagreements on what government should do in the future by focusing on their mutual opposition to what Democrats and the Slave Power had done in the past when they controlled it. Once Republicans inherited control of the executive branch of the national government, submerged animosities resurfaced.

The first battleground was the composition of Lincoln's cabinet. Former Democrats and former Whigs vied to keep representatives of the other out of it, and both tried to exclude Free Soilers, who just as insistently demanded a voice in the incoming president's official family. Free Soiler Salmon Chase and ex-Whig Seward were the chief targets of these brickbats.

The movement toward secession in the Deep South immediately after Lincoln's election complicated this competition. Opponents of secession in the Upper South pleaded with Lincoln, Seward, Thurlow Weed, and other Republicans to abandon the Republican party and its antislavery, anti-southern stance and to combine with southern anti-secessionists in a new Union party that eschewed South-bashing and the slavery issue and focused on the need to avert disunion.[40] As a result, where potential cabinet members stood on this issue of consigning the new Republican party to an early grave and replacing it with a bisectional Union party also played a central role in the jockeying over Lincoln's cabinet.

Lincoln, for example, was warned not to appoint Seward, his eventual secretary of state, because Seward favored the "abandonment" of the Republican party and "the early formation of new combinations, under the name of Union party, or something of the kind." Similarly, Lincoln was frantically urged not to appoint his ultimate choice for postmaster general, Montgomery Blair, a former Democrat rather than a former Whig, because the Marylander Blair favored "a *de*-republicanizing of the party and a coalition administration," "a sort of 'Union' party to take the place of Republicans."[41]

In short, the Republican party may have won the presidency, but to many people inside and outside Republican ranks, it still seemed an ephemeral coalition, not a permanent major party. Conducting the North's war effort against Confederate disunionists between 1861 and 1865 would enhance the case that it should be preserved, even as that effort persuaded others in and outside the party that it should be fundamentally reoriented, reorganized, or displaced by a bisectional Union organization. The survival or endurance of the Republican party, in short, remained no sure thing. Justifying its continued existence remained a continuing necessity for the politicians committed to it. And that necessity influenced much of what Republicans did during the war and Reconstruction. In this way, the perceived plasticity of American politics between the mid-1850s and the mid-1870s shaped much that happened during those years.

CHAPTER THREE

War Is the Health of the Party: Republicans in the American Civil War

Phillip Shaw Paludan

Abraham Lincoln dominates discussion of Civil War Republicanism.[1] Influenced, perhaps, by a modern world in which the presidency shapes party goals and rhetoric, historians have undervalued the significance of his party and concentrated on Lincoln's actions as emancipator, master strategist, master diplomatist. Works that study Lincoln's relationship to his party are entitled *Lincoln and the Party Divided, Re-electing Lincoln, Lincoln and the Radicals, Lincoln and the War Governors,* and, most recently, in a study of the Congressional Joint Committee on the Conduct of the War, *Over Lincoln's Shoulder.*[2]

Of course, Lincoln mattered profoundly in shaping the war and influencing his party. His decisions moved armies, freed slaves, jailed opposition, protected and armed freedmen. Above all, his inspirational and well-calculated rhetoric led the nation toward its better angels.[3]

But in the long run, especially the run of the mid-nineteenth century when legislatures dominated government and politics, the Republican party was equally significant and at times more important. For one thing, getting right with Lincoln was not likely to be the number one priority with lawmakers. He didn't have long coattails. In many states the party was more popular than the president. In the election of 1860, in eleven of the fourteen largest northern states, Lincoln got a smaller percentage of the popular vote than did congressional Republican candidates. Four years later it was a similar story. In 1864 in New York and Indiana, two of the larger northern states, party candidates for governor outpolled Lincoln. In most of the races congressional candidates in Iowa and Massachusetts outpaced Lincoln in 1864. In New York even the

PORTRAIT OF ABRAHAM LINCOLN, PRESIDENT ELECT OF THE UNITED STATES OF AMERICA, WITH SCENES AND INCIDENTS IN HIS LIFE.—Phot. by P. Butler, Springfield, Ill.

Figure 3.1. "Portrait of Abraham Lincoln, President Elect of the United States of America, With Scenes and Incidents in his Life, Phot. by P. Butler, Springfield, Ill.," *Frank Leslie's Illustrated Newspaper*, March 9, 1861 (Alexander Hesler's photograph, misattributed to Preston Butler). The new president is portrayed as a free-soil exemplar, surrounded by vignettes showing his rise from laborer to middle-class professional to president of the United States. The Lincoln image and biography was ready-made to appeal to the laboring classes and farmers; it also served the interests of businessmen and others who preached self-willed independence as the way to wealth.

lieutenant governor, canal commissioner, and inspector of prisons won more popular votes.[4]

Lincoln's leadership mattered but, as he often said, events also controlled him, and the nation. Many of those events were the work of other Republicans. While Lincoln can take much of the credit for emancipation and for bringing the war to a successful end, Congress helped and at times led him in these efforts. The first official action taken by the United States against slavery was the First Confiscation Act, which Congress passed August 6, 1861. Seven months later, on March 6, 1862, Lincoln asked Congress to help states end slavery by compensating them for their loss of human property. After that the two branches of government leapfrogged each other with laws and proclamations attacking human bondage. And toward the end of the war, it was Congress's Wade-Davis bill and not Lincoln's plan of reconstruction that promised the most protection of the former slaves from their masters. It would be a postwar Congress, without Lincoln's help, that passed the Fourteenth and Fifteenth Amendments.[5]

Congress flexed its muscles in part because Lincoln was usually too busy to oversee events beyond his stated constitutional authority: to execute the laws, to act as commander in chief of the armed forces, to make treaties and appoint officials. The president focused his attention on choosing generals, suggesting strategy, negotiating with lawmakers about emancipation and Reconstruction. But Congress was the dominant body in gathering resources, creating an infrastructure that not only won the war but also reshaped the American economy for a century or more. It was thus the Republican party as much as Lincoln, and at times more than Lincoln, that (in a large sense) won the war. How did they do that? And what did they do?

This was the Republicans' war. Their campaigning had created it; by dividing the house their philosophy had demanded it. Of course they wanted a peaceful triumph for their ideals. They promised in their 1860 platform not to attack slavery where it existed, to let states control their own domestic institutions, as the Constitution provided. They condemned John Brown. They wanted to place slavery in the course of *ultimate* extinction. But they built their party on criticism of the South and slavery. Republican success precipitated the secession movement, and that led ultimately to war.

They did not do it alone. Southern fire-eaters, southern nationalists caused the war too, and at Fort Sumter rebels fired the first shot that

turned sectional debate into a battle cry of freedom. But now, with battle before them, the war became the Republican war in another sense: it
became a war that would allow them to create a Republican America, to
enact their view of what the nation should be.

Wartime Republicans had the votes to achieve these goals in almost
every northern state and especially in Congress. In 1861 the Grand Young
Party, as we might call it, held fourteen of eighteen governorships above
the Mason Dixon line. By 1862 there were three Democratic governors;
by early 1864 only two northern states had Democratic governors, New
Jersey and New York. The next year it was down to one. In 1860 Republicans controlled all but three state legislatures. By 1864 they retained
their heavy majority.[6]

Republicans also dominated Congress. The thirty-seventh Congress
contained 31 Senate Republicans, 7 Unionists (all from border states), and
10 Democrats. In the House 106 Republicans outvoted 42 Democrats
even if all 28 Unionists joined the Democrats. The thirty-eighth Congress
had 102 House Republicans and 75 Democrats, and 36 Republican senators overwhelmed the 9 Democrats. For the years of the war the United
States arguably became a party state, a one-party polity. The party was
doing something right.[7]

Or, to put it more accurately, it was doing many things right in
different places, for Republicans were not all of one mind. They looked
united behind their president and his vague symbolism as Railsplitter.
But despite this unifying symbol, Republicans were hardly unanimous
on all questions. The party divided over the tariff. Free traders like
Salmon Chase clashed with protectionists, especially the "Iron and Coal
Men" of Pennsylvania. Important senators such as the chairman of
the Senate Finance Committee, William Pitt Fessenden, voted against a
Pacific railroad; so did Pennsylvania's radical chairman of the House
Ways and Means Committee, Thaddeus Stevens. Fessenden voted "Nay"
because he wanted the government to build it so that private interests
would not prevail over public good. Stevens wanted more government
regulation of railroad construction.[8] But Stevens and Fessenden parted
company on the money question: Stevens advocated greenbacks, Fessenden feared that they would destroy the economy. The necessities of
war would, however, unite Republicans behind the cause of preserving
the Union and its corollary, freeing the slaves, and, as the war continued,
unity on other issues grew. Congress would pass and Lincoln would

sign bills that set in place the entire Republican platforms of 1860 and 1864.

Civil war produced the best environment possible to unite a diverse party. It united them because the full range of economic interests could be satisfied and justified in the greatest of causes: saving the nation. The Republican economic package corresponded almost perfectly with the needs of war. The infrastructure of warmaking demanded railroads, a banking system and national currency, protection of industry, immigration of workers, internal improvements, higher education, and new land opened to grow the meat and grains that fed hungry soldiers and the workers who were supplying them. Republicans justified them all as imperative for victory.

And they faced a heavily handicapped opposition Democratic party. Divided from the South, its base of support, and opposed to a war where nearly two million men were risking and losing their lives, the party of Jefferson and Jackson was easily tarred with the stigma of treason. To have your favorite economic development schemes anointed with patriotism is every politician's dream. The Republicans dreamed well between 1861 and 1865, and those dreams echoed for decades.[9]

Patronage helped unite the party. Lincoln replaced almost every Democrat who worked in the more than 1,500 jobs directly under executive control. It was the biggest political purge in the nation's history to that time, but well suited to providing roots for a party that was less than seven years old in 1861. Lincoln removed more men from their jobs than Andrew Jackson, the reputed master of spoilsmanship, had. But Lincoln did not demand a unified vision from his appointees. He was a loyal party man, but he respected local and state conditions and built party infrastructure by letting congressmen and senators influence appointments in their states and districts. (Even in this area of executive initiative the influence of congressmen was evident.) He balanced factions in more national places; a more radical man might receive the collectorship of a port, but second in command there would likely be a moderate Republican. A look at his cabinet reveals his understanding of party diversity: Secretary of State, William Henry Seward, former Whig from the middle states; Secretary of the Treasury, Salmon Chase, former Democrat and Free Soiler from Ohio; Secretary of War, Simon Cameron, former Democrat and tariff advocate from Pennsylvania, replaced by another former Democrat from Pennsylvania, Edwin Stanton; Secretary of the Navy, Gideon Welles, former Democrat from Connecticut; Attorney General, Edwin Bates, former Whig from Missouri; Postmaster General, Montgomery Blair, former Democrat from Maryland; Secretary of the Interior, Caleb Smith, former Whig from Indiana. Vice President Hannibal Hamlin was a former Democrat from Maine.

Party rewards went to faithful servants of political necessity. For example, when Hamlin was asked to step down from the vice presidency, his reward was the collectorship of the port of Boston, one of the richest plums in the patronage pot.

Leading Republicans controlled large numbers of the jobs in their state. They made patronage a family affair. Seward hired his son to be his secretary. Senator Fessenden had four brothers and a sister in patronage jobs. In addition, two brothers were congressmen from Maine, and two sons who entered the army with no military training somehow managed to become brevet generals by the end of the war.[10]

While Republicans argued over economic directions, they stayed united on the greatest issue of the day, slavery. They were the party of emancipation, the first major party in American history that unequivocally advocated the end of slavery. Republicans had family fights about emancipation, but these were fights about speed more than destination, about means, seldom about ends. During the war the party emancipated slaves, armed them, expanded their rights at the state and national level, and protected them with the force of arms. By the end of the war many Republicans were calling for black suffrage. Race issues most fundamentally divided the parties. In 1862 the Congress voted on slavery-related questions: emancipation in the District of Columbia, outlawing slavery in the territories, ordering soldiers not to return runaway slaves, and a confiscation act freeing slaves of disloyal masters. On these issues 96 percent of the Democrats voted "No"; 99 percent of the Republicans voted "Yes."[11]

But even while expanding liberty for former slaves, the party was careful not to stir up the racism of voters. Republicans focused voter attention on saving the Union more than on emancipating the slaves. Party campaign broadsides and pamphlets in 1864 emphasized that the party was the Union party much more than the emancipation party. Of 213 pamphlets and broadsides issued that year, only 28 made emancipation their primary argument.[12] The election strategy of 1864 was described by James G. Blaine: "The struggle for the presidency demanded harmony and by common consent agitation on the [emancipation] question was abandoned."[13]

And yet African Americans were Republicans too, despite their party's reluctance to affirm full equality. Blacks would have liked their party leaders to hate slavery as a moral evil and to believe in the basic equality of all humankind. But, lacking that chimera, they foresaw a better future for themselves inside the Union than in a separate nation dedicated to the preservation and expansion of slavery. They had zero interest in supporting any organization that rested on the "cornerstone," as the Confederate vice president declared, that "the negro is not equal to the white man . . . [and that] slavery, subordination to the superior race, is his natural condition."[14] Blacks would also benefit from Republican policies generating economic growth and the ideal of free labor. And they looked with gratitude on a Republican party that voted for ending discrimination in voting, civil rights, and public accommodations when these issues were voted on at the state and national level in the war-era North.

Civil War Republicans were thus the most effective nineteenth-century advocates of racial justice. Most historians of recent years have applauded them for that. But the party's other great contribution has gotten mixed reviews. They were the party of economic growth and development. They passed the laws that helped create the Gilded Age, an age symbolized not by Lincoln but by Ulysses Grant and his cronies, by bearded, overweight men in dark suits, smoking cigars at lavish banquets, eating ten-course meals while their minions crushed strikes, swindled farmers, and displaced workers. The Robber Barons threatened to eclipse the Railsplitter.

The Civil War moved the party from its small-producer, middle-class origins toward becoming the party of big business. Perhaps this was almost inevitable, for Republicans rose as the advocates of the market revolution and industrialization. The regions of the North most supportive of the war, the Republican base, were the regions most deeply involved in industrializing the nation. Since the time of Henry Clay, even of Alexander Hamilton, pro-southern Democrat legislators had blocked the economic legislation that gave government the power to assist private enterprise. Federalists, Whigs, and now Republicans had been stifled by southern fears that use of government power to develop the economy forecast using that power to meddle with slavery. But when war began, Republicans had overwhelming majorities. And they had a war and the lives of "our boys" and the survival of the Union to justify the program of economic development.[15]

Building a wartime economy intimately linked the Republican party with the capitalists who controlled and developed an industrialized America. Free Labor Republicans bound themselves to the monarchs of the Gilded Age. Heather Richardson's book, *The Greatest Nation of the Earth*, on Republican economic policy during the war, describes this evolution as grounded in an evolving ideology. Republican free-labor doctrine inspired hostility to slavery in large part because slave labor was seen as hostile to the free-labor world where men could rise freed of the economic control of others. War against slavery required laws that built the strength of large-scale enterprises. These enterprises gained relatively free reign with the victory of the free-labor North over the slave-labor South.

But Richardson undervalues other factors that also generated the Gilded Age from the small producer goals of Lincoln's party. Republicans went to bed with capitalists because they needed them to win the war. They needed them because, for decades, dominant Democratic rhetoric and years in office had built a tradition of limited national power. Ironically, Democrats had helped shape the world they attacked, for the national government lacked the experience and knowledge to organize the nation's resources on the eve of war.[16]

When war began, the United States did not have its own currency. There was no income tax, no national banking system. When Treasury secretary Chase needed to sell bonds, he could not call on the bond division of the Treasury Department. There was no such thing. The experts on money-raising were the bankers of the nation, men like Jay Cooke of Philadelphia who organized profoundly successful bond sales. Railroads got built and ran on time because private citizens like Tom Scott and David McCallum and Herman Haupt knew how to run railroads. When Democrats attacked him for giving government power to a private banker, Chase defended his use of Cooke to sell bonds by explaining that the Treasury lacked nationwide branches and an infrastructure to sell anything on the necessary scale.[17]

Public perception of the links between private money and government and politics were quite different in those days. This is not to say that Democrats didn't attack the connections between private capital and government power, but it was well known that wealthy men supported candidates who advocated their economic goals. Jay Cooke financed the

campaigns of Chase and John Sherman in Ohio. They could be counted
on to repay him with their votes in Congress. People, Republicans especially, objected very little to the fact that government helped build private fortunes when those fortunes were used to develop the economic
commonwealth. When Cooke made commissions on selling government
bonds, many people saw him as earning a reasonable commission for
performing a public service. Cooke was a patriot, not the shady symbol
of an interest group.

The influence Republicans had and the prestige they gained while
saving the Union became a weapon against what modern politicians
might call class-warfare politics: attacks by workers on concentrations
of wealth and power. When draft riots exploded from worker neighbor-
hoods throughout the North, their bosses argued that rioters helped the
Confederacy. Miners who rose up in eastern Pennsylvania met the same
accusations. One owner wrote to Lincoln in 1863 equating striking for
higher wages with disloyalty: "a large majority of the [miners]" were defy-
ing the draft and "making unsafe the lives and property of Union men."[18]

Urban labor protests were answered not with conciliation and nego-
tiation but usually with accusations of disloyalty. The wartime bloody
shirt was a useful Republican tool not only in helping former slaves
but also in stifling urban protests. Several strikes during the war were
put down by Union generals insisting that strikes helped the enemy and
that workers were disloyal. Two companies of soldiers were sent to Cold
Springs, New York, in March 1864 to stop a strike. They threw four leaders in jail for seven weeks without a trial, and the strike collapsed. In St.
Louis, General William Rosecrans treated strikers the same way. He prohibited picketing, meetings, and even refusal to work. General Stephen
Burbridge followed Rosecrans's example in Louisville.[19]

Republican capitalists also challenged urban protest by appealing
to nativism. That branch of the party with Know-Nothing roots had
long proclaimed that Irish Catholic immigrants were loyal to the Pope,
not to their new nation. The loyalty of the essentially urban Irish to the
Democratic party had thus raised suspicions about alien influences in
Democratic cities. Wartime strikes fed these doubts, real and/or partisan.
Strikes were depicted in city Republican newspapers and magazines as led
by brutish Irishmen, the major source of Democrat George McClellan's
city support, it was claimed. In 1864 Thomas Nast pictured respectable
gentlemen voting for Lincoln, while dirty apelike Irishmen cast McClellan

ballots. Part of the anti-Irish feelings arose from the atrocities committed by Irish workers in the draft riots: castrating blacks and burning
them and burning down a black children's orphanage. But by attacking
Irish workers of all kinds as brutes (a well-established practice before the
war) the Republican party changed the subject from economic inequality to disloyalty by less than human workers. (It was a Republican varia-
tion on playing the race card.)[20]

Did the Republicans know that they were forcing the social costs of
economic change on working-class people, that they were making what
radicals might call class warfare on labor? Historians frequently go into
denial on the subject. They place the growth of economic inequity after

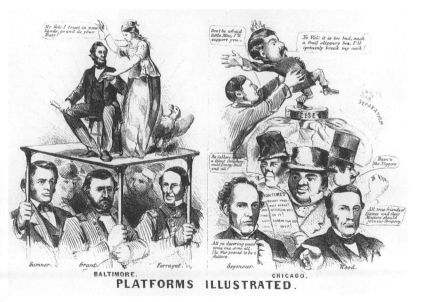

Figure 3.2. *Platforms Illustrated*, lithograph (n.p., 1864). This lithograph was one
of many Republican political tracts and illustrations painting Democrats as
treasonous while casting Republicans as champions of the Union and liberty.
In this campaign lithograph, the Democrats are supported by Confederate
sympathizers Clement Vallandigham and Fernando Wood, New York's
anti-war governor Horatio Seymour, rioting Irishmen, and a Copperhead
guard. Supporting the Republicans are political and military heroes counseled
by Liberty.

the war; they practice "innocence by association" by pointing out that Lincoln was empathetic to striking workers and noting that he was dead by the Age of Grant. The latest study of the wartime Congress downplays the costs of wartime inflation and ignores entirely worker protest against the war and the Republican party. In Heather Richardson's work there are no strikes, no riots, only the Republicans "Unwitting[ly] . . . lay[ing] the groundwork for the turmoil of the late nineteenth century."[21]

But the party would have had to have lost its wits not to see the protests against economic change that went far back into the prewar years and continued through the war. Even before there was a Republican party there had been labor protests against economic changes that accelerated in the 1820s and 1830s. Between 1852 and 1860, six national unions were created. The rise of the Republican party corresponded with the rise of these unions. In February 1860, the largest strike in the nation's history to that time involved 20,000 strikers, men and women. When Republicans said "go west young man" to provide a safety valve against eastern inequality, they knew that some sort of safety valve was necessary. But they were able to direct attention to a greater evil in the public mind—the Slave Power conspiracy.

Still, when the war came there was substantial evidence that workers faced enemies in the North as well as the South. Anyone who read the wartime labor press in New York City surely knew that. Indeed, the labor press itself grew. Between 1863 and 1873, 120 journals appeared. *Fincher's Trades Review* in Philadelphia expanded its circulation from 5,000 in 1863 to 11,000 in 1865, reaching thirty-one of the thirty-five states. William Sylvis of the Iron Workers union protested that the Republicans were passing laws that crushed the workers. Thousands of industrial workers, Sylvis said, were "sunk to a degree of mental, moral and physical wretchedness horrible to contemplate." Meanwhile, the capitalists, "the worst enemies of our race . . . make commerce of the blood and tears of helpless women and merchandize of [their] souls. In the poverty, wretchedness and utter ruin of their helpless victims they see nothing but an accumulation of gold." The number of strikes in New York City escalated during the war, covering trades all over the city. The strikes that Union soldiers crushed surely suggested the costs of the economic juggernaut that the northern economy was forging.[22]

Evidence accumulated that industrialization hurt people. In Massachusetts an investigation into child labor conditions in the state's textile factories revealed children of seven working fourteen hours a day in these mills. In Pennsylvania 22 percent of the textile mill workers were under sixteen. Women workers protested to Lincoln that their wages had been cut and that "We are unable to sustain life for the prices offered by contractors, who fatten on their contracts by grinding immense profits out of the labor of their operatives." There were protests against economic consolidation from the West too. Rural and small-town Democrats decried the consolidation of economic power in the East, forecasting the Granger protests (1867–71) that began only two years after the war. There was evidence that the free-labor system might be creating wage slaves just as slavery created chattel slaves. Just after the war the *New York Times*, in a story on labor discontent, noted that "The capitalists or masters are becoming fewer and stronger and richer. . . . The laborers or slaves are becoming more numerous or weaker and poorer."[23]

Lincoln occasionally could be quoted in sympathy of suffering laborers: "I know the trials and woes of workingmen. I have always felt for them," or "in almost every case of strike I know the men have just cause for complaint." But the party as a whole had less sympathy. When the president in his first annual message warned about "the effort to place *capital* on a equal footing with, if not above *labor*," the House did not refer that section of his message to a committee. It was customary to do so, but Thaddeus Stevens mocked the section by saying "There is no appropriate committee on metaphysics in the House." Of course, the party as a whole could always insist that the economic race was open to the hard-working and strong, could assert honestly that many Republicans themselves had risen from poverty. But there were many signs that the world where they had allegedly made themselves was not as open as it had once been. Reflecting this sentiment, Horace Greeley's *Tribune* often attacked strikers as lazy, and then played its trumps, echoed in practically every party paper, that labor protests were inspired by Democratic disloyalty.[24]

Republicans gained cover also from the fact that many workers in the industrializing economy supported the Republican party, especially during the war. Skilled workers were more likely to be Republicans than unskilled colleagues. One Philadelphia union symbolized many worker feelings in 1861 when it closed its activities with the words, "It having been resolved to enlist with Uncle Sam for the war, this union stands adjourned until either the Union is safe or we are whipped."

Newburyport, Massachusetts, had boiled with labor protest in 1860 and 1862, organizing a dominant "Worker Party" that won elections in those years. But by 1863 Republicans won the city election, and in 1864 no votes at all, zero votes, were cast against Republican candidates. A diverse economy diffused worker protest as did the proclaimed struggle of "free labor" versus the Slave Power.[25]

Not only did Republican economic programs advance under the mantle of winning the war; opposition to that program could be branded disloyalty. The strong temptation was to overestimate and exaggerate the disloyalty of the Democrats. As Jean Baker has shown, Democrats usually voted for military supplies even as they attacked other Republican policies. But Republicans yielded to temptation. They cranked up a propaganda machine led by Philadelphia's Board of Publications of the Union League and New York City's Loyal Publication Society. The two groups produced millions of copies of nearly two hundred pamphlets and shipped them around the country. Most of these pamphlets targeted Democrats as traitors and conspirators.[26]

Republicans had a substantial advantage in that they were able to use government resources to attack Democrats. A report by Judge Advocate General Joseph Holt that came out in 1864 (not coincidentally) declared that at least 500,000 midwestern members of a subversive organization called the "Organization of American Knights" stood ready to undermine the Union war effort. The report vastly overestimated the size and danger of this organization but took pains to designate Democrat anti-war representative Clement Vallandigham as its leader. The report was widely quoted during the 1864 campaign.[27]

Republicans took low as well as high roads to achieve their goals. They used public buildings to distribute party propaganda. "You can hardly go into a public office or store," one Democrat protested, "but you will see . . . [Union League] documents on tables, counters, and even *posted* as handbills." Enforcement of pro-war measures was partisan. The draft system was, among other things, a patronage opportunity. The provost marshal's office, charged with enforcement, was a special Republican preserve. In Iowa, for example, the linkage between party and draft enforcement was so tight that the party central committee assessed provost marshal boards $100 each for the 1864 presidential campaign. Even some Republicans thought this went too far. One wrote to Stanton from Cleveland that the marshals there were "as corrupt as hell." And

"While the Cat is away, the Mice will Play."

About this time a PEACE PARTY is organized who present *little* UNREADY a mansion not "in the skies," but in New York, where his indecision of character is illustrated by the story of the

CARPENTER'S JOB.

Napo. Why did you not cut two openings, as you were directed?

Carp. Why, you see, General, I feared you might come here sometime "taken short," being unable to decide which "hole" to patronise, you might meet with a serious disaster.

Napo. Your explanation is so far satisfactory, I shall recommend you to the President for a Brigadier's commission? But why have you put up that odious picture, in this private room, visited by no one but myself?

Carp. Why, you see, General, that's more of "my strategy." If you are costive at any time, that picture will make you evacuate quicker than anything else.

Figure 3.3. *"While the Cat is away, the Mice will Play"* (n.p., 1864). This scatological and scurrilous handbill was part of the Republican smear campaign ridiculing the Democrats and their candidate in 1864.

some Republicans also criticized Lincoln for being too aggressive against Democrats. When Vallandigham was arrested, Horace Greeley wrote, "Freedom of speech and of the press are rights which like everything else have their limitations. The license of speech and press which men like Vallandigham indulge in calls for the suppression of neither."[28]

Although Republicans outvoted Democrats and at times repressed them, they could never fully suppress them. McClellan's party got 45 percent of the popular vote in the 1864 presidential election. Democratic vote totals went up in some northern states. Both New York and Pennsylvania saw a 56,000-vote increase in each state. In the bloc of states from Connecticut to Illinois the Democrats increased their percentage of the presidential vote from 1860 to 1864. Throughout the wartime North the electoral process burgeoned and continued to churn. In the North overall, the number of voters increased by 3.1 percent between 1860 and 1864, this at a time when thousands of soldiers could not get to ballot boxes. Whatever the protests about the dangers of party in wartime and accusations of Democratic treason, Republican leaders were not able to stifle that opposition; Democrats were not so intimidated that they ceased to campaign.[29]

One reason Democrats stayed vigorous was that Republicans alienated many white workers. Republican emancipation policies had economic consequences. In places like New York City, where lower-class black and white laborers competed for jobs, white workers at least had the psychic wages of believing themselves superior to blacks. But the Republicans' equality agenda—the party's growing interest in emancipation, in civil equality, and in black soldiers—slapped the faces of many lower-class whites, some of whom had lost hope of ever entering the ranks of the shopkeepers and small farmers that Republican economics allegedly favored. The divide between working class and employers that was implicit in Republican ideology continued to grow.

Republicans were passionate partisans during the war. Their propaganda unfairly stigmatized Democrats as traitors. The party also nurtured the development of Gilded Age America, where lower-class workers often paid the price for the prosperity of their employers. And yet overall the party contributed mightily to the profoundly important goals of saving the Union and freeing the slaves, and it did so with the support of large numbers of American voters. We get some idea of that by looking at the election of 1864.

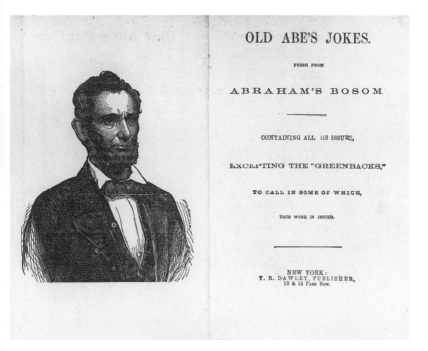

Figure 3.4. *Old Abe's Jokes: Fresh from Abraham Lincoln's Bosom* (New York: T. R. Dawley, Publisher, 1864). Lincoln was well known for his sense of humor and love of jokes. This pamphlet compilation of Lincoln's wit and wisdom helped portray him as the candidate of the common man and, used as a campaign tool, masked his silence on workingmen's rights, civil liberties, conscription, and other divisive issues.

In this election the Republicans more than held their ground with their established constituency. Lincoln and Johnson carried twenty-two of the twenty-five states. Lincoln received 55 percent of the vote from the same places and people who had voted for him four years before. New England again went hugely for Lincoln, although he lost five counties there; in 1860 every New England county had been for Lincoln. The Upper North, settled from New England, also went for Lincoln and his party. The people who voted Republican tended to be native-born and Protestant farmers, professionals, and skilled workers. Democrats won below modern highway 40 in the Older Middle West, areas settled from Dixie, and they won among unskilled workers and immigrant Catholics.

Republicans tended to win in places benefiting from and integrated into the ongoing market revolution; Democrats won where the social costs of industrialization were most obvious. But in this wartime national election clear class divisions were muted. While urban workers in New York and Brooklyn gave McClellan a huge margin in New York City (in New York 73,709 to Lincoln's 36,681, in Brooklyn 25,726 to Lincoln's 20,838), the president carried Philadelphia, the nation's second largest city, 55,791 to McClellan's 44,032. Lincoln also swamped McClellan by 22,318 to 9,597 in Boston. And in nineteen of the twenty largest cities (New Orleans excluded) the Republicans actually did better during the war than before Sumter: in 1860 the party carried eight of the nineteen, in 1864 it carried twelve. Most workers in these cities believed that the party that supported free labor shared their ideals.[30]

What did this Republican victory mean? Consider the consequences of a McClellan victory in '64. If McClellan had won, the promises of emancipation and equality Republicans had made to blacks would have been in jeopardy. The Democratic platform was silent on emancipation. But at that time about one-eighth of all Union soldiers were black, most of them former slaves. These troops were indispensable to the Union. What kind of effort would have to be made to send how many of these men back to slavery? How many black soldiers would there have been after this retreat from equality? Could the Union have continued to fight, could it win without these troops? Did a McClellan victory mean the war was lost? Since Confederates had been praying for the repudiation of Lincoln, would their morale have improved? Would deserters have returned to Confederate armies, swelling their size as Union armies diminished? Is a restored Union imaginable under these circumstances? Of course, it is possible that, given large congressional Republican majorities a President McClellan might have been impeached for retreating, but could a war be fought while an impeachment was underway? Anyway, the Republican party won, and emancipation and Union were won, too.[31] Because Republicans won, they were able to pass along a truly priceless heritage.

Civil War Republicans institutionalized the struggle for equality in the United States. They incorporated abolitionist ideals into the constitutional process that at least two million northerners had fought for. The "government of the people, by the people and for the people" now included within its constitution the end of slavery and promises that states could not deny American citizens life, liberty, property, or the equal protection of the laws. Early Republican laws of 1866 and 1872 even protected freedmen from private discrimination. And they made black people American citizens. The postwar Constitution also stopped racists from using the heritage of slavery as a legal excuse to deny former slaves the vote.

In securing these rights within the Constitution, the Republican party of the war era also made the national government the guarantor of those rights. Most of the states had failed miserably to secure racial justice; "state rights" had been the shibboleth for slavery and oppression. So the Republican-dominated Congress, opposed often bitterly by war-era Democrats, placed at the coda of the three Civil War amendments the words, "Congress shall have the power to enforce this amendment by appropriate legislation." Congress used the momentum of wartime national power to promise a future of equality. That future was a long way off, and it contained the turn that for several years made Democrats, more than Republicans, the civil rights party. But Republicans had begun the process about a century before. And both parties came to see that for some problems government was the solution, not the problem. Equally, post-Civil War blacks quickly recognized that when the era of big government was over, so was protection for their rights.

An inescapable part of emancipation was the exercise of government power. Without national authority, freedmen would have been kept as close to slavery as their former masters could keep them. But the Republican party had other uses for national power. It supported government aid for economic growth, government protection of minority rights, a stronger national government. The party was much more likely than the Democrats to favor expanding rights for women, for minorities. Lincoln's party established a new permanent national government bureau, the Department of Agriculture. It set up for a temporary period (1865–72) the Freedmen's Bureau, which in several ways anticipated the New Deal. The Bureau provided relief for blacks and whites in Dixie who suffered from war's devastation. It helped black veterans of the Union Army, built schools, and provided for courts where minority Americans could claim their rights against their former masters.

The Republican party also used national power to grow a national economy. Although the market and industrial revolutions had been under way for years before the war, the conflict brought national legislation to shape its direction. Republicans were the party of government help, not

Figure 3.5. *On the March to the Sea,* engraving by A. H. Ritchie after F. A. O. Darley (Hartford, Conn.: L. Stebbins, 1868). General William Tecumseh Sherman promised Lincoln he would "make Georgia howl." Sherman's capture of Atlanta and subsequent "March to the Sea" not only carried the war directly to southern civilians but also secured Lincoln's reelection. During the war, military success decided elections and superseded all other issues, save perhaps emancipation.

government regulations. There was no national regulatory agency before 1887 (twenty years after the war). But inspired by war necessity, Republican support nurtured national economic growth. The Pacific railroad, the national banking system, the Homestead Act, the federal income tax, a national currency, land grant universities, protective tariffs—all provided federal support for economic choices resting on expansion into (and exploitation of) western and eastern resources. War necessity energized and justified these actions and made Republicans the midwives of a modern America.

It wasn't all roses. Republicans also midwifed the social costs of this new economy. Urban workers increasingly lost control of their economic destiny; Native Americans were swept brutally off their homelands (a policy that Democrats rarely protested). Perhaps one can argue that, in the long run, this economic growth capitalized job creation and new opportunities. But the labor violence of the late nineteenth century came

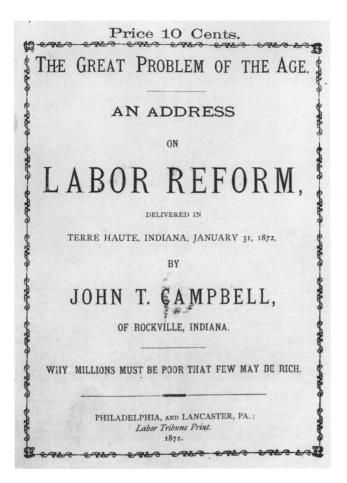

Price 10 Cents.

THE GREAT PROBLEM OF THE AGE.

AN ADDRESS

ON

LABOR REFORM,

DELIVERED IN

TERRE HAUTE, INDIANA, JANUARY 31, 1872,

BY

JOHN T. CAMPBELL,

OF ROCKVILLE, INDIANA.

WHY MILLIONS MUST BE POOR THAT FEW MAY BE RICH.

PHILADELPHIA, AND LANCASTER, PA.:
Labor Tribune Print.
1872.

Figure 3.6. John T. Campbell, *The Great Problem of the Age.
An Address on Labor Reform, Delivered in Terre Haute, Indiana,
January 31, 1872. Why Millions Must be Poor that Few May
be Rich* (Philadelphia and Lancaster: Labor Tribune, Print.,
1872). After the war, the major parties' preoccupation with
Reconstruction, race, railroads, and even reform of the political
system left laboring men and women and others feeling
abandoned in an age of intense political consciousness. Third
parties sprang up to address particular needs ignored by the
major parties. In 1872 the Labor Reform party organized to
"fight monopolies" and defend labor's interest—a harbinger of
the shift to economic issues that would drive politics by the
end of the century.

from workers who were hardly placated by hypothetical benefits to future generations. Farmers who saw railroads, eastern bankers, and market middlemen as unbridled masters of the agrarian world also could thank Republicans for their fate.

These challenges to Republican hegemony were rebutted by reviving war memories. Indeed, the party waved the bloody shirt for years to enlist and energize its base.[32] Blacks benefited immensely from this sanguinary flag because the Republican party was their sole protector. But labor protestors lost power when the war was recollected. They were tarred as the revived mobs who had challenged the Union and brutalized and murdered its defenders. Agrarian protest could be painted as the echo of Copperhead defiance spawned while loyal young men had gone off to war.[33]

But the power of Republican defenses and rebuttals arose from what had been accomplished during the great Civil War. Those accomplishments were immense: a restored and now permanent Union, the salvation of the political process, and the emancipation of over 4 million men, women, and children.

If we believe that saving the Union and its political-constitutional processes and freeing the slaves were two of the nation's greatest triumphs, perhaps it is not out of line to see the Civil War as the Republican party's finest hour. To put it more cynically, quoting Senator Fessenden, "So far as the Republican party is concerned, the war [was] a godsend."[34] Maybe not just for the Republicans.

The Genesis and Growth of the Republican Party: A Brief History

In the mid-nineteenth century the old political party system fell apart and a new one arose. Slavery was the issue, freedom the cause that led many northerners in the 1850s to seek a new political home in the Republican party, an unlikely melange of former Whigs, Democrats, nativists, Free Soilers, and others who agreed only on "no further extension of slavery into the territories." When southerners seceded from the Union rather than accept a Republican presidential victory in 1860, civil war came. The new party became the "majority" party, for the moment, as it waged war to save the Union and, then, to end slavery. Republicans also enacted legislation that expanded freedom by opening the West and providing land and learning for its settlers. Defining freedom in political, economic, and even social terms became the great challenge of the Republican party, and the country, during Reconstruction after the war. Both blacks and women demanded inclusion in the reconstructed nation. By 1872 the first generation of Republicans was passing from the scene, weary of wrangling over issues of who got the franchise and the rewards of office. A new generation assumed the stage dedicated to building the nation and the party in support of commerce and industry rather than Reconstruction. Such in brief is the "history" of the first generation of the Republican party.

The Republican party was born in the hothouse of sectional politics in the 1850s. It sprang from several sources that became bound together to fight a common cause, even as they disagreed among themselves on other issues. That cause was checking slavery's advance. That time was a period when many northerners were growing frustrated with

Figure 1. "Republican Convention—Announcement of the Nominations at Musical Fund Hall, Philadelphia," *Frank Leslie's Illustrated Newspaper*, July 5, 1856.

southerners' dominance of the federal government, much, they thought, to northern economic disadvantage, and with gasconading politicians threatening disunion unless they had their way on the slavery issue. But the slavery question proved ever less negotiable and ever more volatile. It consumed all political discussion and forced people to choose sides. Once Americans became engaged in the question they could not escape it. Events forced a rapid reordering of political loyalties. The Compromise of 1850, with its Fugitive Slave Act, led many northerners to fear the southern "Slavocracy," which threatened the liberties of free whites. The Kansas-Nebraska Act of 1854 evoked an instant chorus of protest, fractured political alliances and a Whig party already straining over sectional divisions, led to the bloody Kansas conflict that would dominate the rest of the decade, and gave rise to a new political force, the Republican party.

Promising free soil, free speech, free labor, and free men, in 1856 the Republicans nominated their first presidential candidate, John C. Frémont,

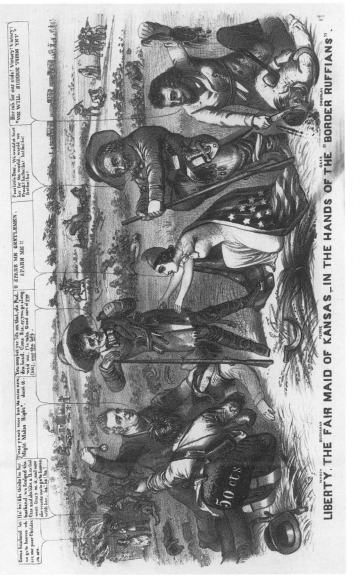

Figure 2. *Liberty, the Fair Maid of Kansas—In the Hands of the "Border Ruffians"*, lithograph (n.p., 1856). Free soil advocates and Republicans used images of Democrats raping and plundering a virgin Kansas, shown here as a flag-draped woman, to stir outrage over slavery's advance into "free territory."

the "Pathfinder." Although the Republicans lost the presidential contest, the Frémont ticket carried eleven free states and Republicans won many seats in state legislatures and Congress. As such, the Republicans, though almost wholly a sectional party, emerged as the major opposition party to the Democrats and seemed poised to win the White House in 1860 should they hold onto their gains of 1856 and take Pennsylvania and either Indiana or Illinois.

Sectional turmoil increased after 1856. Civil War broke out in Kansas, and violence erupted in Congress when Preston Brooks, a U.S. representative from South Carolina, caned Senator Charles Sumner of Massachusetts for his verbal assaults on southern honor and integrity amid the Kansas troubles. The 1857 *Dred Scott* decision by the Supreme Court threatened to expand slavery throughout the Union, or so Republicans charged. Abraham Lincoln's "House Divided" speech echoed earlier warnings of an "irrepressible conflict" over slavery. In 1859 John Brown's raid convinced white southerners that "black abolition" had taken over the North and that secession was inevitable if the Republicans ever took national power. Amid the frenzied, and constant, political agitation and crises of the 1850s, Americans had little time to reflect dispassionately on issues, and men seeking public office inflamed sectional feelings as a sure way to get attention, and votes.

In 1860 the slavery issue tore apart the Democratic party along sectional lines, almost assuring Republican victory, but also making disunion a likely prospect. The Democrats were the last national institution in the country that appealed to people across sectional lines. The principal Protestant churches had split over slavery and doctrinal issues, and sectional suspicions weakened intersectional comity and commerce. Republicans seized the moment. Sensing the chance for national power, moderate Republicans pushed through Lincoln's nomination and presented a party platform emphasizing economic progress more than attacks on the slave power. In the ensuing campaign, Republicans exploited Lincoln's log cabin origins and image as a rail-splitting yeoman to underscore the party's free-labor principles. Democrats, in turn, warned that social chaos and disunion would follow a "Black Republican" win. When Lincoln was elected, "fire-eating" secessionists in seven states in the deep South made good their threat to leave the Union rather than submit to Republican rule.

When the southern states left the Union in 1860–61, the Republicans

SOUTHERN CHIVALRY—ARGUMENT versus CLUB'S.

Figure 3. *Southern Chivalry—Argument versus Club's*, lithograph (Philadelphia: John L. Magee, 1856). While seated at his desk in the Senate Chamber franking copies of his "Crime Against Kansas" speech, Massachusetts senator Charles Sumner was attacked and beaten by South Carolina representative Preston Brooks. Republicans pointed to the incident as evidence of slavocracy's tyranny and threats to free speech.

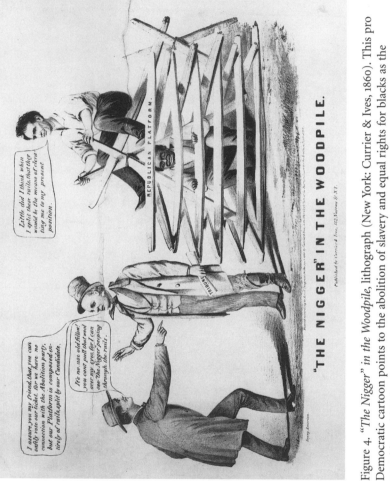

Figure 4. *"The Nigger" in the Woodpile*, lithograph (New York: Currier & Ives, 1860). This pro Democratic cartoon points to the abolition of slavery and equal rights for blacks as the Republicans' hidden agenda.

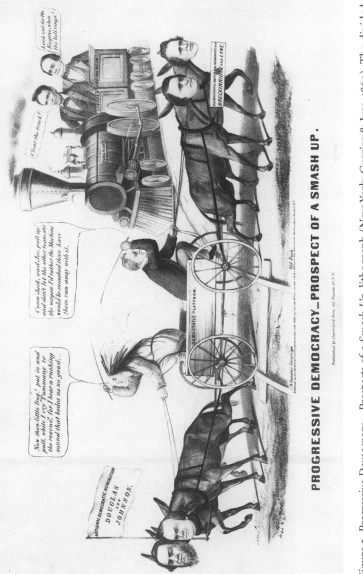

Figure 5. *Progressive Democracy—Prospects of a Smash Up*, lithograph (New York: Currier & Ives, 1860). The divided Democrats face a united Republican opposition on its way to certain victory.

immediately became the majority party in the new Congress that assembled in March 1861. Compromise failed to reverse the secession of the deep southern states; the firing on Fort Sumter brought civil war, and Lincoln's call for troops to suppress the rebellion caused the secession of four more southern states. Although Lincoln, as war president, reached out to Democrats and Republicans alike to rally support for the Union cause, Republicans in Congress moved to enact the various parts of the 1860 Republican platform promises to provide more freedom for economic and social mobility to white Americans, some of which proposals had been blocked by Democratic majorities in the 1850s. Congress approved the route and funding of the transcontinental railroad; revised the tariff to promote industry and protect the working man; reformed the currency and banking system to facilitate commerce; and imposed new taxes to finance the war.

But the war dragged on, and Republican fortunes were hitched to military success in the field as much as legislation in Congress or state assemblies. Radical Republicans and black and white abolitionists pressed Lincoln to convert the war to save the Union into a war to end slavery and expand freedom. Slaves fleeing bondage by running away to Union lines further forced the slavery issue on the nation. Military necessity soon led Lincoln to accept blacks offering their services to the cause. By the summer of 1862, Lincoln believed that the time had come when "slavery must die so that the Union might live." Emancipation, though, cost Republicans at the polls. Democrats charged them with the double tyranny of promoting racial mixing and suppressing Democrats' civil liberties during the war. But the bravery of black troops temporarily silenced many critics of black freedom, though it did not deliver Republican victories in local elections in 1863 and 1864.

The drawn-out war seemed never to end. Mounting casualty rates, political losses due to Republican emancipation policy and war measures, and public doubts about Lincoln's leadership haunted the party. Fearing they might lose the 1864 elections. Republicans recast themselves as the National Union Party and nominated Tennessee Democrat Andrew Johnson as vice president to court a broader "Union" constituency. They also enlisted military heroes to thump for the Lincoln ticket and used every means of propaganda and mass rallies to build support for the cause and the party.

PRESIDENTIAL COBBLERS AND WIRE-PULLERS MEASURING AND ESTIMATING LINCOLN'S SHOES.
INCLUDING BENNETT, HUDSON, GREELEY, RAYMOND, WEED, SEWARD BROOKS, SUMNER, FORNEY, AND MISS ANNA DICKINSON

Figure 6. "Presidential Cobblers and Wire-Pullers Measuring and Estimating Lincoln's Shoes," *New York Illustrated News*, March 5, 1864. Lincoln's Lilliputian Republican critics measure his shoes in their hunt for a replacement candidate. The cartoon illustrates the power of the press: eight of the figures identified are newspaper publishers, along with William Henry Seward, Charles Sumner, and the popular antislavery orator Anna Dickinson.

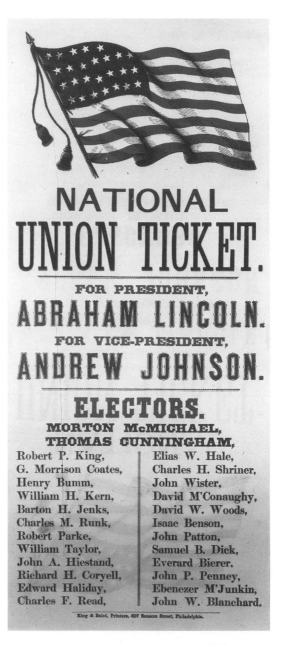

Figure 7. *National Union Ticket,* poster (Philadelphia: King & Baird Printers, 1864).

The Democrats named General George McClellan as their presidential candidate and ran him on a supposed "peace platform." While the Democrats beat up Republicans on the issues of civil liberties and race, the Republicans charged the Democrats with selling out to the Confederacy and giving up on the brave Union soldiers. Getting out the soldier vote proved crucial to Republican success. So, too, did timely victories on the battlefield, especially General William Tecumseh Sherman's taking of Atlanta. In the afterglow of Sherman's "March to the Sea" and Confederate reverses, Lincoln won reelection and Republicans held on to key governorships and state legislatures across the North. But the Republican triumph at the polls and the Union one on the battlefield ended in gloom when Lincoln was assassinated soon after his second inauguration. What to do about reconstructing the defeated South remained unanswered at his death. With the meaning of northern victory, southern defeat, and black freedom all in doubt, the Republicans, and the nation, confronted Reconstruction.

With the war over, Americans were forced to define what the expanded freedom resulting from black emancipation meant in law and practice. At the national level, Republicans fought for ratification of the Thirteenth Amendment, which ended slavery, and, in its enabling clause, empowered Congress "to enforce this article by appropriate legislation"— to define freedom. But the Republican definitions of freedom coming from Congress waited on Andrew Johnson, the new president and lifelong Democrat until his support for the "Union" ticket in 1864.

Johnson ignored the Republican party's needs and interests and initiated a policy of easy restoration for the former Confederate states that resulted in white rule, "black codes" severely restricting the freedpeople's civil rights and economic opportunity, and violence directed at Unionists and blacks in the South. The "unreconstructed" South's intransigence angered those Republicans who demanded control of Reconstruction for reasons of principle and party. At minimum, they wanted to extend Republican beliefs into the South and secure basic rights to the freedpeople. And they wanted the chance to build Republican strength in the South before the former Confederate states returned to Congress with their representation increased because of the abolition of slavery. Blacks, meanwhile, rushed to define freedom for themselves. They founded churches, started schools, gathered in conventions to lobby for basic civil rights, and bargained for the best labor arrangements possible.

Figure 8. "Andrew Johnson's Reconstruction, And How It Works," *Harper's Weekly*, September 11, 1866. Republicans criticized Johnson for failing to protect freedpeople's basic rights and for restoring former Confederates to power in an as yet unreconstructed South.

Once Congress reconvened in December 1865, Republicans began drafting their own Reconstruction policy, which was premised on the belief that federal intervention in southern affairs would be temporary and that, with basic freedoms established, the freedpeople would be accountable for their own work and lives. The Civil Rights Act, the Freedmen's Bureau bill, and the Fourteenth Amendment, which defined citizenship to include the freedpeople and guaranteed the equal protection of the laws, summed up the definitions of freedom and federal obligations for most Republicans—in 1866.

Johnson blocked Republican Reconstruction at every turn, campaigned against the Fourteenth Amendment, and accused the Republicans of "treason" for their attacks on him and their efforts to enfranchise blacks and "force" Republican principles on the South. Democrats rallied to Johnson's side, and Johnson and his supporters claimed the "Union" label in 1866 by seizing control of the National Union Party. Johnson's policies forced erstwhile "Union" Republicans to become more Republican. The issue shifted from "Union" to Reconstruction. When Johnson persisted in undercutting congressional will, Republicans impeached him for abuse of power in 1868. He escaped conviction by one vote, but was chastened enough to end his obstructionism. Finally, Republican Reconstruction might be implemented.

Americans did not wait on the president or Congress to define freedom for them in the postwar period. Emancipation had unleashed hopes for expanded freedom across America. Reformers hitched the freedom struggle in the South directly to struggles in the North, arguing that equal rights should know no bounds. The contagion of liberty that grew from the freedom struggle of the antislavery movement in the 1830s, and the rise of the Republican party in the 1850s, gained new energy and purpose during and after the war. Equal rights before the law now meant breaking down discriminatory laws and practices that kept blacks from equal access to public transportation and accommodations and to the ballot box. It also spread to include the idea of universal, or impartial, suffrage. Women, too, insisted on the vote. The freedom, or Reconstruction, amendments—the Thirteenth, Fourteenth, and Fifteenth—charted the direction and dimensions of those freedoms for the nation. But, as women discovered when they were left out of specific enfranchisement provisions in the law, securing their own freedom to vote and participate more fully in public affairs would demand further organization and

Figure 9. "Pardon . . . Franchise. Shall I Trust These Men and Not This Man?"
Harper's Weekly, August 5, 1865. The question of black enfranchisement and
the disfranchisement, and reenfranchisement, of former Confederates
defined political categories in Reconstruction.

FRANCHISE.

"AND NOT THIS MAN?"

HOW IT WOULD BE, IF SOME LADIES HAD THEIR OWN WAY.

Figure 10. "How It Would Be, If Some Ladies Had Their Own Way," *Harper's Weekly*, May 16, 1868. Women reformers seeking the vote in freedom's ferment after the war faced ridicule as well as political opposition. Many critics of woman's suffrage mocked women's aspiration by suggesting the enfranchisement of women would "de-sex" both men and women.

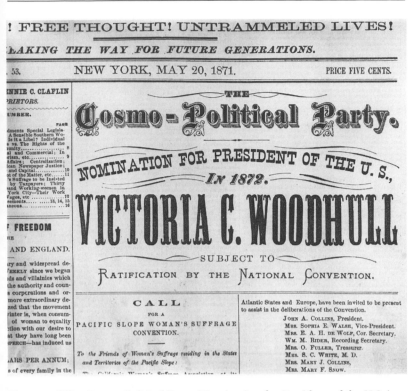

Figure 11. "The Cosmo-Political Party, Nomination for President of the U.S. in 1872. Victoria C. Woodhull," *Woodhull & Claflin's Weekly*, May 20, 1871. Failing to get support from Republicans, woman's suffrage advocates organized their own lobbies and, in the case of radical women's rights agitator Victoria Woodhull, launched a presidential campaign in 1871. Although Woodhull's campaign collapsed before the 1872 election, her candidacy and woman's suffrage lobbying kept the issue before the public.

persistent struggle. Native Americans continued to be excluded from the body politic of the Constitution. Chinese immigrants were denied citizenship, although their children born in the U.S. were deemed citizens. Freedom's bounds remained contested and confused.

The meaning of emancipation and the Civil War was immediately relevant to the "reconstructing" efforts in the postwar South. What happened there also had a profound effect on expectations and definitions of freedom elsewhere. Crucial to the process of rebuilding the South and defining freedom in the South was restoring, and maintaining, law and order and opening the political process to others than former Confederates and Democrats. Republican efforts to secure a place in a "new South" were short-lived and bitterly opposed. The Republican governments that came to power following black enfranchisement rested, one observer wrote, on a "three-legged stool" of "carpetbaggers, scalawags, and Negroes"—an unsteady alliance of northerners who had come south, native white southerners (mostly Unionists and former Whigs), and freedmen in which whites controlled the party and the governments but depended on black votes.

The Republicans in office tried to build a "new South" by underwriting railroad construction, establishing public school systems, reforming tax codes, and promoting industry and agriculture. The increased costs of government, and the inexperience of so many new men in office, led to Democrats charging Republicans with incompetence, injustice, and corruption. But more than anything else, conservative whites used the presence of blacks as voters and officeholders as proof that Republican governments were illegitimate and justified any means to overthrow them.

The rise of and widespread support for the Ku Klux Klan revealed the extent to which white southerners endorsed violence as the final say as to who should rule. The governments begged for federal intervention, but the Republican mantra of the Grant administration, elected in 1868 in part on a promise of bringing order to the troubled postwar world, was "let us have peace." And by 1868 many northerners had tired of Reconstruction and had turned to concerns about the emerging new industrial order. Southern Republicans were left to themselves. The combination of northern apathy and southern white terrorism toppled Republican regimes across the South.

For the Republican party the postwar period became a time of internal party reassessment and realignment. The party in power groaned under the tugs of competing interests, which often revealed the resurfacing of antebellum identities. Thus, for example, low-tariff former Democrats tilted against high-tariff former Whigs. And patronage quarrels wracked the party at every level. Also the enforced unity of purpose Johnson's and the unreconstructed South's intransigence had given Republicans from 1866 to 1868 was lost once Johnson was out of office and Republican Reconstruction was finally instituted in the South. Democrats capitalized on Republicans' internal problems and on whites' fears about race and

"THIS IS A WHITE MAN'S GOVERNMENT."

" We regard the Reconstruction Acts (so called) of Congress as usurpations, and unconstitutional, revolutionary, and void."—*Democratic Platform.*

Figure 12. "This Is a White Man's Government," *Harper's Weekly*, September 28, 1868. In a typical Republican campaign image linking Democrats with lawlessness, disunion, and threats to laboring classes, this Thomas Nast cartoon caricatures an unholy alliance of Democrats—a violent Irishmen from the 1863 draft riots, an unrepentant southern rebel, and a New York capitalist standing united over the body of a black man.

the industrial economy. The Republicans struggled to keep their house in order.

Stung by a string of defeats in northern state elections in 1867 and embarrassed by the failed impeachment of Johnson, Republicans wanted a certain winner in 1868. They nominated Ulysses S. Grant, the hero of Appomattox. Deflecting accusations of corruption and favoritism toward blacks, Republicans ran on Grant's reputation of personal honesty and courage. They also discovered they could get more votes by tarring Democrats as disloyal than by discussing substantive issues. Grant won, but without the votes of newly enfranchised blacks in key states he would have lost. That reality moved the party to embrace national black suffrage, which the Fifteenth Amendment was intended to provide.

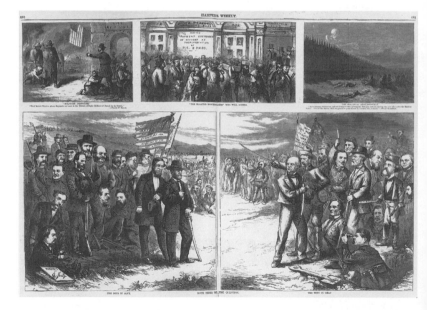

Figure 13. "Both Sides of the Question. The Boys in Blue. The Boys in Gray," *Harper's Weekly*, October 24, 1868. Although Grant campaigned on the slogan "Let us have Peace," the Republican campaign "waved the bloody shirt" of Civil War passion, denouncing the Democrats as traitors. In this cartoon, Democratic presidential candidate Horatio Seymour and his running mate are allied with the resurgent rebels against Grant and Henry Wilson, who are supported by Union forces.

THE REPUBLIC ON THE BRINK

U. S. G.—"*Push her off, boys. I'll kick this thing over. We must have things our own way.*"

Figure 14. "The Republic on the Brink," *Frank Leslie's Illustrated Newspaper*, November 9, 1872. Grant won handily in 1872, getting 286 Electoral College votes against 63 for all his opponents and none for Greeley. The defeated reformers likened Grant's victory to the burial of honest government, claiming that ballot-stuffing and machine politics delivered the vote to Grant and his allies but gave them a dubious claim to legitimacy. Whatever divisions persisted among Republicans over government ethics and obligations to extend and protect freedom in the South or elsewhere, among several divisive issues, the 1872 election marked the coming of age of the Republican party. A new generation of Republicans, in many cases indifferent to the reform interests of the party's founding generation, stood ready to take command.

In 1872 one wing of the Republican party, the "Stalwarts," renominated Grant. Disaffected members of the party, calling themselves "Liberal Republicans," angered by scandals in the Grant administration and the disarray of Republican governments in the South, broke from the party and nominated Horace Greeley, editor and former abolitionist, on a separate Liberal Republican ticket. The Democrats, still disorganized from their 1868 defeat, could do no better than endorse Greeley. The Stalwarts denounced Greeley as an apostate and distracted voters from Republican wrongdoing by "waving the bloody shirt," painting the Democrats as the party of treason and Republicans as saviors of the Union. Grant and the Stalwarts won overwhelmingly, without the need for the black vote.

Thereafter, Republicans turned away from Reconstruction and toward business capitalism. And coming into office and control of party machinery were new men, with new interests, who had not fought the early battles for Republicanism and "a new birth of freedom." The party's abandonment of the remaining Republican governments in the South in order to win the 1876 election was the most obvious indication of a new tack. Despite continued internal strains and stiff opposition from Democrats, which, though, also served to keep Republicans together during elections just to stay in power, the Republican party was firmly established. It had a history and party faithful. It was accustomed to power, and it had the infrastructure and machinery to stay in power. Indeed, the one-time sectional party remained the dominant party in the national government for much of the next half-century. It was now the "Grand Old Party."

CHAPTER FOUR

Politics Purified: Religion and the Growth of Antislavery Idealism in Republican Ideology During the Civil War

Mark E. Neely, Jr.

In the aftermath of the shocking defeat at the Battle of Bull Run in the summer of 1861, Republicans found it difficult to take a philosophically long view of the country's situation. It helped, of course, to live far to the north of the nation's capital and not to witness the frightening and humiliating arrival of the panicked and rain-soaked Union soldiers who had thrown their shiny new equipment away to speed their flight from the victorious rebel army. But Republican members of Congress, present for a special session called by the president to pass essential war legislation, recognized the threat posed by the Confederate victory to the perilous loyalty of the border slave states and hastened to reassure them that they had no designs on the institution of slavery.

Seemingly as stampeded as the pathetic Union soldiers pouring in from Virginia, members of the House of Representatives voted 117 to 2 (and the Senate 30 to 5) for what came to be called the "Crittenden Resolution," declaring:

> That the present deplorable civil war has been forced upon the country by the disunionists of the southern States, now in arms against the constitutional Government, and in arms around the capital; that in this national emergency, Congress, banishing all feelings of mere passion or resentment, will recollect only its duty to the whole country; that this war is not waged on their part in any spirit of oppression, or for any purpose of conquest or subjugation, nor for the purpose of overthrowing or interfering with the rights or established institutions of those States, but to defend and maintain

the *supremacy* of the Constitution, and to preserve the Union with all the dignity, equality, and rights of the several States unimpaired; and that as soon as these objects are accomplished the war ought to cease.[1]

Republicans owned great majorities in Congress, so the vote represented a cringingly practical party sentiment for them.

In Boston, on the other hand, New England's intellectuals could afford to take a longer view of the situation, and Charles Eliot Norton, for one, did. In an important article written quickly for the *Atlantic Monthly*, Norton attempted to convince his readers of "The Advantages of Defeat," not something easily appreciated in Congress with "disunionists . . . in arms around the capital," as the Crittenden Resolution so vividly expressed it. Norton could frame the Battle of Bull Run as an incident in a greater struggle:

> God has given us work to do not only for ourselves, but for coming generations of men. . . . We are fairly engaged in a war which cannot be a short one, even though our enemies should before long lay down their arms; for it is a war not merely to support and defend the Constitution and to retake the property of the United States, not merely to settle the question of the right of a majority to control an insolent and rebellious minority in the republic, nor to establish the fact of the national existence and historic unity of the United States; but it is also and more essentially a war for the establishment of civilization in that immense portion of our country in which for many years barbarism has been gaining power. It is for the establishment of liberty and justice, of freedom of conscience and liberty of thought, of equal law and personal rights, throughout the South. If these are not to be secured without the abolition of slavery, it is a war for the abolition of slavery. We are not making war to reestablish an old order of things, but to set up a new one.[2]

By pointing to God's mission in the war, Norton echoed the message some northern clergymen had been asserting for months. Thus Henry Whitney Bellows, pastor of All Souls' Church in New York, had preached an immediately popular sermon less than two weeks after the fall of Fort Sumter, published in pamphlet form as *The State and the Nation—Sacred to Christian Citizens*. It was "important to understand," Bellows said, "that the contest before us is one in which some long-rooted and deeply-bedded errors fatal to our peace, our national morals, our religion and our power and prosperity, are to be exterminated—it may be with bloody hands." "It is no longer to be said with bated breath only," he added, invoking an old Free Soil political slogan, "Freedom is national, Slavery is sectional; that is to be thundered with constitutional cannon upon the deaf and deluded ears of those who have refused to listen to the ballot-box."[3] He characterized the rebellion as one "against the Ballot-box, the most sacred possession of modern civilization." "The ballot-box is more vital to our interests as Americans," he insisted, "than mints and forts and bank-vaults and treasuries and armories." He had quickly stirred nationalism, antislavery sentiment, and the principle of majority rule into a fervent patriotism inseparable from religious duty. Bellows maintained his emphasis on "reform" when he learned of the results from Bull Run some three months later. He insisted that the battlefield defeat was a "moral necessity" that alone "could thoroughly arouse the country to the efforts, the reforms, and the spirit essential to the proper and vigorous conduct of this war."[4]

When I read Norton's famous article and Bellows's sermon in preparation for this essay, I was surprised to see the direction that they took—toward revolution and reform and away from the shortsighted concern of the Crittenden Resolution merely with saving the Union—because the reigning interpretation of ideology in the North during the Civil War indicated the opposite.[5] Historian George M. Fredrickson in his influential book *The Inner Civil War: Northern Intellectuals and the Crisis of the Union*, where I first learned about Norton's *Atlantic Monthly* article and about Bellows's sermon, depicted Norton's work as that of an "exuberant conservative" who was "[s]triking at the humanitarian reformers" and Bellows's as that of a man with a "basic distrust of democracy."[6]

We know that in the end the Republican party followed the course predicted by Norton and Bellows and not by the Crittenden Resolution, and such a development seems more easily explained if the influential clergymen of the North were not preaching against humanitarianism and democracy. Indeed, one of the persistent questions raised by the party's early history is how did radicalism triumph during the war?

The presence, power, and growth of the radical wing of the Republican party have attracted attention for decades. In past times, the central drama of the political history of the North during the war has been depicted as a struggle between President Lincoln and the radicals in Congress.[7] In more recent writing on the subject, with the agenda of the Radical Republicans—emancipation, African American soldiers, and confiscation—looking more attractive to modern historians, there has been a tendency to draw the president and the radical wing of his party closer together, and to contrast their ideology more sharply with that of the Democratic party.[8] Biographies of conservative Republicans, thus, remain scarce, whereas the Radical Republican Salmon P. Chase has benefited from revisionist interpretation and from a major archival project.[9]

The problem of Republican history during the war arises from our knowledge of the prewar history of the party and from established models of party behavior. We know that, despite the eventual triumph of radicalism during the Civil War, racism among northern white voters had strictly restrained Republican radicalism in the antebellum period. We know, too, that the logic of party competition in a vigorous two-party system should be to adopt moderate platforms and to drive ideologies toward the center.[10] Noting the persistence of two-party competition in the North has become one of the salient features of Civil War history as written since the 1960s.[11] During the war, nevertheless, the radical antislavery platform of the party triumphed among the same northern electorate, essentially, and with more or less the same voters going to the polls as eagerly and, to judge by the continuing competitiveness of the parties, from the same motives. How can that be?

The answer to this large and longstanding question cannot be provided in an essay of the length allotted here. But it should constitute a key part of the enterprise of writing on the Republican party during the Civil War to help explain the triumph of radicalism—its origins and the sources of its strength and growth despite the prejudices of the northern electorate and despite the normal dynamics of two-party competition.

We do not know exactly what happened in the Republican party during the war for two principal reasons. One is that Eric Foner's definitive study of Republican ideology, *Free Soil, Free Labor, Free Men: The Ideology of the Republican Party Before the Civil War*, ends in 1860. Foner's widely accepted scheme has never been systematically extended to the war period. The other reason is that, in lieu of such direct study of Republican ideology during the war, the description of northern political and social ideas developed a generation ago by George Fredrickson—on which I had to rely for key sources at the beginning of this essay—has quietly held sway. But Fredrickson's scheme, however accurate it might be for explaining intellectuals in the North, does not and cannot explain political ideology as well.

What *The Inner Civil War* tells us about dominant ideas in the North during the war is essentially this: an easy and uncritical identification with government and even military authority grew among intellectuals. Fredrickson maintained that intellectuals generally supported the government by forging what he called "the Doctrine of Loyalty." He depicted the war as a moment of crisis seized on by clergymen and other professional men to assert authoritarian ideas that would counter trends toward individualism and democracy in American society with which they had long been uneasy.

But if we examine the sources anew, documents like Norton's article and Bellows's sermon hold surprises for which *The Inner Civil War* does not prepare us. Characterized there as an argument that pioneered a "tough-minded" Darwinian view of war and "a formidable weapon against philanthropy and reform," Norton's "Advantages of Defeat" in fact contained many traditional, even chivalric sentiments. Steeling northerners for the necessary cruelties of war and sacrifice of life, Norton was nevertheless careful to point out that the North was not motivated by "vindictiveness," that this was "a religious war," and that it could therefore "be waged only mercifully, with no excess, with no circumstance of avoidable suffering." Finally, he said, "Though the science of war has in modern times changed the relations and the duties of men on the battlefield from what they were in the old days of knighthood, yet there is still room for the display of stainless valor and of manful virtue." And among the model soldiers he mentioned were Lancelot and Bayard.[12]

As for the Unitarian minister Bellows, he appears throughout *The Inner Civil War* as one of "those intellectual figures within the Republican camp who had least sympathy with the party's strain of humanitarian idealism" and who "looked forward to a war which would re-establish the rights of authority."[13] His sermon on *The State and the Nation*, Fredrickson maintained, hinted "at the supreme heresy—the idea that all recognized nationalities and established governments rest on the same solid religious basis as that of the United States. He spoke of nationalism as 'sublimely . . . exhibiting itself' in Czarist Russia."[14] In fact, however, Bellows argued a different point altogether. In calling his congregants to the defense of the nation, he carefully pointed out that "In the old world, . . . nationality—always and under all circumstances beautiful and glorious—has been more or less in rivalry with civil liberty." But times had changed, and "Russia has just achieved undying glory, by an

THE BATTLE OF ANTIETAM. MD. SEP? 17ᵀᴴ 1862.

Figure 4.1. *The Battle of Antietam, Md. Sept. 7th 1862*, colored lithograph (New York: Currier & Ives, 1862). The Battle of Antietam, in which Union forces stopped Lee's northern advance and from which a victory-starved Union gained a much-needed boost in confidence, encouraged Lincoln to issue his preliminary emancipation proclamation on September 22, to take effect on January 1, 1863. However much pressed for by abolitionists and many Republicans, the Emancipation Proclamation hitched the party to the promise of freedom and opened it to charges of favoring black interests over white, which Democrats exploited ruthlessly in nakedly racist appeals to northern white voters.

act surpassing even British emancipation in courage and fidelity to conscience. Her splendid enfranchisement of the serfs is perhaps the greatest tribute ever paid by a natiosn to moral convictions." Though often thought of as a "barbarous people," the Russians had now "laid down the intoxicating but corrupting and damning pride of *man-owning*, at the feet of a Christian throne."[15] The lesson for American nationality was surely lost on no one sitting in a pew in All Souls' Church.

*   *   *

It is time to recognize that the Civil War was liberating and not notable for its conservative effects on northern Republicans. Republicans could not have moved from the Crittenden Resolution to the Thirteenth

Amendment in three years if the increasingly dominant ideas in the North undermined humanitarianism and democracy. We need not only to reinterpret the arguments of the northern intellectuals but also to find the ideas and organizations that helped steer the Republicans from the conservatism of the Crittenden Resolution to the triumph of their radical wing. This essay will focus on some of the leading indicators of advanced public opinion—heretofore neglected by historians—that reached the Republican president. These sources, religious in origin, suggest that Republicans, once the border states were secure after the summer of 1862, quickly caught up to the idea of a religious war glimpsed in Norton's and Bellows's early statements of war aims.

Lincoln sampled many sources of public opinion in his office. He read newspapers and felt the sting of their criticisms of administration policy. Politicians from all over the country corresponded with him and visited him. And he received mail from groups not as closely tied to the Republican electioneering organization. Much of it was aimed at proving to Lincoln that Norton's contention was right: he was embarked on a "religious" war.

As the editors of the *New York Times* put it in 1864, it was "a most significant thing that the religious and moral element of the nation is precisely the element which is strongest for the war."[16] It frustrated the leaders of powerful denominations in the country that this support seemed to go unacknowledged by the Republicans. Thus the Reverend George H. Hepworth of Boston pointed out to the president in October 1864, "You have never said it is a very significant fact that the American Clergy are as loyal as their ancestors. The exceptions are very rare. The men whose professions lead them to take the highest view of national affairs, are, with an unanimity that is very significant, on your side because they believe that you are on God's side."[17] In fact, by that election autumn of 1864, many Protestant denominations had made abundant efforts to be sure the president knew they were on his side and what he must do to remain on God's side.

We are no better prepared to appreciate these surprising expressions of religious patriotism than we were for the revolutionary meaning of Charles Eliot Norton's article, for the reigning paradigm of interpretation causes us to expect from the clergy's call to battle what we were told to expect from the other intellectuals in the North: conservative authoritarianism.

George M. Fredrickson naturally featured Protestant clergymen like Henry Whitney Bellows among the prominent and representative intellectuals he studied, and what he wrote about the rise of Protestant patriotism in *The Inner Civil War* focused on its reactionary and authoritarian message. James H. Moorhead's *American Apocalypse: Yankee Protestants and the Civil War, 1860–1869* focused directly on the clergy, but his argument was by his own admission "indebted to that of George Fredrickson."[18] Moorhead generally found in the doctrines of the Protestant clergy in the North "an authoritarian note inimical to free institutions."[19] And Fredrickson has himself returned to his subject in recent years, also focusing directly on the religious response of the North to the Civil War.[20] He reiterated his earlier position, maintaining that the movement to support the government in the war constituted essentially a conservative coup by an elite profession, the clergy.

To Fredrickson, the "sympathy of recent historians for the side that clergymen espoused in the debate over the expansion of slavery may have obscured the extent to which the clerical activism of the Civil War era concealed quasi-theocratic ambitions and threatened the Jeffersonian view of the relationship between church and state."[21] The clergy's sermons, he argued, did not embody sympathy for the African American victims of slavery: "forthright condemnations of racial inequality as the essence of slavery's sinfulness," he said, were not "the dominant themes in this emancipationist discourse."[22] On the contrary, the "biblical justification of the 'divine right' of rulers to compel obedience of their subjects became the single most popular text of the war sermons that have come down to us in printed form."[23] The pastors, Fredrickson argued, put "the philosophy of the Declaration of Independence . . . under attack, and few ministers would have shared Lincoln's view that the spirit of the Declaration informed the Constitution. What they, in fact, stood for was a conservative republicanism that, especially in times of crisis, would give the preservation of order a higher priority than democratic procedures and the rights of individuals."[24]

Protestant patriotism was a mainstay of the war effort in the North as in the Confederacy, and it was too important to leave misinterpreted, as I think it has been for a generation.[25] Fredrickson's reiteration of the essential conservatism and authoritarian stamp of the Protestant ministers' sermons should not be the last word. A wider sampling of what Protestant clergy and lay people wrote and said suggests a different view.

Such a reading is important to understand not only "public opinion" but also the cultural and social context of thought. Republicans ignored these opinions at their peril.

Despite his reticence in acknowledging it publicly, President Lincoln surely noticed the contribution of religious bodies to the cause. No reader of the White House mail during the Civil War can long remain unaware of it. There, cheek by jowl with the many letters of office-seekers and patronage manipulators lie the handwritten resolutions sent to the president from religious organizations. Sometimes they were the work of a single church. More often, they came from the annual meeting of a regional denominational conference. In the season of such meetings— late summer and early autumn—they constituted a significant part of the president's mail. They reached high tide in the summer and early autumn of 1863, when the president received them at the rate of two sets of resolutions per week.

They came from Baptists, Methodists, Presbyterians, Congregationalists, Universalists, United Brethren in Christ, Christians, and a scattering of other denominations. With minor exceptions they were favorable to the president and his policies and usually ardently supportive. Apparently, denominations unhappy with the Republicans kept their counsel or sent their resolves to Democrats, though I have never seen any. Radical denominations were overrepresented, the United Brethren, for example, and the Reformed Presbyterians (or "Scotch Covenanters"—self-described as radicals and antislavery). Yet well over 40 percent of the sets of resolutions came from the largest mainstream Protestant denominations, Baptists, Methodists, and Presbyterians. The upper North— Massachusetts, New Hampshire, Rhode Island, Connecticut, Wisconsin, and Michigan—was overrepresented, but groups in California, Oregon, Illinois, Indiana, Ohio, Pennsylvania, New Jersey, New York, Delaware, and Tennessee also sent resolutions to the president.

I have examined seventy-six different sets of religious resolutions and petitions sent to Lincoln during the Civil War. These constitute all such documents surviving in the Lincoln papers from four key periods of religious meetings during the war: August 13–December 6, 1861; July 28– November 12, 1862; August 7, 1863–January 27, 1864; and July 4, 1864– March 2, 1865. A few came from single congregations or small missionary outposts abroad, but others represented substantial numbers of citizens, including by far the largest organization represented, the Presbyterian

Synod of 1862, whose ministers claimed to speak for 444 ministers and 57,313 communicants. In between were many conference-wide meetings representing all the churches of a particular denomination within a certain geographical area. Elites likely dominated the meetings. Typically, they were made up of clergymen, and the resolutions sent to the president had been agreed to by unanimous consent expressed by "rising vote" of the people present. Still, lay people sometimes participated in the conferences, and resolutions from individual congregations were often signed by women members. Short of polling, Lincoln had hardly a better or broader index of public opinion between elections, and this index indicated that the American electorate, under the stress of rebellion, was changing its attitudes.

*   *   *

From beginning to end the religious resolutions, like Charles Eliot Norton after the Battle of Bull Run, focused on the theme of emancipation. The first batch of them was prompted largely by the president's revocation of General John C. Frémont's emancipation proclamation for the slaves of Missouri rebels in the summer of 1861.[26]

Of the ten sets of resolutions Lincoln received in 1861's season of religious meetings, four explicitly endorsed Frémont's proclamation. Such opinions were, of course, either explicitly or implicitly critical of the president, who had countermanded the general's proclamation.[27] The Church of Christ of Stockton, in Ford County, Illinois, for example, maintained "reverence" for Lincoln as their "ruler," but nevertheless asked allowance "to express . . . deep regret" that, before countermanding Frémont's order, the president had not stopped to read and ponder "the XVI & LVIII Chapters of . . . Isaiah."[28] Those texts, Lincoln knew now if he had not before, included the language of "breaking the yoke from the neck of the oppressed."[29]

Perhaps the most remarkable resolutions came from the United Presbyterian Church Synod. Presbyterians did not have a reputation for radicalism. The tone of their resolutions was moderate, yet the practical position they took coincided with Frémont's and with Congress's in its legislation aimed at confiscating rebel property. "We regard those who are identified with the system of slavery," the Presbyterians concluded, "& have placed themselves in the attitude of rebellion against the Govt. as

having thereby forfeited all claim to the protection of their peculiar institution." In the end the Presbyterians recommended "the manumission by
military proclamation of the slaves of all persons, who are found in arms
against the Govt, [and] the confiscation of their property."[30]

All the remaining sets of resolutions from 1861 mentioned slavery as
a sin or a cause of the war to be eliminated if possible. Baptists in central
New Jersey pledged "our lives, our fortunes and sacred honors" to the
government's cause and vowed "if the rebels raise the issue between slavery and the constitution that we will support the Government in sweeping from the country that infamous outrage on the rights of man."[31]

Lincoln saw thirty-three sets of resolutions from religious bodies in
the season of religious meetings in 1862, twenty of them sent to the president before the announcement of the preliminary Emancipation Proclamation on September 22. Twelve of those twenty urged the issuance of
some such proclamation, and two more urged the next-best thing: vigorous enforcement of Congress's acts of confiscation. Some took advanced
ground on race. Christians in Lamoille, Bureau County, Illinois, criticized "the Anglo Saxon," who "in his pride has robbed the African—a
human being from the hand of God as well as himself—of the natural
right given him by his Creator."[32]

The religious petitioners tended to invoke the biblical idiom, but, as
the Illinois Christians' mention of "natural right" reminds us, they proved
adept as well at connecting with important secular sources in America's
past and at embracing the practical powers available under the Constitution, a document that notoriously did not invoke God's blessing.[33] New
Hampshire's General Association of Congregationalist and Presbyterian
ministers entreated Lincoln "to wield that majestic power with which he
is invested as commander-in-chief of the army and navy of the Republic,
and . . . destroy . . . Slavery."[34] And Chicago Christians declared that "the
time has come of which Jefferson solemnly warned his country"; slaves
indeed were enduring "a bondage one hour of which is fraught with
more misery than ages of that which occasioned the war of the Revolution."[35] Even the more cautious Christians, like the Baptists of Clarion,
Pennsylvania, who could "not see how our Government can interfere
directly with the system of Slavery in the revolted, more than in the Loyal
Slave States" and were "glad of its uniform and steadfast refusal to do so,"
nevertheless could "rejoice in the indications, that God . . . is about to
make this wanton outbreak of Slavery propagandism, a great step toward

the removal of a system which Washington deplored, and Jefferson declared, likely to bring on us the displeasure of a God, not one of whose attributes can take part in its defence."[36]

After Lincoln issued the preliminary Emancipation Proclamation on September 22, 1862, thirteen sets of resolutions arrived. None was critical of the proclamation, and nine supported it. The Reformed Presbytery of Chicago celebrated African Americans' "inalienable rights to life, liberty, and the pursuit of happiness" and pressed the president for such "moral and religious education as shall qualify them for the performance of the duties of freemen."[37]

Those who were silent on the proclamation felt other more pressing concerns. Religions that were finding it difficult to gain complete acceptance in American society tended to seek modest goals and not to advise the president broadly on national policy. Thus the Board of Delegates of American Israelites sought the appointment of Jewish chaplains in the army.[38] And Lincoln received no sets of resolutions from Roman Catholics.[39] Some denominations, like the Episcopalians, were more chary than other denominations of involvement in political questions. Even so, the Episcopalians urged investigation of the nation's Indian affairs.[40] They proved to be deeply concerned about conscription of clergy for military service, and Lincoln more than once received communications from Episcopalians on that subject.[41]

*   *   *

For the resolutions the president saw in 1863, the label "Doctrine of Loyalty," devised by Fredrickson, is more apt than for the earlier ones. For example, the Damariscotta Mills, Maine, Baptist Association, resolved that "the powers that be are ordained of God."[42] In addition to these Baptists, the United Brethren's Sandusky, Ohio, Conference and the New York State Missionary Convention of the Baptist Church invoked the familiar language of biblical authoritarianism from Romans 13: "the powers that be are ordained of God," and from Matthew 22: "render unto Caesar."[43]

The religious petitioners offered other vigorous assertions of the necessity of loyalty to the government and the administration. The 1863 resolutions from the Stephentown Baptist Association came from H. A. Guild, the pastor of the Baptist Church of Berlin, New York. He praised

Head Quarters Jewish Union Republican Association,

New York, Pennsylvania and Indiana,   1864.

To our Jewish Brethren :

Owing to our peculiar tenets and opinions, we, the Jews of America, have ever been and are still a united body in all matters wherein our religious and social interests are concerned; but in the political affairs of our adopted country very few members of our persuasion have hitherto been led to take an active part. The reasons for this, which apply equally to other classes not professionally political, are self-evident and do not require enumeration here.

Nearly four years of desperate and bloody war with our misguided fellow-countrymen of the South have, however, changed the face of all things, and the crisis is approaching when it becomes imperative upon every honest-minded responsible Jew as well as Gentile, in the interests of humanity, patriotism and the preservation of the National existence, to well and impartially weigh the respective merits of the two candidates for the Supreme Executive Power in the American Republic,—the grandest in the worlds' history,—but which, if allowed to remain divided against itself, must inevitably follow the fate of its fore-runners in Rome and Greece, and end in shame and ruin, to the satisfaction and profit of the despotisms and aristocracies of Europe.

The spirits of innumerable martyrs to the cause of liberty are watching anxiously for the end of this great struggle, and the noble hearts of thousands of brave devoted patriots are pulsating hopefully in unison with the Union-loving North. Every Federal victory, every step toward the annihilation of the rebellion, is one more guarantee of the final triumph and prevalence of republican self-government throughout the universe.

One more effort, strong, united and determined, and the Champion of Freedom, the Emancipator of the Slave and preserver of his country will be re-elected to the power he has so wisely and justly wielded during four years of civil war and political disorganization. We call earnestly upon our Jewish brethren to bring heart and soul, influence and wealth to this great movement, without the success of which, the American republic, the country's national greatness and unparalleled prosperity must sink into wreck and ruin.

Unity is strength—Combine strongly, act energetically and unitedly, and the votes of the immense number of Jewish citizens will go far to determine the re-election of Abraham Lincoln to the presidency in November next, in other words, the salvation of the republic.

Not only has the Military Career of General McClellan been a failure and therein strengthened the rebellion, but in none of his political acts or manifestoes has he given evidence of the exalted and unswerving patriotism and statesmanship required of the President of this republic in the present terrible crisis, and which Abraham Lincoln, despite the slurs and slanders of his political enemies, has constantly displayed in so high a degree during the term of his administration.

Has Mr. Lincoln executed the trust confided on him by the American people ? Look at the map of the United States and you will find that the soil now held by the rebels in arms is but a speck, in contrast with the area of territory overrun by them in 1861.

Making due allowance for all disadvantages, inexperience and obstacles, never in the history of the world has so numerous and formidable a force, led by skilful generals, and animated by the false enthusiasm of accomplished demagogues, and stimulated by the moral and material aid of European sympathisers, been more speedily and completely reduced to almost subjection than the rebellious Confederacy under Jeff. Davis has been defeated and driven to the last extremity by the patriotic and Union-loving armies of the North, under the wise and determined administration of Mr. Lincoln.

Let us act wisely. Should the nominee of the Chicago Convention be elected, disintegration will follow, and two nations occupy that land over all of which once waved the glorious stars and stripes. With the division of the republic, there will come, as sure as night follows the day, utter financial ruin, discord and anarchy.

On the other hand, should Abraham Lincoln again be elected President, the high hopes of liberty will be realized. The country desires peace, not a peace destructive to its interests and dishonorable to the nation, but a peace which shall maintain the Constitution and the Union in all its integrity. Abraham Lincoln will submit to none other. With his re-election the olive branch of peace will soon wave over the land, the finances of the country will be restored, harmony and prosperity will prevail, and the nation will again move on in its career of greatness and grandeur.

Lincoln and Union! McClellan and Disunion !
" Choose ye this day whom ye will serve."

ELIJAH MIERS, N. Y.	ISAAC HYNEMAN, Phila.
H. ALEXANDER, N. Y.	HERMAN VON BEIL, Penn.
JOHN WOLF, N. Y.	REV. JULIUS SALINGER, Penn.
S. MYERS, N. Y.	LEON HIRSH, Pa.
B. DAVIS, N. Y	WM. LONESTATTER, Pa.
REV. E. MIERS, Ill.	WM. EPSTEIN, Pittsburgh.
H. DEBOOR, Penn.	CHAS ARNSTAHL, "

Figure 4.2. Jewish Union Republican Association, *To Our Jewish Brethren* (n.p., 1864). Religion and politics mixed openly and vigorously during the war. Some northern Jews lined up for the Union and supported the Republican party, in part because Lincoln and Republicans listened to their concerns and courted their votes.

the Emancipation Proclamation and fused religion and patriotism, finding it "irreconcilable in consistency in being loyal to God without at the
same time being loyal to country, Freedom and Humanity." Guild followed up the resolutions with his own request for an appointment as an
army paymaster—likewise fusing the two great traditions of writing to
the president, the pious and the patronage-seeking.[44] In fact, a majority
of the sets of resolutions, like those of the Indiana Methodists, for example, specifically endorsed government policies, and those that did not do
so expressly surely did so by implication when they sent their encourag-
ing resolves to the embattled President of the United States.[45]

The resolutions generally asserted the necessity of loyalty to the
government, but such assertions did not make them conservative or
authoritarian. Being loyal to the government by this time meant fealty
to a policy of emancipation as well, and the religious resolves adopted
from Maine to California, with few exceptions, forthrightly supported
emancipation. The Sandusky Brethren, for example, noted that "human
government" was "ordained of God, for the preservation of order in society," but they also opposed "all compromises with slavery and rebellion,"
insisting that no peace would be permanent without the destruction of
slavery altogether.[46]

The religious resolutions as a whole must be characterized as fervent in their message of social reform—as well as consistent—and several
went well beyond mere endorsement of the government's Emancipation
Proclamation and approached racial equalitarianism. Back in the summer of 1862, the Spring Street Congregational Church of Milwaukee had
resolved: "We love the Constitution and the Union, but not with a blind
devotion that would sacrifice for them all that would make them valuable; . . . we love them because we believe they mean *Freedom.*" And these
Congregationalists went on to denounce the "reasonless and unchristian
prejudice against the African race."[47] In 1863 the Beaver Baptist Association, of Lawrence County, Pennsylvania, included from the resolutions
of one church in the association resolves that advocated "confiscation of
Rebel property" and "justice to *all* the inhabitants of the land."[48] The
North Ohio Conference of the Methodist Church went further and wider
when it expressed regret that in the Emancipation Proclamation "all the
oppressed of the nation were not made free."[49] Urging the president to expand the proclamation in particular or its spirit in general provided the
message of several resolutions. Methodists of the California conference

Figure 4.3. "Morning Mustering of the 'Contraband' at Fortress Monroe, On their Way to Their Day's Work, Under the Pay and Direction of the U. S.," *Frank Leslie's Illustrated Weekly*, November 2, 1861. Several Union officers in 1861 declared slaves coming into Union lines as "contraband" of war, refusing to return them to their former masters and setting them to work for the army. The practice encouraged slaves to run to Union lines, crowding army camps in Virginia. But the action spurred efforts not only to find uses for the fugitives but also to enlist them in the Union cause and to move against slavery altogether.

affirmed their support of the Emancipation Proclamation as well as the president's recent proclamation "to extend the same protection to colored soldiers, under the laws of war, which is extended to the white soldiery of the government."[50]

The Universalists' general convention did not cite the familiar texts of loyalty from the Book of Romans but the text "break every yoke and let the oppressed go free," from Isaiah 58.[51] The Universalists expressed enthusiasm for the use of African American soldiers and invoked a vision of "the blessing of a common freedom" for black and white people alike. The Auglaize Conference of the United Brethren, from northwestern Ohio, not only advocated arming African Americans for the war but also denounced the racism revealed in the draft riots of the previous summer in New York: "the injustice, barbarity, and inhumanity so long practiced against an innocent and unoffending race reached their climax in the recent riots in New York, and other Northern cities."[52] Unitarians sought the "privilege of individual freedom . . . to all, irrespective of color, as a religious right."[53] And the Baptists of the New York State Missionary Convention were bent on "securing to all the dwellers in our land, regardless of class, complexion or color" the "inalienable right to life, liberty and the pursuit of happiness."[54]

*   *   *

The language of New York's Baptists, echoing the phrases of the Declaration of Independence, offers another important revision of the "doctrine of loyalty" thesis; for most Americans invoking national loyalty did not call into question traditional libertarian American political values derived from the Declaration of Independence. The resolutions drew on several traditions of rhetoric, biblical and secular, but the Declaration of Independence appeared as often in the resolutions as specific quotations from the Book of Romans.

The California Methodists mentioned their "inalienable rights."[55] The Rhode Island and Massachusetts Christian Conference carefully affirmed their belief "in a government whose members are elected by its subjects, and which secures to them, 'life, liberty, and the pursuit of happiness.'"[56] The Sandusky United Brethren, after invoking the Book of Romans and insisting that "human government" was "ordained of God," could not help expressing as well their debt to the American Revolution. They affirmed their belief "that in the struggle of our revolutionary fathers, for freedom from the oppression of England, and in the formation of a free and independent government" God had been with them.[57]

*   *   *

Like the nation's political shibboleths, political party considerations figured in the religious resolutions. Several of the resolves, especially those sent from Ohio in 1863, when there was a closely watched gubernatorial contest between peace Democrat Clement L. Vallandigham and Republican John Brough, had high partisan content. The Ohio conference of the United Brethren in Christ praised the president's Emancipation Proclamation and the suspension of the writ of habeas corpus and resolved as well:

That we cannot recognize any patriotism or Christianity, or even manhood in any man who will sustain Mr. Vallandigham, or any of his measures, in the present issue, either by vote or otherwise.

That in the present crisis, it is the imperative duty of every loyal man, to exercise the right of suffrage, and to vote for men who sustain the present Administration.[58]

Such resolutions were virtually indistinguishable from those that were adopted at mass political rallies.

The annual convention of the United Brethren of the Western Reserve, meeting in Mayfield, Ohio, likewise endorsed the Emancipation Proclamation and the suspension of the writ of habeas corpus and then declared: "That it is incompatible with the principles and spirit of the U.B. church for any of its members . . . to vote for C. L. Vallandigham, . . . a traitor to his country [and] . . . an advocate of American slavery."[59]

Party context allows us to see that the patriotic political views of the pastors and their lay supporters were not conservative by any practical measure of American politics. The conservative party during the Civil War was the Democratic party. In fact, Democrats during the war took to calling themselves "conservatives." Had the Protestant activists aimed at assertions of truly conservative doctrine, they would likely have been sending their resolutions of support to Clement Vallandigham and not to Abraham Lincoln. Thus, the religious resolutions were more partisan than systematically philosophical or theological, so that supporting the suspension of the writ of habeas corpus was less a matter of authoritarianism than of taking a political position against Vallandigham, who had been arrested by military authority and denied a writ of habeas corpus. Likewise, their ultimate partisan purpose helps to explain the anomalies of formal political philosophy found in them; Jefferson and Caesar were jumbled together to win the war and abolish slavery so that there would be no more civil wars in the country.

In choosing political sides in the Civil War, Protestant denominations, the Baptists most strikingly, had fused the Bible and the Declaration of Independence into a form of "civil religion" that, however incongruous it may appear to us now, seems to have caused nineteenth-century Americans no intellectual discomfort. The ideas were not necessarily conservative or authoritarian.[60] In the context of the Civil War, they proved to be as liberating as the Republican party's rhetoric in general had always been.

Perhaps the most striking example was the resolutions sent to Lincoln after Christmas 1863 by the Pennsylvania Baptist Convention. Representing some 40,000 people, the annual meeting offered a version of American history that blended the sacred and profane in a great liberal consensus. The "history and progress of Baptists," the Pennsylvanians pointed out, "is interwoven with the history and triumph of civil and religious liberty." In fact, the republic was modeled on "Baptist polity," and it was "a little Baptist church, near the residence of Thomas Jefferson, from which he declared he derived his first ideas of a Republican form of government."

The Pennsylvania Baptists also insisted on public witness of patriotism: "a minister, who, purposely, go[es] through the religious services of a Sabbath, without any allusion to the present state of his country, is either too disloyal, or too insensible, to be tolerated in a Christian pulpit." Such patriotism in the context of civil war dictated "unqualified support of our National and State Governments." They celebrated "recent victories at the ballot-box"—the election triumph of Pennsylvania's Republican Governor Andrew G. Curtin over peace Democrat George W. Woodward was surely in their minds—as "exhibiting the loyalty of the people." And they celebrated the Emancipation Proclamation. The steady loyalty of the liberal Protestant denominations and congregations was rooted more in the traditional liberties associated with Thomas Jefferson and the Declaration of Independence than in old New England doctrines derived from seventeenth-century Puritanism.[61]

Conservative and anti-Jeffersonian ideas are more difficult to find in the Republican "doctrine of loyalty" than in the ideas of the Democratic party. While Republican clergy were urging a new birth of freedom to live up to the standards of the Declaration of Independence, the Democratic leadership in Philadelphia was inviting the Episcopal bishop of Vermont, John Henry Hopkins, to allow them to reprint his famous prewar pamphlet *The Bible View of Slavery* for the 1863 canvass in the state.[62] Hopkins devoted over a fourth of his essay to an attack on the Declaration of Independence, arguing that its self-evident truths were not "truths at all," that all men were certainly not created equal, and that rights to life, liberty, and the pursuit of happiness were not "unalienable" but "alienated" by original sin.[63] Hence he "utterly discard[ed] these famous propositions of the Declaration of Independence."[64]

*   *   *

It is tempting to leap from these fervent resolutions embodying sentiments of religious reform to the conclusion that Abraham Lincoln was influenced by them to move ever further and higher toward purely moral denunciations of slavery. The temptation is especially strong because of the accident of timing of Lincoln's death. The last formal public address he made before his murder was his famous Second Inaugural Address, which was replete with religious language.[65] Otherwise, he spoke only from the balcony of the White House, answering a serenade with a statement on Reconstruction policy. Lincoln's life so resembles a structured drama that it seems to culminate in the Second Inaugural. Such a conclusion would give this article a dramatic conclusion and shape, and I should very much like to invoke it.

But we must keep in mind that if John Wilkes Booth had not shot Lincoln about a month after hearing the inaugural address himself, Lincoln might have gone on to give other public statements on questions of Reconstruction, land policy, economic development, civil rights and suffrage, and the role of former Confederates in the polity. He would eventually have been involved, perhaps, in promoting or discouraging the presidential aspirations of his vice president, Andrew Johnson, and the immensely popular Ulysses S. Grant, not to mention the ever-ambitious Salmon P. Chase. He would surely have criticized the Democrats' national leaders like Horatio Seymour and Francis P. Blair, Jr. Amidst pronouncements on these controversial and partisan questions, perhaps the Second Inaugural Address would not loom so large in our memory and in the conclusions of biographies and other studies of the Republican president's life.

Moreover, Lincoln, like the Republicans in Congress in the days after the Battle of Bull Run, felt constrained to make practical compromises that clergymen drafting religious resolutions did not. It is perhaps an irony that one rhetorical compromise Lincoln made was to retreat from his expressions of commitment to the political philosophy of Thomas Jefferson. For Lincoln, as President of the United States after 1860, Jefferson became not only the author of the Declaration of Independence but also the inspiration of secession in the Virginia and Kentucky Resolutions of the Federalist era. Lincoln referred to Jefferson directly only three times after the Civil War began, once in 1861 fondly as the author of the phrase "all men are created equal," once again perfunctorily as the author of the Declaration of Independence in a brief answer to a serenade just

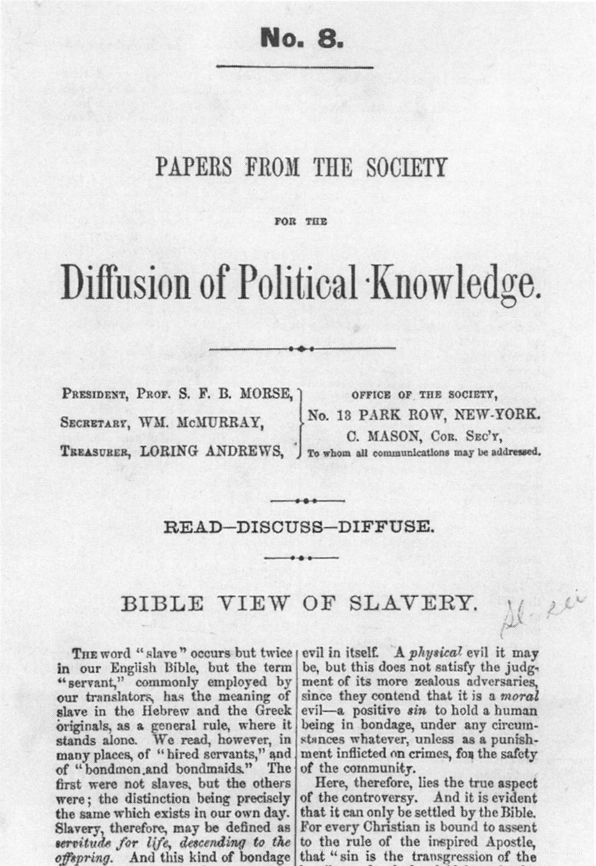

PAPERS FROM THE SOCIETY

FOR THE

Diffusion of Political ·Knowledge.

PRESIDENT, PROF. S. F. B. MORSE,
SECRETARY, WM. McMURRAY,
TREASURER, LORING ANDREWS,

OFFICE OF THE SOCIETY,
No. 13 PARK ROW, NEW-YORK.
C. MASON, COR. SEC'Y,
To whom all communications may be addressed.

READ—DISCUSS—DIFFUSE.

BIBLE VIEW OF SLAVERY.

THE word "slave" occurs but twice in our English Bible, but the term "servant," commonly employed by our translators, has the meaning of slave in the Hebrew and the Greek originals, as a general rule, where it stands alone. We read, however, in many places, of "hired servants," and of "bondmen and bondmaids." The first were not slaves, but the others were; the distinction being precisely the same which exists in our own day. Slavery, therefore, may be defined as *servitude for life, descending to the offspring.* And this kind of bondage appears to have existed as an established institution in all the ages of our world, by the universal evidence of history, whether sacred or profane.

This understood, I shall not oppose the prevalent idea that slavery is an evil in itself. A *physical* evil it may be, but this does not satisfy the judgment of its more zealous adversaries, since they contend that it is a *moral* evil—a positive *sin* to hold a human being in bondage, under any circumstances whatever, unless as a punishment inflicted on crimes, for the safety of the community.

Here, therefore, lies the true aspect of the controversy. And it is evident that it can only be settled by the Bible. For every Christian is bound to assent to the rule of the inspired Apostle, that "sin is the transgression of the law," namely, the law laid down in the Scriptures by the authority of God—the supreme "Lawgiver, who is able to save and to destroy." From his Word there can be no appeal. No rebellion can be so atrocious in his sight as that which dares to rise against his

117

Figure 4.4. John Henry Hopkins, *Bible View of Slavery* (New York: Society for the Diffusion of Political Knowledge, 1863) and *The Voice of the Clergy* (Philadelphia, 1863). To whip up opposition to emancipation, the Society for the Diffusion of Political Knowledge, the Democratic party's pro-southern propaganda machine, published this edition of Vermont Episcopal Bishop Hopkins's biblical defense of slavery. Hopkins's work evoked an outpouring of protest pamphlets, including the above condemnation from Pennsylvania's Episcopal clergy.

The Voice of the Clergy.

Among the extraordinary incidents of the times is the fact that the Democratic State Central Committee has circulated through Pennsylvania, as a campaign document, the Letter of BISHOP HOPKINS, of Vermont, in which it is maintained that Slavery, in the language of Judge WOODWARD, is an incalculable blessing. The sentiments of Bishop HOPKINS on this subject are so atrocious, and their adoption and promulgation by men professing to be Christians is so scandalous, that the Episcopal clergy of Philadelphia have felt themselves constrained to define their position, as they have done in the following manly and outspoken

PROTEST:

"The subscribers deeply regret that the fact of the extensive circulation through this diocese of a letter by

'John Henry Hopkins, Bishop of the Diocese of Vermont,'

in defence of Southern Slavery, compels them to make this public Protest. It is not their province to mix in any political canvass. But as Ministers of Christ, in the Protestant Episcopal Church, it becomes them to deny any complicity or sympathy with such a defence.

"This attempt not only to apologise for slavery in the abstract, but to advocate it as it exists in the Cotton States, and in States which sell men and women in the open market as their staple product, is, in their judgment, unworthy of any servant of Jesus Christ. As an effort to sustain, on Bible principles, the States in rebellion against the government, in the wicked attempt to establish by force of Arms a tyranny under the name of a republic, whose 'corner stone' shall be the perpetual bondage of the African, it challenges their indignant reprobation. Philadelphia, September, 1863."

Alonzo Potter,	L W Smith,	George Leeds,	J W Robins,
John Rodney,	S Appleton,	J A Childs,	Thomas B Barker,
E A Washburn,	Phillips Brooks,	Thomas C Yarnall,	S Tweedale,
Wm Suddards,	Daniel Washburn,	E Lounsbery,	M A Tolman,
D R Goodwin,	D O Kellogg,	H M Stuart,	George Bringhurst,
G E Hare,	Kingston Goddard,	J G Maxwell,	G W Shinn,
M A DeW Howe,	J L Heysinger,	J A Vaughan,	C W Duane,
W W Spear,	R Newton,	E S Watson,	J H Drumm,
Jacob M Douglass,	Chas A Maison,	Samuel Edwards,	S Hall,
H S Spackman,	John Long,	Joel Rudderow,	G B Allison,
P Van Pelt,	Ormes B Keith,	Geo A Durborow,	J N Spear,
C D Cooper,	A B Atkins,	R J Parvin,	Jos N Mulford,
W F Paddock,	Samuel E Smith,	A Beatty,	G G Field,
R D Hall,	H Hooker,	T S Yocum,	L C Newman,
J D Newlin,	W N Diehl,	J R Moore,	R C Evans,
B W Morris,	B Watson,	W J Alston,	E C Jones,
D S Miller,	Chas W Quick,	A Elywn,	J De W Perry,
B T Noakes,	Treadwell Walden,	G M Murray,	R G Chase,
R A Carden,	H T Wells,	C A L Richards,	T G Clemson,
R C Matlack,	H J Morton,	G A Strong,	H W Duchachet.
D C Millett,	J S Stone,		

after the Fourth of July 1863, and once in 1862 because Lincoln was considering the acquisition of territory by purchase and Jefferson offered the vivid precedent of Louisiana.[66] The ironic effect was that the resolutions of the American clergy during the Civil War showed more fervent indebtedness to Jefferson than Lincoln did.

Finally, the historical sources simply will not permit concluding this paper with a ringing final reference to the Second Inaugural Address, as though it were the culmination of Lincoln's political thought and of Republican ideology in the Civil War. The religious resolutions fall off in number in the Lincoln Papers the nearer we get to the Second Inaugural Address. Lincoln received or his secretaries retained only eight such communications between the Fourth of July 1864 and his second inauguration. It seems from the available record that the White House grew more preoccupied with reelection of the president in 1864, and the political letters squeezed out the religious ones in the White House office record-keeping system. Had Lincoln written the inaugural address in late 1863 rather than early 1865, the argument might be persuasive, but he did not. The sources, therefore, do not sustain such a dramatic direction.

The Second Inaugural, when compared to the First, reveals that other strands of argument had, for the time being at least, fallen by the wayside in Lincoln's address to the nation. For example, not only are Jefferson and the Declaration of Independence not in evidence in the speech, republican political ideas, as historian Nicholas Parrillo brilliantly pointed out, are altogether absent. "This speech," Parrillo said, "could be given by an absolute monarch just as easily as by an American president."[67] Instead, Lincoln delivered a speech that could aptly be called, as Ronald White did, a "sermon."

The form of the Second Inaugural may be as important as its actual content. Lincoln meant in the speech, as he explained privately later, to show Americans "that there has been a difference of purpose between the Almighty and them."[68] But by casting the address in the form of a sermon, with a biblical text, and expressing it in religious language, Lincoln suggested equally strongly that righteousness was the realm of Republicans' work.[69] Lincoln did not know, as we do in retrospect, how near the war was to its end, and he had already remarked in the address on the astonishing duration of the conflict. So when he saw that "to finish the work we are in" might entail further gigantic sacrifice, his statement about the future of the war still had real sting in it for Americans: "Yet, if God

PRESIDENT LINCOLN TAKING THE OATH AT HIS SECOND INAUGURATION, MARCH 4, 1865.—PHOTOGRAPHED BY GARDNER, WASHINGTON.—[SEE PAGE 164.]

Figure 4.5. President Lincoln Taking the Oath at His Second Inauguration,"
Harper's Weekly, March 18, 1865.

wills that it continue, until all the wealth piled by the bond-man's two
hundred and fifty years of unrequited toil shall be sunk, and until every
drop of blood drawn with the lash, shall be paid by another drawn with
the sword, as was said three thousand years ago, so still it must be said

'the judgments of the Lord, are true and righteous altogether.'"[70] Charles Eliot Norton's point back in 1861 had been to warn that the war would last long enough to accomplish this essentially moral purpose.

By the time of Lincoln's Second Inaugural Address, reformist Protestant denominations no longer had cause to lament, as the United Brethren of Sandusky, Ohio, had in 1863:

> one of the errors of the American people, has been that of divorcing political, from moral obligation; and consequently the politics of our nation has become awfully corrupt; and since it is not in the power of the press alone to correct this error, there must be a large infusion of the religious element in order to this purification.[71]

The Republican party had witnessed a large infusion of that religious element.

Although they did not throw their weight around in correspondence with the president, the clerical elite who addressed resolutions to the White House obviously carried influence with a great body of American voters. To know what the clergy preached, of course, is not necessarily to understand the lesson the flock took to heart—if the flock listened at all. But the reformist Republicans sought conviction and signs that public opinion was changing. Republicans like Lincoln obviously took some interest in these expressions. The resolutions of the religious bodies were retained in the president's mail, when not every piece of incoming mail to the White House was. The religious resolutions may have had less impact in the presidential election year than earlier, but they had impact. Otherwise, it is difficult to explain the course of the Republican party toward radicalism in the Civil War.

And, otherwise, it is difficult to understand the language and world view of the Republican politicians. Like the president's mail, with its mixture of political considerations and moral ones, the letters of the Republican leaders revealed a mixture of concerns. Henry Wilson, the wily Massachusetts senator, provides a good example with which to end this chapter. Christened Jeremiah Colbath, the penniless boy changed his name to Henry Wilson on his ambitious search for improvement. He was nicknamed the Natick Cobbler, but in fact was a wealthy owner of a shoe factory. His pathway to the reformist Republican party had wound deviously through the ranks of the anti-Catholic and anti-immigrant Know-Nothing party in the middle of the 1850s and showed him to be, in addition to a sincere antislavery reformer, in historian William E. Gienapp's words, "a master at political intrigue."[72] He has been the object of scornful depiction as a hypocrite in modern literature.[73]

But when Wilson read President Lincoln's public letter to James C. Conkling of August 26, 1863, he recognized what had drawn him to politics and to the Republican party. In that letter, written by Lincoln as an early bid for renomination for 1864 and as a keynote for states holding important elections in 1863, the president offered essentially a brief and inspiring essay—of some 1750 words—in defense of the Emancipation Proclamation and the employment of African American soldiers in the Union armies.[74] Wilson dashed off a note of support to Lincoln. "May Almighty God bless you for your noble, patriotic and Christian letter," Wilson said.[75] So purified had Republican politics become that it is difficult to distinguish the letters written by "masters at political intrigue" and religiously inspired reformers.

CHAPTER FIVE

Defining Postwar Republicanism: Congressional Republicans and the Boundaries of Citizenship

Jean H. Baker

The period after the Civil War afforded the Republican party both the opportunity and the necessity of renegotiating the basic legal, constitutional, and political principles of American society.[1] In a national government they dominated, the Republicans framed and implemented new policies and structures for all blacks—newly freed slaves in the South and border states as well as free Negroes throughout the United States. At the same time, Republicans rejected the argument that voting was an entitlement of citizenship and thereby refused to expand the rights of women. Republicans also legislated the temporary arrangements defining the degree of political inclusion for their former enemies, the Confederates.

By 1865 the Republicans, the super-majority party from 1865 to 1870, comprised a loose coalition of believers and voters as well as opinion makers such as editors and writers. It had none of the formal national machinery or committee structures that between elections sustain our parties and coordinate party functions today, although it did have a fundraising national congressional committee. And it boasted a patronage army of thousands of zealous partisans, especially in the Post Office and Treasury departments, available to contribute money and work to the party. But most important, it included a group of experienced representatives and senators at a time of great political malleability when changes in the status of various groups, most obviously African Americans, were necessitated by the results of the war. In many ways, it was to these experienced legislators that the process of redefining the meaning of American public life fell.

The questions were endless and unavoidable. Which categories of individuals would be included as the equals of white adult males? What measure of equality would be permitted black freedmen in the South? What was the meaning of emancipation? Did it carry entrance into the body politic in terms of voting, office holding, jury serving, and participation in legal rights? And what of the white southerners who, in Charles Sumner's contested definition, had committed treason, whose states had engaged in an act of state suicide, and who were therefore no longer Americans? What should their immediate and future status be? And what of Asians who were denied political liberty on the West Coast, or for that matter, immigrants, many of whom had fought in the Union army?

And after two decades of women's conventions and political activism by leaders like Susan B. Anthony, Lucy Stone, and Elizabeth Cady Stanton, what about women? What level of "belonging" would they have in this postwar civic community that members of the majority party in Congress would establish in their efforts to begin the nation anew? And once a civil right was legislated and the boundaries of citizenship expanded as they would be for black males, how would the new dimensions of citizenship be enforced? "Victory was nothing," warned the Philadelphia *Press*, "unless you secure its fruits."[2]

This chapter considers the extensions and limitations on the boundaries of citizenship as defined by congressional Radical Republicans from 1865 to 1870 for two of these groups—black males and women of both races.[3] In these two cases decisions made for one group were intertwined with policies developed for others—for example, what the Republicans legislated for black males had an impact on their decisions about the definitions of citizenship for women. Certainly, the actions of former Confederates influenced future policies for black males. In the most obvious example, the inclusion of blacks in the body politic as persons, not three-fifths of a person, meant that the representation of the Confederate South would increase by at least fifteen seats in the House of Representatives—hardly a supportable result of victory after a bitter civil war. Such a partisan imperative affected the decision of Republicans to extend voting rights to black males, although politics should not obscure the principled commitment of Republicans to protecting blacks through their enfranchisement. As Representative William Kelley, who was committed to black male voting before some of his colleagues, concluded, "Party expediency and exact justice coincide for once."[4]

Republicans also were convinced that black suffrage would help black males defend their economic rights. They subscribed to the republican ideal that every man was endowed by God with the power to support and improve himself through hard work. Some contended as early as 1866 that the acknowledgment of any right, in this case the right to work, implied the power of Congress to protect it. On a trip to the South in 1867, Representative Kelley encouraged audiences of freed people "to practice industry, be just to all . . . and get independence . . . by mechanical pursuits and by acquiring land." The first generation of post-slavery black leaders concurred, supporting in their meetings suffrage and the right to hold office, which they linked to the protection of their right to hold property.[5] Even before the end of the war, the Republican Congress, using the power of the federal government, had passed a bill incorporating the Freedmen's Savings and Trust company, which Lincoln signed on March 3, 1865.

ELECTIONEERING AT THE SOUTH.—Sketched by W. L. Sheppard.—[See Page 467.]

Figure 5.1. "Electioneering at the South," *Harper's Weekly*, July 25, 1868. Blacks in the South did not wait to exercise the franchise and speak to their own interest, as this illustration attested.

*   *   *

Republicans did not deal with issues concerning civic inclusion in a vacuum. While they made decisions based on republican, egalitarian principles to extend the boundaries of civil rights to former slaves, there were numerous constraints. First, there were the precedents and customary ways of doing things that had emerged during and even before the war. Republicans were committed to the doctrine of federalism and did not want to subvert state power entirely.[6] Furthermore, like most Americans, Republicans held sharply defined ideas about social space and its division into a public sphere—largely off limits to women—and private space, the latter closed off to government interference.

There was the constraint of public opinion and the importance of developing policies acceptable to the constituents of thirty-seven states (a figure that includes the eleven states that had seceded from the Union and Nebraska, which was admitted in 1867) and the nearly two hundred house districts of the period. By 1868 Republicans knew that black suffrage, having failed in four northern state referendums (Connecticut, Kansas, Wisconsin, and Ohio, as well as in the territory of Colorado), was not a popular cause. Certainly, the minority Democrats must be consulted, even though the Republicans held nearly three-quarters of the seats in Congress. This majority proved essential for the party's disciplined efforts to overturn frequent vetoes of congressional legislation during Andrew Johnson's administration. (In his forty-seven months in office, Johnson vetoed a record twenty-one bills and pocket-vetoed another eleven.) Throughout the period Democrats provided an electoral alternative for American voters, who in 1874 voted out the Republican majority and returned, for the first time since before the war, a Democratic majority in the House.

Republicans were also affected by the Reconstruction policies that Lincoln already had formulated and installed in order to restore the civilian government of three Confederate states. His plan, by implication, could define the appropriate future status of blacks and former Confederates and was at least a possible limit on the Republican representatives' programs. As for any proposed changes in the status of women, there was the heavy weight of convention and standard practice that had for so long placed them outside the boundaries of any meaningful public participation so that their petitions for the vote seemed as radical

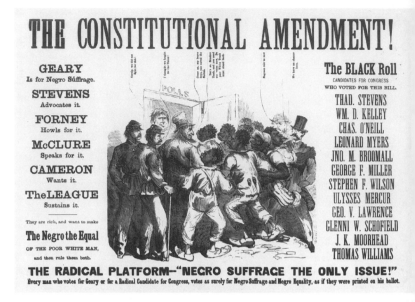

Figure 5.2. *The Constitutional Amendment! The Radical Platform—"Negro Suffrage The Only Issue!"* broadside with woodcut (Philadelphia?, 1866). For the election in 1866, Pennsylvania Democrats launched an intensive racist campaign against Republicans and their support for the Fourteenth Amendment. This is one of several such broadsides issued to raise white fears in the Democrats' campaign against Governor John W. Geary and the congressional Republicans.

to most northern Republican males as did black civil rights to white southerners.

While there were limits on the degree of inclusiveness extended to various segments of the population by the postwar Congress, there is no doubt that the degree to which the national government considered policy in categories of persons—of black, of female, and of southern white former Confederate—increased. Before the war most legislators thought in terms either of individuals or of residents of states. Reconstruction set the nation on its way to overturning Hector St. John Crèvecoeur's famous eighteenth-century concept of individuals who left their prejudices behind and became a new nationality of assimilated Americans. Instead, Reconstruction made Americans think in more pluralistic terms and encouraged what historian Arthur Schlesinger, Jr., has called the decomposition of the United States into groups.[7]

Figure 5.3. *Practical Illustration of the Virginia Constitution,* lithograph (n.p., 1868). White racist thought, as expressed in this cartoon, was an all-or-nothing proposition—freedom for blacks meant white subordination. There could be no middle ground, which, in the calculus of white conservatives, meant anyone who stood with blacks was against whites. Republicans were thus illegitimate "rulers" to whom no whites owed respect or obedience.

Compared to their congressional predecessors, and despite these inherited limitations on their policies, this first generation of Republican legislators had extraordinary powers, partly because the fighting of a civil war had ineffably centralized powers in the national government unheard of two decades before. The public landscape had changed for Americans who in both the North and the South had learned to accept, however grudgingly, the authority of the federal government in formerly private aspects of their lives. Examples in both the Confederacy and the Union accumulated during the war in the form of a national draft, new forms of taxation, and the increased powers of the federal government over those of the state. What the war had transformed was not just what the government did, but who in the federal system that divided powers between states and the federal government did it.

Representatives of the national Republican party might be first generation members of a party that was only ten years old, but they were also veterans of the battles of wartime congresses that had necessarily extended legislative powers. The process of redefining the citizenship entitlements guaranteed by the state and, in turn, the obligations and duties of citizens to the state were familiar to them in a way that was unknown to previous generations. After all, they had drafted the Confiscation Acts, the Enrollment Acts, and the Habeas Corpus Acts as well as the Thirteenth Amendment that had first been voted on in Congress in 1864 and that included, besides its abolition of slavery, the pledge that Congress had the power of its enforcement. Of fifteen members of the Joint Committee on Reconstruction, nine had held office before the war; four were elected during the war, and only two were freshmen. In sum, these experienced Republicans were the victors, and they commanded the electoral support of a majority of Americans.

The Republicans did not redefine citizenship and civil rights alone, although they were the majority party in the 39th, 40th, and 41st United States Congresses that are the primary focus in this paper. The Republicans held 149 seats in the House during the 39th Congress in 1865-67, compared to 42 for the Democrats. In the Senate party representation was as unbalanced—42 Republicans to 10 Democrats. In the 41st Congress, 1869-71, House Republicans numbered 149 compared to 63 Democrats, and in the Senate there were a disproportionate 56 Republicans to 11 Democrats. To be sure, there were always factions within the majority party—super-majorities encourage such factionalism—and some conservative Republicans voted with Democrats.[8] With limited success, historians have attempted to establish categories for these factions within the Republicans such as Centrist, Moderate, Conservative and the name that is still used to describe the most progressive Republicans of the period—Radical.[9] More significant than these categories is the amount of agreement among Republicans at the national level as they wrote what has been called the "peace treaty ending the war" (see Table 1).[10]

TABLE 1. Party Representations in Congress, 1865–71

House of Representatives

39th Congress	149 Republicans	42 Democrats
40th Congress	143 Republicans	49 Democrats
41st Congress	149 Republicans	63 Democrats

Senate

39th Congress	42 Republicans	10 Democrats
40th Congress	42 Republicans	11 Democrats
41st Congress	56 Republicans	11 Democrats

In fall 1865 and spring 1866, Republicans in Congress began to define the future status of black freedmen. In so doing, they enlarged the civic community to include black males whose civil rights would now be guaranteed by the federal government. According to the Republican pamphleteer Marvin Warren of Ohio, it is "the duty of the National Government to stand between the authorities of a State and one or more of its citizens . . . whenever the constitutional rights of either of these parties is without any other redress."[11]

Earlier, the Thirteenth Amendment prohibiting involuntary servitude had transformed the federal system by extending to the national government the authority to protect personal liberty and by giving to Congress the power of passing "appropriate" enforcement legislation. For the first time in a political culture in which state authority had been primary, freedom had become national, but what exactly did freedom mean in terms of behaviors and practices? As would be their habitual response to changes in the status of blacks, white southerners who held to a minimalist view that freedom meant mobility and little else, and sometimes not even that, challenged the Republican party's redefinition of public and private space.

Republicans, believing in a free-labor system, passed the Southern Homestead Act to grant land to settlers. In this model blacks were viewed as potential Horatio Algers, enacting what Booker T. Washington descriptively titled his autobiography—*Up from Slavery*. "The result of free labor," according to the *Cincinnati Daily Gazette*, which applauded the industry of the freedpeople, "will be the doubling of the aggregate wealth of the South."[12] What congressional Republicans considered as infringements of the spirit and intention of the law—that is, apprenticeship systems and "black codes"—produced a ratcheting effect in terms of their legislative efforts.

In December 1865, Republicans established a Joint House and Senate Committee on Reconstruction whose fifteen members included some of their most dominant figures. Among the members were Thaddeus Stevens, Elihu Washburne, John Bingham, and Roscoe Conkling.[13] But Charles Sumner, the great egalitarian senator from Massachusetts, was excluded because of his supposed extremism. It was from this committee that the statutory and constitutional changes of this first generation of Republicans emerged. Under their leadership in March 1866 the Republicans passed the Civil Rights Act that gave national citizenship to blacks and explicitly asserted the right of the United States government to intervene in state affairs to protect citizens' rights. In the language of its author, Lyman Trumbull, senator from Illinois, "All Persons born in the United States except Indians not taxed are citizens of the United States and are entitled to various rights." These were defined as the right to sue, to be part of the judicial system as jurors or plaintiffs in civil actions, to own property, and most important, to have laws equally applied to them.

Enforcement rested in the second section of the 1866 Civil Rights Act that made violation of any person's civil rights subject to punishment. Understanding that southern courts, under the control of former Confederate slaveholders, would pay little attention to transgressions by either state or local governments of their white neighbors and friends, U.S. district courts received jurisdiction. Federal officers were given the authority to institute proceedings against violators. But in a feature lost on neither Democrats and white southerners nor black leaders, the act restricted prosecutions of those who violated blacks' rights to state and local officials. Acts by private individuals such as requiring tenant farmers to have work cards or violating sharecropping contracts were not covered.

In fact, the denial of black male citizenship by noncomplying white southerners had already begun in the reenslavement of blacks through the Black Codes passed by Mississippi, Louisiana, and Alabama. Despite its revolutionary shift of power from the states to the federal government—"calling in the giant," as it is sometimes called—and its definition of the public meaning of civil rights, the 1866 act was a slender reed for guaranteeing the civil rights of freedmen in the face of local opposition.

It might be overturned by another statute. It was not a constitutional amendment. Only nine years before the *Dred Scott* decision had stated forthrightly that blacks were not citizens of the United States and could never be. The Civil Rights Act of 1866 made no such affirmative claim and did not positively state that blacks were citizens of their states and the United States. Most southerners, many Democrats, and a few border state Republicans believed that only by a constitutional amendment could blacks become citizens.

Mainstream Republicans came to agree with them. By 1867, after extensive debate, the constitutional amendment crafted by the Joint Committee on Reconstruction—an amendment that had originally dealt primarily with the issue of the political status of former Confederates—

passed both houses of Congress by the two-thirds majority that reveals this first generation of Republicans' consensus on civil rights for blacks. What became the Fourteenth Amendment contained a citizenship and civil rights section similar to that in the Civil Rights Act, along with four other sections that answered some of the political problems that Trumbull's original Civil Rights Act had not.[14]

As a statement of black rights, the Fourteenth Amendment—a pillar of American liberties—has been called cryptic, conservative, and ineffective. Certainly, its original meaning has been a source of endless controversy among jurists, lawyers, historians, and constitutional scholars, some of whom argue that the privileges and immunities clause was not meant to apply to such elemental rights as jury service, suffrage, or anti-miscegenation and segregation statutes.[15] Yet given its abstract language, later courts would rule that it barred discrimination based on class, ethnicity, sex, place of residence, and religion. And in a section partly immobilized by the conservative Supreme Court in the 1870s and 1880s, it delegated to Congress the authority to secure the status and civil rights of blacks. Of this titanic shift the Republican senator from Ohio John Bingham proclaimed the authority to secure the rights of citizens "belongs to every sovereign power and is a subject of national jurisdiction."[16] Indeed, Republicans fully appreciated the significance of their work and acknowledged, according to representative Jehu Baker of Illinois, that "we are framing an amendment of our fundamental law which may exist for centuries without a change."[17]

Still, Republicans were too wedded to the concept of federalism to believe that the national government would define exactly and completely which privileges and immunities were protected; only states and local political bodies could do that in this state-acknowledged nationalism. "Although the states," writes historian Robert Kaczorowski, "were expected to continue in their traditional function of securing civil rights, their authority was to be shared with Congress and the federal courts. Because federal law was supreme, Congress and the federal courts could supplant all state authority over personal rights. The framers' legal theory of citizenship and congressional authority over the rights of citizenship held the potential of ending federalism and establishing a unitary state."[18] But however much citizenship and civil rights were nationalized on paper, in the daily lives of black Americans the practical power of the nearest local authority constrained their freedom.

Republicans also empowered the Freedmen's Bureau to protect freed-people's rights as citizens. In the Freedmen's Bureau Act of 1865 (extended in 1866, vetoed by Andrew Johnson, and then passed over Johnson's veto), Republicans led by Ohio's Robert Schenck entered the domain of private rights, previously considered beyond the reach of public officials. First they focused entirely on freed men who were black, but then Republicans were challenged on the basis that they were affording preferential treatment to one race. So they included white "refugees" in the bill.

Given the laissez-faire culture of a period without previous federal welfare programs protecting individuals, Democrats and even Frederick Douglass objected to efforts "to prop up the Negro," who in Douglass's unique view should simply be given equal rights with white males and left alone. But many blacks in the South who had joined the Republican party dissented from Douglass's position and believed in the necessity of the Bureau. Meanwhile, congressional Republicans accepted a guardianship role. As Representative William Kelley from Philadelphia argued, "We are to guide them, as the guardian guides his ward for a brief period, until they can acquire habits and become confident and capable of self-control." But that meant limited protection, according to many Republican congressmen.[19]

As eventually defined, the Freedmen's Bureau provided food for the destitute of both races; it established schools and hospitals for freedmen; it supervised labor contracts entered into by blacks, and at least in the beginning it placed some black families on the abandoned and confiscated land the federal government controlled in 1865. The second Freedmen's Bureau extended this protective function in more explicit ways.[20] In practice, the agents who supervised this program sometimes failed to protect blacks in the face of local hostility, but congressional Republicans remained more worried about discrimination against blacks than white southerners' resentment of a policy that placed federal agents in their midst. Moreover, through the Freedmen's Bureau the Republicans stretched previous understandings of the scope of government to incorporate welfare provisions for citizens under the powers of the federal government. Republicans also proposed manual education for blacks in the form of the National Farm School, which primarily offered primary education and agriculture courses. They encouraged blacks in the South to join local Republican Union Leagues as well.

During the war a few Republicans had argued that voting, the essential act of American political identity and ever the most precious of liberties in the national political culture, must be guaranteed to black males. Voting, it was believed by leaders like Charles Sumner and Frederick Douglass, was a concomitant of citizenship as well as a protection; it was also a means of expanding the Republicans' partisan base. In 1867 the Reconstruction Acts initiated black suffrage in the former Confederate states. Under their aegis, blacks in the former Confederacy voted for the first time for constitutional delegates, served as such, and then participated as officeholders and voters in newly established state governments. But these acts covered only the Confederate South, and they might be repealed by another Congress. Moreover, demonstrating the limits of their progressivism, when black registration in ten former Confederate states outnumbered that of whites (many of whom were boycotting the election), conservative Republicans began to worry that the South would be controlled by former slaves with radical ideas.

By the late 1860s the partisan motives of Republicans coincided with their egalitarian commitment to expand and protect black rights. There is a complicated legislative history of twenty-four roll-calls involved, but in February 1869 the Fifteenth Amendment passed the Senate by a vote of 39 "for" and 13 "no," and in the House by 144 "for" and 44 "against," with 31 not voting. This was, with only five exceptions, a straight party vote. The amendment did not affirm the right of blacks to vote; its negative language only barred states from making race a qualification for suffrage, facilitating the white South's later successful campaign to limit black voting through statutory legerdemain such as grandfather clauses and poll taxes applied on paper to all males.[21]

Many northern Republicans interpreted the passage of the Fifteenth Amendment as the end of the federal government's role in Reconstruction. This was largely the case, although Republicans did pass the Enforcement Acts of 1872 and 1873. The latter were intended to protect blacks from private acts violating their civil rights. "It is the general feeling," wrote one Ohioan to Republican Senator John Sherman, "that we have done enough, gone far enough in governmental reconstruction, and that it is best for all that the southern communities should be left to manage themselves." According to the *New York Times*, "The work of the Republican party . . . ends with the adoption of the Fifteenth Amendment."[22] Wrote the editor of the *Chicago Tribune*, "The freedman has been raised as high as he can be. Nothing more is possible. The rights of the Negro

Figure 5.4. *Extract from the Reconstructed Constitution of the State of Louisiana. With Portraits of the Distinguished Members of the Convention & Assembly. A. D. 1868*, lithograph (n.p., 1868). Shown here are the black delegates to the Louisiana Constitutional Convention who were later elected to the state legislature, with text from the constitution outlawing discrimination in schools and public accommodations. At the bottom is a fiery statement from one member, Pinckney B. S. Pinchback, threatening black reprisal against any further white violence. Pinchback's warning was added in type some months after this lithograph was published, following an assassination attempt on him. As expressed in the fact of their election and their insistence on respect, black Republicans expected to be part of the political structure thereafter.

can never be an issue again in our national politics."[23] Here then were
the limits of this first generation's definition of republicanism for black
males.

*   *   *

One group of Americans did not think that these should be the limits. Accordingly, black and white women, acting through first the Equal
Rights Association and later the National Woman Suffrage Association
and the American Woman Suffrage Association, tried to seize an opportunity for universal suffrage. In logic analogous to that propelling Republicans toward black male suffrage, women argued that they had provided
important service to the Union during the Civil War. They had, after
all, served as nurses, spies, and even soldiers; they had organized the
local auxiliary associations that collected clothes and medicines for the
U.S. Sanitary Commission; they had run farms and businesses and had
worked, under the direction of the Woman's National Loyal League, to
free the slaves.

Yet for the most part women activists in the immediate postwar
generation made their case in the name of natural rights and on the
comparative grounds that, as Susan B. Anthony argued, "disenfranchise-
ment in a republic is as great an anomaly, if not cruelty, as slavery itself.
It is therefore the solemn duty of Congress in guaranteeing a republican
form of government to every State of this Union to see that there be no
abridgment of suffrage among persons responsible to law, on account
of color or sex."[24] Her lifelong friend and collaborator Elizabeth Cady
Stanton agreed: "Now in the reconstruction is the opportunity, perhaps
for the century, to base our government on the broad principle of equal
rights to all. The representative women of the nation feel they have an
interest and duty equal with men in the struggles and triumphs of his
hour. . . . Has not the time come to bury the black man and the woman
in the citizen?"[25]

In their resolutions and appearances before state judiciary commit-
tees and similar ones in the U.S. Senate and House, women argued that
they needed the ballot to protect their economic interests and their "persons" within marriage at a time in which men possessed their bodies.
"Tyranny on a southern plantation," wrote Elizabeth Cady Stanton, "is
far more easily seen by white men at the North than the wrongs of the
women of their own households."[26] Later some suffragists, especially those

CONSTITUTION

OF THE

IMPARTIAL SUFFRAGE LEAGUE.

THE undersigned, desiring to see the Republic established on those ETERNAL PRINCIPLES OF JUSTICE which will guard against future convulsion and civil war, and insure it stability and enduring peace, promote the industrial development of the South, and the commercial prosperity of the country, — do form ourselves into an IMPARTIAL SUFFRAGE LEAGUE, for the purpose of securing to all men, throughout our entire country, the full enjoyment of EQUAL CIVIL AND POLITICAL RIGHTS without regard to color or race.

To obtain this end we will operate through the following organization subject to the ordinary rules of amendment : —

I. The Officers of this Society shall be a President, not less than five Vice-Presidents, a Recording Secretary, a Corresponding Secretary, a Treasurer, and an Executive Committee of not less than five persons, — each of whom shall perform the duties indicated by their titles, and usually devolving on such officers.

II. The Corresponding Secretary shall officiate as General Agent, and, under the direction of the Executive Committee, shall call meetings and conventions, and organize Co-operative Societies; and shall labor to promote the objects of the League by lectures, addresses, and publications, for which services he shall receive a reasonable compensation.

The Executive Committee may employ such other agents as the exigences of the cause may demand.

III. The Society shall hold an annual meeting, for the choice of officers, and the transaction of other business, at such time and place as the Executive Committee shall determine.

IV. Any person may be a member of the League by signing its Constitution, and contributing to its funds.

OFFICERS OF THE IMPARTIAL SUFFRAGE LEAGUE.

PRESIDENT.
HIS EXCELLENCY ALEXANDER H. BULLOCK.

VICE–PRESIDENTS.

HIS HONOR WILLIAM CLAFLIN,	LEWIS HAYDEN, ESQ.,
EX–GOV. JOHN A. ANDREW,	REV. EDWARD N. KIRK, D.D.,
MARTIN BRIMMER, ESQ.,	REV. A. A. MINER, D.D.,
MAJ.-GEN. BENJAMIN F. BUTLER,	GEORGE R. RUSSELL, ESQ.

RECORDING SECRETARY.
MARSHAL S. SCUDDER.

CORRESPONDING SECRETARY.
WILLIAM L. BURT, 96 Washington Street, Boston.

EXECUTIVE COMMITTEE.

SAMUEL G. HOWE,	ALPHEUS CROSBY,
F. W. BIRD,	GEORGE L. STEARNS,
GILBERT HAVEN.	

TREASURER.	AGENT.
EDWARD S. PHILBRICK,	LORING MOODY,
8 Bromfield Street, Boston.	83 Sudbury Street, Boston.

Figure 5.5. *Constitution of the Impartial Suffrage League* (Boston, 1866). Abolitionists in particular pressed for "impartial suffrage" as the surest way to secure civil and political rights "without regard to color or race." The Impartial Suffrage League formed to advocate enfranchising blacks especially as "the only safe method of Reconstruction through our entire country." But the omission of woman's suffrage from its constitution signaled a break in the alliance of women's rights with black freedom.

in the American Woman Suffrage Association led by Lucy Stone, made the case that women would bring to electoral politics their moral sensitivity along with an understanding of issues such as temperance that affected American households.

To suffragists, their right to vote was granted in Section 4 of Article 4 of the United States Constitution, where the United States, presumptively the federal government, "guaranteed" to every state a republican form of government. Republican government was, in this argument, inextricably linked to citizens' voting. It was not an arbitrary entitlement bestowed by some legislative body. Women had included their call for the ballot as a feature of citizenship since the Seneca Falls Convention of 1848, but Reconstruction, and especially the commitment of congressional Republicans such as Benjamin Butler, Aaron Sargent, and Samuel Pomeroy, encouraged a campaign before a group of men who were making changes in the status of blacks.

In 1866 suffrage leaders Susan B. Anthony and Elizabeth Cady Stanton had rushed to Washington to lobby Republican senators to oppose a regressive constitutional first—that is, the introduction of the word "male" in the second section of the Fourteenth Amendment. Stanton accurately predicted after their failure that, once the word "male" was put into the Constitution, it would take years to remove it.

On the other hand, the Fourteenth Amendment defined citizens as those born or naturalized in the United States. Making her claim to Republican senators and targeting an uninterested Charles Sumner, Anthony insisted that citizenship, an expression of political being, automatically included voting. After all, women were taxed and were subject to the law. In 1869 the addition of one word—sex—to the Fifteenth Amendment along with race, color, and previous condition of servitude would bring women the suffrage. But, as the reformer Wendell Phillips told Stanton, it was "the Negro's Hour." Any alliance with women would "lose for the Negro more than it would gain for women."[27] In the calculus of even the most liberal Republicans, there must be one question—one reform—at a time.

Friends of the past from Frederick Douglass to William Lloyd Garrison denied the urgency of women's suffrage. As Douglass insisted at a convention of reformers in 1866: "With us, the matter is a question of life and death. . . . When women, because they are women, are hunted down through the cities of New York and New Orleans; when they are dragged from their house and hung upon lamp-posts; . . . when they are in danger of having their homes burnt down over their heads . . . then they will have an urgency to obtain the ballot equal to our own." To this, Anthony responded "Is that not all true about black women," and Stanton asked satirically if all blacks were male.[28]

Nearly all congressional Republicans agreed with Douglass. Despite their efforts to expand the boundaries of Republican party inclusiveness, Anthony and Stanton failed to persuade these men to broaden the scope of the Fifteenth Amendment or to support a Sixteenth Amendment that would guarantee the enfranchisement of all women citizens. In the face of such setbacks the suffrage movement split between those in the National Woman Suffrage Association, who believed that women must remain nonpartisan until one party accepted a suffrage resolution in its national or state convention, and those led by Lucy Stone in the American Woman Suffrage Association, who continued to support the Republican party on the grounds that it had led the way in the liberation of slaves and the civil rights of the freedmen. Yet, even in this time of Republican legislative power, the resolution for a Sixteenth Amendment, which was introduced regularly, was tabled or defeated in the Judiciary Committee of both House and Senate until 1887 and was defeated on the floor of the House and Senate until 1917. Not all first generation Republicans opposed women's suffrage, but supporters like Henry Wilson, Thaddeus Stevens, and Benjamin Butler—the true Radical Republicans—were exceptions.

Congressional Republicans were well aware that state referendums on women's suffrage had failed. But so too had referendums on black suffrage, the most important example being a simultaneous vote in Kansas in 1867. Here both black and women's suffrage had lost, women's suffrage by three to one, black suffrage by a lesser margin. But the defeat of black suffrage inspired Republicans to guarantee that right by a constitutional amendment for males. As these feminist leaders argued for the rest of the century, they were the only group in American history who did not have significant support within Congress and who were forced to work alone and outside of the legislative halls in their efforts to get the ballot. Others, from the voteless white male poor to black males, had benefited from the support of those in power.

Overlooked by congressional Republicans, women attempted a new constitutional strategy based on the premise that females already

AN

APPEAL

TO THE

WOMEN·OF THE UNITED STATES

BY THE

NATIONAL WOMAN SUFFRAGE AND
EDUCATIONAL COMMITTEE,

WASHINGTON, D. C.

COMMITTEE.

Mrs. ISABELLA B. HOOKER, Hartford, Conn.
Mrs. PAULINA W. DAVIS, Providence, R. I.
Miss SUSAN B. ANTHONY, Rochester, N. Y.
Mrs. MARY B. BOWEN, Washington, D. C.
Mrs. RUTH C. DENISON, " "
Mrs. JOSEPHINE S. GRIFFING, " "

HARTFORD:
CASE, LOCKWOOD & BRAINARD, PRINTERS.
1871.

Figure 5.6. *An Appeal to the Women of the United States by the National Woman Suffrage and Educational Committee, Washington, D. C.* (Hartford, Conn.: Case, Lockwood & Brainard, Printers, 1871). Angry that they were shunted to the political margins of the Republican party in the rush to pass the Fifteenth Amendment and left out of any explicit suffrage requirements at the federal or state levels, women of the National Woman Suffrage and Educational Committee formed a Washington lobby to continue to press for woman's suffrage. Women reformers knew the ways of politicking and lobbying and used their skills and contacts to keep the issue of woman's suffrage alive.

possessed the right to the franchise guaranteed by the Fourteenth and Fifteenth Amendments. Suffragists argued that since the Fifteenth Amendment prohibited states from blocking citizens' access to their suffrage rights and since the Fourteenth Amendment made all persons born or naturalized *citizens* and since citizenship carried the suffrage with it, women could vote. In what was called the "New Departure," suffragists began registering and voting, only to be arrested, tried, and convicted, in Susan B. Anthony's case as a criminal subject to three years' imprisonment. Just as a conservative Supreme Court would in time narrow the margins of constitutional rights for blacks, so in 1874 in the case of *Minor v. Happersett* the Court ruled that, although women were persons and citizens, the answer to the question of whether all citizens are necessarily voters was "no." Unless Congress passed uniform rules preempting the states' role in elections, states could continue to define privileges and immunities and therefore exclude women from the electorate. After this decision women concentrated their campaign on a federal suffrage amendment, which they expected would be the Sixteenth, but, given the implacable hostility to women's suffrage, turned out to be the Nineteenth.

Certainly, the congressional Republicans of this first generation of the party had extended the parameters of freedom and equality in the United States. They did indeed make history and, as one Republican noted, "lay the foundations for our national building," extensions of the central government that most of their constituents supported.[29] From today's perspective, they are often viewed as partisans with limited vision but immense partisan ambition. Yet it is worth remembering that they provided future generations with an outline of the ways in which civil rights for black males and to a lesser extent black females might be protected from state governments. They made the national government the defender, arguing for what today seems an obvious point. As John Bingham insisted, "the authority to secure the rights of citizens belongs to every sovereign power and is a subject of national jurisdiction."[30] Nearly all first generation Republicans supported a concept that was radical for its day, and in their struggle for the suffrage, women took the same cue, seeking a federal amendment and abandoning for the most part their effort to achieve suffrage by state campaigns.

But operating within the conventional thought of their time that separated society into economic, political, and social categories, Republicans refused to extend the parameters of constitutional protection to women, who must remain in a separate sphere. Thus, while the law remained "wholly masculine, created and executed by men," in the complaint of one suffragist, it did not remain wholly the creation of white males or states.[31] Republican congressmen had expanded the limits of citizenship to include black males and in the process they had enlarged the scope of the national government in order to guarantee, at least on paper, new liberties. But they had fallen short of extending any similar entitlements to women.

CHAPTER SIX

The Reforging of a Republican Majority

Brooks D. Simpson

The story of the Republican party from 1868 through the 1870s is that of an ongoing quest to define identity, ideology, and issues—to reforge the majority first fused together in the 1850s. Party leaders entered the period believing that Reconstruction was coming to a close; they awaited with anticipation what form a new agenda and perhaps even realignment would take. So did their Democratic foes. Yet time and again old issues kept reappearing and old themes were sounded anew. Neither party realized the coherent outlook each sought on other issues: parties remained divided internally when it came to fiscal, monetary, and economic development issues. It would not be until the 1880s that both parties would be able to escape the shadow of war and Reconstruction. But it was not always for lack of trying.

In nominating Ulysses S. Grant for president in 1868, Republicans sought to hitch party fortunes to the appeal of the nation's foremost war hero. The general was a supporter of congressional Reconstruction efforts and had broken with Andrew Johnson over Johnson's continued efforts to wrestle with the Tenure of Office Act. Grant's desire for an end to political strife, especially in the aftermath of Johnson's impeachment, was best summed up in four words, derived from his letter of acceptance, that soon resonated across the land: "Let us have peace." The malleable meaning of the expression represented its chief virtue: peace between North and South, between white and black, between Democrat and Republican, and, most of all, an end to partisan bickering. As Grant put it, "I could not back down without . . . leaving the contest for power for the next four years between mere trading politicians, the elevation of whom, no matter which party won, would lose to us, largely, the results

Figure 6.1. *The Great American Tanner*, lithograph (New York: Currier & Ives, 1868). In civilian life, Grant had been a tanner by profession, among several jobs. In this cartoon he has "tanned the hides" of the Confederates and now prepares to take on the Democrats. The image spoke to both Grant's "common man" background and his military leadership, a sure-fire combination to win votes in the postwar era.

of the costly war which we have gone through." This hardly constituted a ringing endorsement of Republican leadership, although the general preferred just about anything to a Democratic victory.[1]

Ohio Republicans proclaimed that the party's standard bearer would "guide us into a harbor of rest and quiet." In contrast, a Democratic triumph would mean chaos and revolution.[2] Moreover, the Democrats co-operated in allowing Republicans to portray the election as a replay of the war. They passed up an excellent opportunity to redefine party lines in 1868 when that year's presidential convention selected former New York governor Horatio Seymour as its candidate. The party could have turned to several other aspirants, most notably Chief Justice Salmon P. Chase, and it decided to accept black political equality and concentrate instead on economic issues. True, Democrats were almost as divided as

Republicans over the proper course to pursue when it came to green-backs and the tariff, but the difficulties inherent in mounting such a campaign paled in comparison to another attempt to refight the Civil War. Seymour struggled to escape his wartime error in addressing New York City draft rioters as "my friends"; his running mate, Francis P. Blair, Jr., openly courted controversy when he denounced Republican Recon-struction legislation and promised to work for its repeal in a public letter; the platform waxed eloquent about the horrors of continued Republican rule. Disappointed presidential aspirant Chase later observed that the platform as adopted "drove nearly every dissatisfied Republican, many Conservatives & some democrats to vote for Grant & Colfax tickets."[3] The Chief Justice believed that Grant's election was assured and that he would nearly sweep the nation west of the Appalachians, "not because *his* election is desired, but because people are afraid of violent & revolu-tionary measures in the south if he is not elected."[4] Overjoyed by signs that Democrats were quite willing to join battle on the issues of the war and Reconstruction, Indiana senator Oliver P. Morton sounded the rallying cry for Republicans when he declared, "The great issue is the question of overturning the new State Governments by fear, the restora-tion of the power of the rebels, or, as they call it the white man's govern-ment in those states—and all the rest is leather & prunella." He warned voters "that all that is said about greenbacks & bonds & questions of finance is mere nonsense."[5]

In short, the 1868 presidential campaign was much as the Republi-cans wanted it to be, a refighting of the war that linked northern Demo-crats with Confederates and Klansmen. Best for the moment to obscure those issues that might divide party regulars and promote the victor of Vicksburg and Appomattox as the man best able to secure in peace what had been won in war. And yet the election results should have given Republicans pause. A majority of white men who cast ballots in 1868 did so for the ticket of Seymour and Blair. True, Grant would have prevailed in the electoral college due to the distribution of the vote, but that prospect was less than reassuring, and it was worth noting that the gen-eral ran ahead of the ticket, testimony to his personal popularity but a troubling indication of the degree to which Republican voters held fast to the party's principles.

Moreover, the interpretation placed on Republican victory possessed troubling implications. "The election of Grant settles the Southern

Figure 6.2. "The Modern Samson," *Harper's Weekly*, October 3, 1868. Seymour and his rebel allies cheer the shearing of the black voter as they march to undo Reconstruction. This cartoon emphasized the importance of the southern black vote to the Republicans.

question," the New England industrialist Edward Atkinson declared.[6] Others agreed. Grant's triumph did not mark a new opportunity to place Reconstruction on a sound footing but cleared the way to bring the existing approach to a successful conclusion. For years, Republicans had battled the obstructionist tactics of Andrew Johnson to such an extent that a large portion of the Reconstruction legislation passed in 1867 and 1868 was designed as much to tie the hands of the chief executive (however imperfectly) as to construct an environment for the regeneration of civil government in the former Confederate states. Moreover, opposition to Johnson offered Republicans a rallying point that enhanced party unity; that was no longer necessary, and the significant Republican margin in the Senate ironically reduced the need to stand together and carve out compromises.

From the beginning, Republican strategies for building a southern wing were problematic. Although party leaders assumed that blacks would flock to their support, that in itself was not enough to assure the party a majority in more than a handful of states. Reaching out to attract white southern voters presented other challenges. Perhaps they could be induced to support a program of economic development, but would that come at the expense of serving the needs of black constituents? And federal intervention offered its own dilemmas. While vigorous action might be essential to protect Republican officeholders and voters from violence, the very act of intervention left the impression that these Republican regimes could not survive on their own—raising questions about their legitimacy and perhaps creating unstable conditions that required more intervention.

Not all Republicans cared too much about their party's fortunes in the South. More than a few of the party faithful thought it was time to move on to the issues of the future. In the pages of the *North American Review*, political critic Henry Adams told readers it was time to set aside Reconstruction and focus on issues of structural reform, reassertion of executive independence, and introduction of measures looking toward civil service reform and free trade.

Into this uncertain situation walked Ulysses S. Grant, who on March 4, 1869 took the oath of office as the nation's eighteenth president. The new chief executive did not view himself as a representative of the party that elected him. He formed a cabinet that was shaped far more by personal intuition and association than by party preferences, missing what opportunity existed to forge bonds with party regulars. Indeed, for his first year in office Grant seemed oblivious to the need to curry favor with Republicans in order to get his way. It would not be until 1870 that he grasped the need to wage politics as he had waged war.

The new president came to office committed to fostering sectional reconciliation and promoting black equality before the law. The challenge was to frame a policy that would meet both objectives—and to apply that policy successfully across the entire South, where each state's mix of native southern whites, northern emigres, and blacks differed enough to present a distinct challenge. To frame and implement such a policy in the face of ever-dwindling public support for such measures in the North was equally daunting. Finally, in light of the Republican decision back in 1867 to restore civil governments, the chief executive would have to use what limited tools he had rather creatively.

Grant's efforts to promote reconciliation, racial justice, and Republican interests simultaneously failed when he put them to the test during his first year in office. In easing Virginia's way through the reestablishment of civil government by urging the separate submission for clauses disfranchising prominent former Confederates, he ironically paved a path for a conservative victory in state elections. He did not repeat that mistake in Mississippi and Texas, and he moved vigorously to remand Georgia to the status of a military district in light of ample evidence that political terrorism and fraud had determined the outcome of the 1868 election there. At the same time, he worked for ratification of the Fifteenth Amendment, achieving his goal in March 1870. Republicans celebrated the achievement and mused about the future. "The issues of the rebellion and the war pass away," noted one party organ. The reform-minded *Nation* was even more blunt. "The South ought now to be dropped by Congress," it declared. "All that paper and words can do for it have been done."[7]

At first Grant hoped to do a little more, but his plan to annex the Dominican Republic to offer blacks a possible sanctuary from violence and economic leverage against southern whites backfired. Senate Democrats would have nothing to do with a proposed treaty; neither did several prominent Republicans, led by Massachusetts senator Charles Sumner. Reasons for rejecting the treaty ranged from several shady aspects surrounding the negotiations to Sumner's fear that annexation would compromise the independence of the neighboring black republic of Haiti; other foes of the proposal, led by Missouri senator Carl Schurz, asserted that it would be a great error to introduce more people with dark skin to American citizenship by incorporating Dominicans into the American polity.

Grant's foray into imperialism proved pivotal to the course of Republican politics. It drove a wedge between two leading advocates of black rights, as Grant and Sumner became bitter enemies. It alerted Grant to the need to start playing politics, garnering support through the distribution of patronage, rewarding friends and punishing enemies. However weak and ineffectual a politician he may seem to present-day observers, at the time critics claimed that he used what was at his disposal all too well to gain his way. The president commenced building a corps of supporters in both houses of Congress, notably the Senate, to do the administration's bidding, and isolated Republican dissidents.

The debate over annexation also fueled the growth of a dissenting movement in party ranks. Initially, this group was somewhat loosely unified by a desire for civil service reform and free trade; over time, it gained adherents who were dissatisfied with the incumbent. These dissenting Republicans were fed up with Reconstruction. They believed it was little more than an obstacle to the real issues of government reform and policies based on educated principles. In short, they wanted to remake the party in their own image, one way or another.

They were not alone. "There is no doubt that a feeling prevails that the work of the Republican party . . . ends with the adoption of the Fifteenth Amendment," observed the *New York Times*. Perhaps it was time for a major realignment based on new issues. Once again Democrats played a role in helping to define the political environment. Several party leaders called for a "New Departure" based on the acceptance of the Reconstruction settlement and the construction of a new agenda. "It is reconstruction and the issues growing out of it which preserve the Republican party," observed one southern Democrat. "Strip them of the support which this question gives them and their dissolution will speedily follow."[8]

Unfortunately, neither party could take firm hold of new issues, and, as political violence surged upward in several southern states in 1870 and 1871, it became evident that Reconstruction was not exactly over after all. But it was something of a struggle to craft a proper response to the continuing recalcitrance of many white southerners. In May 1870, Congress had passed and Grant had signed the first in a series of what were to become known as the Enforcement Acts, which enhanced federal supervision of elections, but that action did not curb political violence. In April 1871, after Grant specifically asked for increased legislation, Congress passed another enforcement act, usually known as the Ku Klux Act, authorizing the president to suspend the writ of habeas corpus and dispatch federal forces to subdue terrorists. At a time when Grant was trying to bring his struggle with Sumner over Dominican annexation to a close, many party regulars welcomed the return to Reconstruction issues. As Ohio's Rutherford B. Hayes remarked, "Nothing unites and harmonizes the republican party like the conviction that Democratic victories strengthen the reactionary and brutal tendencies of the late rebel states." Nevertheless, many Republicans also believed that they had gone about as far as they could go. Ohio representative James A. Garfield grumbled

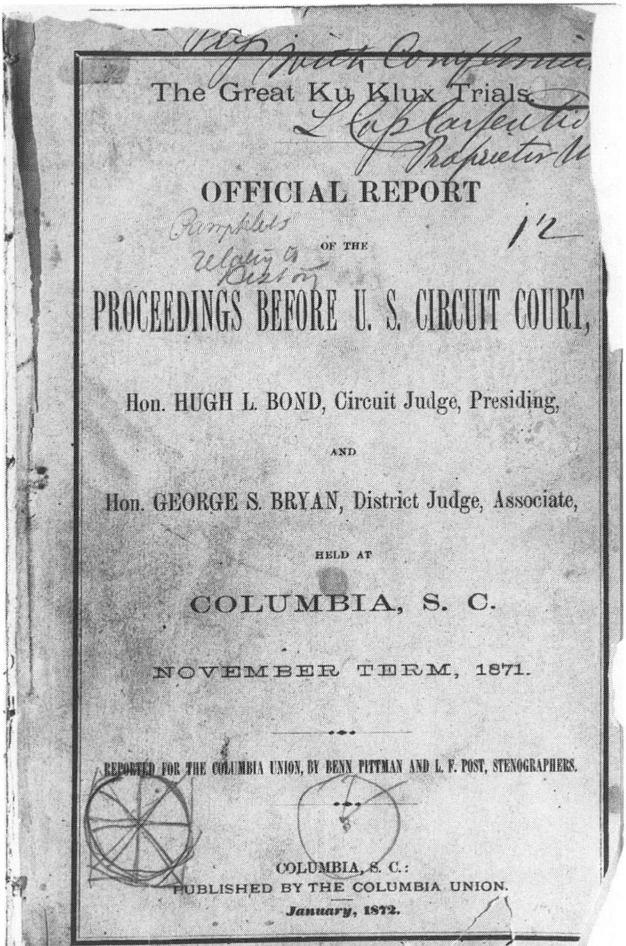

Figure 6.3. United States Circuit Court, *The Great Ku Klux Trials. Official Report of the Proceedings Before U. S. Circuit Court . . . Held at Columbia, S. C. November Term, 1871* (Columbia: Columbia Union, 1872). Reports of Klan activity from the South forced Congress to intervene to protect blacks and Republicans from violence and intimidation and save Republican governments in the South. Congress responded to the Klan terrors by passing the Ku Klux Klan Acts of 1871 and 1872. Federal prosecution of the Klan in several states contributed to its demise, but not before it had undermined Republican rule in the South.

that "we are working on the very verge of the Constitution"; another representative complained, "We have reconstructed, and reconstructed, and we are asked to reconstruct again . . . we are governing the South too much."[9]

As far-reaching as the Ku Klux Act appeared to be on the surface, it was limited in both scope and application. The power to suspend the writ was in force for only a year; Grant invoked the act only once, in South Carolina in the fall of 1871. Enforcement proved problematic and many of those arrested under the act were not prosecuted or were later pardoned; claims that it broke the back of white terrorism were overblown. Moreover, as Attorney General Amos T. Akerman came to understand, even the sensationalism of Klan violence was not enough to compel northerners to renew their concern about southern affairs for a prolonged period. Initially, he believed that the administration could focus public attention "upon the South in such striking matters as the Ku Klux and the rebellious utterances of some of the prominent leaders. . . . All that is necessary to hold the majority of the northern voters to the Republican cause, is to show them how active and cruel the Confederate temper still is in the South." Eventually, he realized that "the real difficulty is that very many of the Northern Republicans shrink from any further legislation in regard to the South. Even such atrocities as Ku Kluxery do not hold their attention, as long and as earnestly, as we should expect. The Northern mind, being active and full of what is called progress, runs away from the past."[10]

Moreover, while intervention shored up Republican prospects in several southern states, elsewhere in the South the party's fortunes were already eroding. Virginia had never really been under Republican rule; Democrats were regaining control in North Carolina, Georgia, and Tennessee. Factionalism within party ranks plagued Republican coalitions in Mississippi, Louisiana, and Alabama, and elsewhere the party's hold on power was none too firm. Nor were either Grant or northern Republicans terribly interested in building up party fortunes in the South through positive initiatives; indeed, they thought enforcement legislation sufficient in itself to offer protection.

If Reconstruction issues continued to energize many Republicans, other members of the party protested that a preoccupation with southern affairs hampered the party's ability to address issues of political and economic policy, which they usually grouped together under the banner of reform. These dissidents first sought to deny Grant renomination, only to discover that the general-president had moved rather skillfully to consolidate his influence with party regulars, until even those Republicans who were not altogether pleased with the president's performance nevertheless conceded the inevitability of his renomination. Unable to effect adoption of either a new political agenda or a new standard-bearer, dissidents began contemplating mounting an independent bid in 1872. They adopted the name Liberal Republicans to distinguish themselves from the main party. Although much of the movement's appeal as a protest against Grant's reelection may have swelled party ranks, that fact also deprived the movement of ideological or programmatic coherence. If movement adherents agreed on anything, it was on the need to adopt a more conciliationist pose toward the white South—a position that kept Reconstruction once more at the center of political debate. Meeting in Cincinnati in May 1872, the movement soon betrayed its earlier commitment to free trade and civil service reform when the mercurial newspaper editor, long-time protectionist, and patronage-seeking Horace Greeley emerged as the Liberal nominee.

The Democratic response to these political developments suggested the troubled nature of that party. The New Departure movement proved stillborn; Democrats preferred to rail against the Grant administration's Reconstruction measures as evidence of the president's commitment to military despotism and overweening power. Yet, in the wake of Greeley's nomination, many Democrats realized that to run their own candidate would assure Grant's reelection; eventually, the party, minus a few protest groups, named the long-time Democratic foe as its standard bearer.

Grant shrewdly responded to the Liberal Republican challenge. He pressed for the adoption of civil service reform and appointed a commission to oversee the framing of rules to administer the policy. He approved a slight decrease in tariff rates; he pushed through a movement to offer a broader amnesty to former Confederates, thus reaffirming his commitment to conciliation where appropriate. These measures blunted Liberal assaults on the administration's record, leaving them to wage what increasingly appeared to be a campaign of personalities rather than issues. But the Republican response was one designed with electoral prospects in mind; the Liberal challenge failed to force a reassessment of priorities.

Republicans determined to run the 1872 campaign as they had the 1868 contest, once more focusing on the questions of war and Reconstruction,

Figure 6.4. "It Is Only a Truce to Regain Power ('Playing Possum')," *Harper's Weekly*, August 24, 1872. Republican apostates Greeley and Charles Sumner encourage a black man gazing on his murdered family to "clasp hands over the bloody chasm" with a Ku Klux Klansman and a racist Irishman. This was among Thomas Nast's most famous, damning cartoons in a graphic war he and *Harper's* waged against the Liberal Republicans. On the other side was Matt Morgan of *Frank Leslie's Illustrated Newspaper*, the other great New York illustrated weekly, who emphasized the corruption of the Grant regime and the good character of Greeley and the reformers.

asserting that a Democratic victory meant the reassertion of southern political influence, repudiating the verdict delivered at Appomattox. In contrast, Greeley promised to foster sectional reconciliation "in the confident trust that the masses of our countrymen, North and South, are eager to clasp hands across the bloody chasm."[11] That was just what some Republican stump orators and publicists wanted to hear. *Harper's Weekly* cartoonist Thomas Nast seized on Greeley's phrase about "the bloody chasm" and recited it mercilessly in a series of cartoons affiliating the newspaper editor with Confederate symbols and personages. To the extent that the campaign became an exercise in personal invective and ridicule, Grant, whatever his foibles and shortcomings, paled as a target in comparison to Greeley, whose varied and contradictory public pronouncements over a long career provided ample ammunition for Nast's attacks. The newspaper editor had made his share of foes as well as friends during his lengthy tenure in the public spotlight: Maine Republican representative James G. Blaine later observed that Greeley "called out a larger proportion of those who intended to vote against him than any other candidate had ever before succeeded in doing."[12]

Often treated as a misadventure in American politics, the Liberal Republican movement, united primarily as it was by the opposition of its members to Grant's reelection, was more than a farcical exercise. Greeley's erratic record on various issues obscured the degree to which the movement represented a questioning of the direction in which the Republican party intended to go. Yet Grant's overwhelming reelection was merely a reprieve from the question of realignment. In summer 1873, New Yorker George Templeton Strong took stock of recent reports of the changing political environment. "There seems to be a prevalent feeling that a new party is wanted," he scribbled in his diary. "Republicanism has grown immoral in its old age and survived much of its usefulness." Observing the widespread discussions about party formation and disintegration circulating in the press, he concluded that "new political combinations are almost certainly forming."[13]

The Panic of 1873 and the ensuing long-term economic depression threatened the Republican party's continued survival in power. It dealt a major blow to the party's chances to persist in its approach to Reconstruction and crippled party-building initiatives in several southern states. "The gospel of prosperity" promised by those Republicans who sought to woo white southerners vanished, as railroad bonds and state treasuries took major hits. As hard times spread across the land, voters in the North wondered why the federal government seemed so much more interested in the fortunes of southern blacks than of northern whites, while in the South impoverished whites protested that their tax dollars were being spent to support programs that advanced the fortunes of the former freedmen. The flight of scalawags from party ranks and the increasing evidence of internal strife, defections, and factionalism played right into Democratic hands, as Arkansas, Texas, and Alabama slipped away from the Republicans for good. Moreover, in the 1874 elections Democrats succeeded in regaining control of the House of Representatives, effectively ending the chances of any additional legislative initiatives to bolster federal intervention efforts in the South.

Yet the crumbling of several Republican regimes in the South and increasing northern criticism of federal intervention in southern affairs were not the only reasons the Democrats claimed victory. In the wake of economic depression Republicans struggled to frame an adequate response. They fell back on tinkering with the nation's money supply; enough Republicans joined Democrats to send to Grant's White House desk a bill that allowed for relatively modest inflation. Grant's decision to veto that bill on April 22, 1874 moved the party in the direction of pro-creditor contraction policies (and eventually led to additional legislation to retire the remaining greenbacks). "Some say this will split the Republican party and destroy it," George Templeton Strong observed. "Never mind if it does. We want a new party founded on hard money, free trade, and home rule. Only let it *not* be called Democratic."[14] It did not quite go that far, but the veto damaged the party's fortunes in the West as well as the South, where debtors looked elsewhere for help; third parties emerged to articulate these new desires.

At least as damaging to the Republicans was the fact that, when most northern whites thought of Reconstruction, their attention was usually directed toward Louisiana. During Grant's first term the political conditions there were at best uneasy as Republicans battled each other as well as their Democratic foes. By 1872 Louisiana Republicans had split into two wings, one led by Governor Henry Clay Warmoth, the other by William P. Kellogg. Grant eventually sided with the Kellogg clique, while Warmoth and his followers embraced Greeley's candidacy and the fortunes of Democratic gubernatorial candidate John McEnery in his race against Kellogg. Both sides claimed victory in a contest marked by fraud, intimidation, and violence; Grant eventually recognized Kellogg's claim to office. During the next two years violence characterized the state's politics as conservative whites mounted a sustained campaign to overthrow the Kellogg regime, culminating in a coup attempt in January 1875. Grant's approval of General Philip H. Sheridan's quashing of the coup attempt was harshly criticized by Democrats and many former Liberal Republicans; even the president's rather passionate special message in which he spoke bluntly about what was going on in the South was applauded primarily because of its usefulness in countering partisan criticism.

Grant had weighed the political cost of a Reconstruction policy based on intervention for some time. "I begin to think it time for the Republican party to unload," he declared in January 1874. "There has been too much dead weight carried by it. . . . I am tired of this nonsense. . . . This nursing of monstrosities has nearly exhausted the life of the party. I am done with them, and they will have to take care of themselves." For several months he was an interested bystander as Virginia Democrats explored the possibility of supporting Grant for a third term at the head of a bisectional party in exchange for an end to federal support of the remaining Republican regimes. In the meantime the president soft-pedaled his support for new civil rights legislation and wondered whether desegregation of public schools might be counterproductive should white southerners respond by closing down the public schools.[15]

By the beginning of 1875, Grant knew that his Reconstruction policy was in trouble. Court decisions were chipping away at his ability to protect black voters; every time he exercised what powers were available to him, he faced charges that he was a tyrant. Only four southern Republican regimes remained (Mississippi, South Carolina, Florida, and ill-fated Louisiana), and in each case the party's hold on power was tenuous. Moreover, northern patience was eroding, as was Republican strength. James A. Garfield noted that the controversy over Louisiana "appears to be the mill stone that threatens to sink our party out of sight"; another Republican concluded that "the truth is our people are tired out with this worn out cry of 'southern outrages'" and that in the face of "hard times & heavy taxes" there was little interest in black aspirations. Grant's strongly worded indictment offered momentary relief and revived old issues once more: a Republican congressman noted that "both parties have resolved to stand or die in the old attitude toward the South." However, Republican willingness to compromise on questions concerning Arkansas and the failure to pass one last enforcement act revealed that congressional Republicans were also unloading the southern question. The retreat from a national party to one based primarily in the North was on.[16]

In short, while waving the bloody shirt might reenergize the party faithful, there was no support for a more vigorous policy of federal intervention, and flawed administration and court decisions were crippling what measures were extant. Grant acted on this understanding in responding to a request for assistance from Mississippi governor Adelbert Ames, who was faced with a well-planned and skillfully waged Democratic campaign of terrorism designed to secure victory at the polls. As he considered the request, Grant heard from Ohio Republicans that intervention might well cost them the day in a contest that was already rather close.

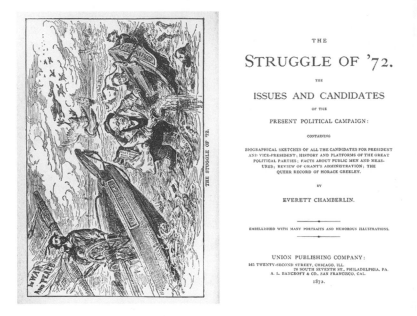

Figure 6.5. Everett Chamberlain, *The Struggle of '72. The Issues and Candidates of the Present Political Campaign* (Chicago: Union Publishing Co., 1872). The Republican party machinery in 1872 cranked out loads of books, papers, pamphlets, hand cards, broadsides, songsters, and any number of printed items drumming up support for Grant and the regular party candidates. Party literature reminded voters that Grant had saved the Union after the Democrats had conspired to destroy it. Chamberlain's *Struggle of '72* was boilerplate Republican propaganda, which showed up in later campaigns as Republicans waved the bloody shirt of Republican patriotism and Democratic disunion, murder of Lincoln, and lawlessness after the war. In 1872 and after, such propaganda covered over fissures within the Republican party with calls to patriotic remembrance and duty.

Wearily, the president confided to his attorney general that "the whole public are tired out with these annual, autumnal outbreaks in the South"; best first to check with Ames to see whether the governor had exhausted all the resources at his command. The governor grumbled, but Grant's forbearance helped Republicans carry Ohio by a mere 5,000 votes in October; the following month Democrats claimed victory in Mississippi.[17]

For a while Grant cast about for alternative ways to rally Republicans. He even explored tapping into anti-Catholic prejudice. Perhaps he could make something of the Catholic Church's efforts to secure public money for sectarian schools. Speaking at a veterans' reunion in Des Moines in September 1875, he predicted that the next contest would be "between patriotism and intelligence on the one side, and superstition, ambition, and ignorance on the other."[18] In his annual message at the end of the year, he remained silent about Reconstruction, preferring to highlight support for public education and the separation of church and state. However, before long he was busily fending off numerous charges of corruption directed at his subordinates; he would have to leave the politics of realignment to others.

At first it looked as if Maine's James G. Blaine would take up that challenge, but Blaine soon cast aside proposals for public education in favor of waving the bloody shirt once more, this time by excluding Jefferson Davis from a measure calling for general amnesty. Republicans then adroitly countered Democratic efforts to feature corruption and reform as the central issues of the upcoming presidential campaign by nominating Ohio governor Rutherford B. Hayes for president. Hayes looked to be reformer enough to blunt the Democratic assault. His own early preference to emphasize issues of church and state and public education soon fell away in light of a resurgence in political violence in the South, and the Republican candidate began to emphasize the importance of securing the fruits of victory at the polls. Should the Democrats come to power, he argued, so would Confederate principles. However, he added that he would not pursue a policy of intervention but would consider other ways of building up the party's tattered fortunes in the South. Once more southern issues had come to define party divisions, with the outcome of the war being determined at the polls.

By now the disputed election of 1876 and the negotiations which led to the so-called Compromise of 1877 are well known. In order to secure Hayes's inauguration without difficulty, Republicans were willing to forego a policy of intervention they were already abandoning; in return southern Democrats made concessions and sought economic assistance, although little came of such promises. Hayes intended to try to rebuild southern Republicanism on the basis of economic development in order to attract former Whigs and other whites to party ranks. He would abandon intervention altogether.

The politics of the Hayes administration offered striking proof of the degree to which reforging Republican identity in the 1870s had been at best a partial success. The president's early hopes at spurring a political realignment in the South proved stillborn. Southern gentlemen of property and standing preferred to stay in the ranks of the Democratic party, sometimes battling in-state foes who pressed for economic change, as in the Readjuster movement in Virginia. Northern Republicans shied away from making common cause with such insurgent movements, aware that to ally with advocates of inflation and debt repudiation would vitiate the party's own stand on fiscal policy. Hayes's own battles for control of patronage and his appointment of several prominent former Liberal Republicans, notably Carl Schurz, to high office alienated many party regulars, who engaged the chief executive in a running two-year battle over appointments; from retirement veteran Radical Republican Benjamin F. Wade groused that the new president "meditates the destruction of the party that elected him."[19]

Yet there was little heart among Republicans for a return to the policy of federal intervention in the South. Such a policy would have depended solely on executive action, as no new legislative initiative would ever survive the Democratic majority in the House of Representatives. As Hayes supporter and *Harper's Weekly* editor George W. Curtis noted, to persist in intervention "would have wholly overthrown the party within two more years. . . . Viewed partywise, the only hope lay in a bold and vigorous change of policy. Not to have made it would have been to destroy the party." Yet the failure of Hayes's own initiative became apparent when Democrats solidified their southern majorities in the 1878 midterm elections. Garfield concluded that the president's policy "has turned out to be a give-away from the beginning"; New York senator Roscoe Conkling chortled that Hayes, "in spite of the fact that he can command no votes in the South . . . seems possessed of the delusion that he is able to create a party of his own there." However, it was less than clear what the alternative should be, for, as Garfield noted, "The man who attempts to get up a political excitement in this country on the old sectional issues will find himself without a party and without support."[20]

Once more the Democratic party rode to the rescue of Republican political misfortunes. In the wake of their victories in the 1878 contests, in which the party secured control of both houses of Congress, Democratic leaders overplayed their hand when they struck at what remained of federal enforcement capability by attaching mischievous riders to appropriation bills. Always proud of his commitment to shoring up executive independence, Hayes resisted such efforts, issuing a series of vetoes. While the president labored to disassociate his actions from any effort to revive Reconstruction—"The present controversy is in no sense partisan and it is not a question of race or color. . . . No present interest of a Sectional character is involved," he asserted—it was clear to other observers that once more it was time to wave the bloody shirt. "The coming of Hayes saw the shirt folded and laid away," remarked one Ohioan; "and then the question was, what rag shall we now brandish before the eyes of the North to excite the necessary fury? As far as I can see, the new 'rag' is 'conspiracy,' 'revolution'; the South capturing the Capitol,' etc."[21]

Reminding voters and each other of wartime allegiances drew Republicans together and revitalized party morale. The controversy even refurbished Hayes's popularity in some quarters of his own party. "I have no doubt that the President's position has been productive of good," concluded James Garfield, "for it has demonstrated, more clearly, the real character of the Southern people than the old policy could have done."[22] In fact, the riders controversy illustrated the political utility of waving the bloody shirt. It enabled Republican leaders to sound again the battle cries of years gone by without forcing them to propose legislation or to take action to support black voters in the South. It revived anti-southern sentiments and effectively linked them to opposition to Democratic initiatives, raising again the question of whether that party could be entrusted with control of the presidency. And it united the Republican party faithful in ways that no other issue or appeal could do. In the fall elections of 1879, Republicans triumphed in the traditionally bellwether state of Ohio and elsewhere, sparking hope that the party would do the same in the presidential contest the following year. Meanwhile, some southern blacks, fully aware that this upsurge in Republican chances presaged no change in policy, voted with their feet and began migrating elsewhere.[23]

In the end, Republicans and Democrats alike still found something of importance in the issues of the war and Reconstruction. Efforts at realignment did not produce the revolutionary changes promised because Republicans could not agree on a common economic platform if it went too far beyond general principles. To be sure, there was some alteration in the party's membership, but the Liberal Republican movement proved abortive and other cries for realignment went unheeded. Instead, Republicans, wrestling with the consequences of retreating from a national to a sectional party, found reviving issues associated with the war to be the surest way of rallying the troops enthusiastically for yet another campaign. Waving the bloody shirt may have been a cynical manipulation of voters' emotions, but more likely it touched party allegiance at the core, and in any case it served as a means to build support for Reconstruction measures where a straightforward appeal to offer additional safeguards for African Americans against violence in the South fell short. Eventually, the party would move on to other issues, notably economic development, and realize more fully its identity as the party of big business. But it took a long time for Republicans to break old habits and to wean themselves from the security offered by waving the bloody shirt.

Afterword

James M. McPherson

From its first days in the troubled 1850s, the Republican party has been a contentious subject. The party drew together, in fits and starts, previously competing interests of free soilers, nativists, anti-nativists, anti-Nebraska Democrats, conscience Whigs, and others. Defining the party was no easy matter as events moved rapidly and Republicans organized to win elections and, once in power, to act on avowed principles and promised advantages. Then, too, those who opposed Republicans also defined them, forcing Republican responses to such charges as being "black abolitionists," "disunionists," nativists, friends of capital and enemies of labor, and so much more. The first generation of Republicans wrestled with winning a war and securing a peace, all the while bringing order to a party of many parts. Republicans argued among themselves on a host of issues and even on the direction the party should go in war and peace. Later, as the party had become a fixture on the American political landscape, Republicans still contended among themselves on such issues as tariffs, civil rights, sabbatarian laws, and the regulation and promotion of business. And in the emerging mythology about its origins the Grand Old Party even argued about its birthplace.

This book on the genesis of Republicanism reflects the contentiousness of the first generation of the party and the age. Just as Republicans disagreed on many details and directions, so too scholars are not of one mind regarding the history and meaning of the party. This book brings together historians of various perspectives and interests with the expectation that they will contend among themselves and point to several different directions that discussion about the Republican party might go. The various perspectives on the early history of the Republican party offered by the six essays in this book provide a dynamic, and sometimes contradictory, multidimensional portrait of the first generation of the "Grand Young Party" that by the 1880s was becoming the Grand Old Party. And it is good that it is so, for varied perspectives are the lifeblood of historical scholarship. Consensus among historians is rare indeed, and when it exists the result is often bland and uninteresting. These essays are neither bland nor uninteresting.

Eric Foner and Mark Neely see the Republican party of the 1850s and 1860s as an agency of radical reform animated by a genuine anti-slavery ideology and an egalitarian impulse that achieved the greatest sociopolitical transformation in American history embodied in the Thirteenth, Fourteenth, and Fifteenth Amendments to the Constitution. Foner views this credo as mainly secular, growing out of the antebellum free-labor ideology that he has done so much to elucidate. Neely emphasizes its religious origins in the "slavery as sin" creed of the abolitionists that broadened into radical emancipationism when the war opened the opportunity to end slavery.

Jean Baker and, possibly, Brooks Simpson implicitly go part way with this interpretation. But Baker notes that Republican accomplishments fell short of equal rights for half the population, thus calling into question the genuine quality of Republican egalitarianism. Simpson appreciates the remarkable nature of Republican achievements, but finds the dominant theme after 1868 to be a tilt toward Hamiltonian economics that was temporarily delayed by southern violence in the 1870s until, after 1876, the party could "realize more fully its identity as the party of big business."

Phillip Shaw Paludan sees the party moving from "its small-producer, middle-class origins toward becoming the party of big business" as early as the war years. Nevertheless, writes Paludan, the war was "the Republican party's finest hour" because it preserved the Union and freed four million slaves, "two of the nation's greatest triumphs." Michael Holt might agree, but his essay focuses less on the ideological or reform or even nationalist economic impulses of the party than on its political pragmatism. For Holt, political parties (especially in election years) define themselves more by what they are *against* than what they are *for*. Their main goal is to attain and retain power; policy achievements are byproducts of this goal.

The principal variance of interpretations occurs between Foner and Neely on the one hand and Holt on the other. For Neely and Foner the main thrust of Republican ideology before the war was anti-*slavery*; for Holt it was anti-slave *power*. Once the war began, Foner and Neely emphasize the movement of Republicanism from negative opposition to slavery toward a positive commitment to freedom and even to equality before the law. "The Civil War," writes Foner, "elevated 'equality' to a status in the vocabulary of freedom it had not enjoyed since the Revolution." For Holt, however, Republicans stood not so much for freedom and equal rights as against the South and its roughshod violation of northern republican rights. "South-bashing" more than reformism or egalitarianism characterized Republican rhetoric.

Drawing on my own memory and experience, I would like to suggest that these apparently antagonistic interpretations are in fact quite compatible. During the civil rights movement of the 1960s, many of us indulged in a certain amount of "South-bashing" in our sometimes unprintable comments about Orval Faubus, George Wallace, Ross Barnett, and other antediluvian southern political leaders. But we liked to think that this bashing was consistent with positive and even idealistic support for the goals of Martin Luther King, Jr., Thurgood Marshall, and other civil rights leaders. It just might be that, similarly, the South-bashing of Holt's Republicans a century earlier was consistent with the emancipationist goals of Foner's and Neely's Republicans.

Whatever their other apparent disagreements, the authors seem to concur that the Republican party retreated from its "broad definition of equality and national power" (Foner) during the war and early Reconstruction years to become "the party of big business" (Simpson) by the 1880s if not earlier. I would like to raise some questions about this thesis. The party of Lincoln and Thaddeus Stevens did not change into the party of Ronald Reagan and Newt Gingrich overnight. Three times during the 1880s the Republican Senate passed a bill sponsored by New Hampshire's Republican Henry W. Blair for large-scale federal aid to education that would have benefited most of all black public schools in the South. Three times the Democratic House killed the bill. In 1890 the House (now Republican) passed a bill sponsored by Massachusetts Republican Henry Cabot Lodge to enforce black voting rights in the South only to see it blocked by Democrats (and a handful of Republicans) in the Senate. After that, Republicans did retreat from federal enforcement of the Fourteenth and Fifteenth Amendments—but never as far as the pre-1950s Democratic party. A proposed anti-lynching law in the 1920s and 1930s attracted more Republican than Democratic support. So did the 1957 and 1960 civil rights bills enacted by Congress and signed by a Republican president. And of course the author of the 1954 *Brown* decision was a Republican chief justice appointed by a Republican president—the same president who was the first since 1877 to send federal troops into the South in 1957 to enforce the Fourteenth Amendment.

As for becoming the "party of big business," that too may require some modification. Republicans could not have won all the elections they did in the North without support from many workers and farmers, who after all vastly outnumbered the Robber Barons. And the opposition of the labor movement today to free trade, low tariffs, and NAFTA suggests that Republican appeals to American workers to support high tariffs in order to protect their jobs and wages from foreign competition in the 1880s and 1890s were not simply a cynical manipulation of false consciousness. If we define big business to include bankers and merchants as well as manufacturers, Democrat Grover Cleveland may have gotten as much "big business" support as did his Republican opponents. William McKinley and Theodore Roosevelt got more labor votes than their Democratic opponents. And until at least 1913 the foremost Progressive leaders were Republicans Robert LaFollette and Theodore Roosevelt. To borrow Phillip Paludan's terminology, the "Grand Young Party" of the 1850s and 1860s did not become the Grand Old Party of Calvin Coolidge and Herbert Hoover as early or as completely as the stereotype created by an earlier generation of Matthew Josephson-influenced historians would have it.

In surveying the various interpretations of the Republican party in these essays, readers may be tempted to compare historical scholarship to the proverbial blind man trying to describe an elephant from the various parts of the beast that each of them touched. All know an elephant is afoot—a Republican party in this case—but they do not agree as to its full shape or direction. But that is the nature of historical scholarship; even with twenty-twenty hindsight, historians will never be able to agree on the exact features and dimensions of such a large and complex animal as the elephant—which of course is the symbol of the Republican party— especially when (and because) it kept growing and moving about. These essays limn the story of the youth of that elephant in all its complexity and variety with a stimulating vitality that maintains the unfailing interest of specialists as well as novices in the field.

Notes

Introduction

1. Allen Nevins, *The Emergence of Lincoln: Prologue to Civil War, 1859–1861*, 2 vols. (New York, 1950), 2: 468

Chapter 1. The Ideology of the Republican Party

1. Eric Foner, *Free Soil, Free Labor, Free Men: The Ideology of the Republican Party Before the Civil War* (New York, 1970).

2. *The Collected Works of Abraham Lincoln*, ed. Roy P. Basler, Marion Dolores Pratt, and Lloyd A. Dunlap, 9 vols. (New Brunswick, N.J., 1953–55), 2: 405, 492, 499–500; 3: 95; 4: 24; Paul M. Angle, ed., *Created Equal? The Complete Lincoln-Douglas Debates* (Chicago, 1958), 111–12.

3. Eric Foner, *Reconstruction: America's Unfinished Revolution, 1863–1877* (New York, 1988), 1–7.

4. Ibid., 7–9, 49; *Works of Lincoln*, 7: 243.

5. *Works of Lincoln*, 6: 301–2.

6. David Potter, *The South and the Sectional Conflict* (Baton Rouge, La., 1968), 56; *Congressional Record*, 43d Cong., 1st sess., 4116; Frank Freidel, *Francis Lieber: Nineteenth-Century Liberal* (Baton Rouge, La., 1947), 302; Edward Everett Hale, *The Man Without a Country, and Other Stories* (Boston, 1898).

7. Philip S. Foner, *The Life and Writings of Frederick Douglass*, 4 vols. (New York, 1950–55), 3: 214; *Congressional Globe*, 38th Cong., 1st sess., 523.

8. V. Jacques Voegeli, *Free but Not Equal: The Midwest and the Negro During the Civil War* (Chicago, 1967), 162–63; Carl Schurz, *For the Great Empire of Liberty, Forward!* (New York, 1864).

9. *The Works of James Abram Garfield*, ed. Burke A. Hinsdale, 2 vols. (Boston, 1882), 1: 86.

10. Foner, *Reconstruction*, 176–227.

11. Ibid., 228–32.

12. Ibid, 241–54, 446.

13. Ibid., 24; *Speeches, Correspondence, and Political Papers of Carl Schurz*, ed. Frederic Bancroft, 6 vols. (New York, 1913), 1: 487–88.

14. Philip S. Foner and Daniel Rosenberg, eds., *Racism, Dissent, and Asian Americans from 1850 to the Present* (Westport, Conn., 1993), 223–24; Luella Gettys, *The Law of Citizenship in the United States* (Chicago, 1934), 62–69.

15. Ellen C. DuBois, "Outgrowing the Compact of the Fathers: Equal Rights, Woman Suffrage, and the United States Constitution, 1820–1878," *Journal of American History* 74 (December 1987): 846; Ellen C. DuBois, ed., *Elizabeth Cady Stanton and Susan B. Anthony: Correspondence, Writings, Speeches* (New York, 1981), 132; Amy D. Stanley, "Conjugal Bonds and Wage Labor: Rights of Contract in the Age of Emancipation," *Journal of American History* 75 (September 1988): 471.

16. Foner, *Reconstruction*, 460–511.

17. Jacob D. Cox to James A. Garfield, March 27, 1871, James A. Garfield Papers, Library of Congress.

18. Foner, *Reconstruction*, 523–34.

19. Ibid., 564–82; 46th Cong., 2nd sess., Senate Report 693, pt. 2, 108; *Proceedings of the Republican National Convention Held at Cincinnati, Ohio* (Concord, N.H., 1876), 26–27.

Chapter 2. Making and Mobilizing the Republican Party, 1854–1860

1. The 1854 Michigan Republican platform is reprinted in Arthur M. Schlesinger, Jr., ed., *History of U.S. Political Parties*, 4 vols. (New York, 1973), 2: 1175–80.

2. Circular dated May 25, 1859, in Edwin D. Morgan Papers, New York State Library, Albany.

3. Schlesinger, ed., *History of U.S. Political Parties*, 2: 1371–73.

4. I expand on this point in "The Mysterious Disappearance of the American Whig Party," in Michael F. Holt, *Political Parties and American Political Development from the Age of Jackson to the Age of Lincoln* (Baton Rouge, La., 1992), 237–64.

5. Michael F. Holt, *The Political Crisis of the 1850s* (reprint New York, 1983), 188, 191.

6. *Washington National Era*, May 22, 1854, quoted in Mark L. Berger, *The Revolution of the New York Party System, 1840–1860* (Port Washington, N.Y., 1973), 36.

7. For more detail on these states, see William E. Gienapp, *The Origins of the Republican Party, 1852–1856* (New York, 1987), 103–27 and Michael F. Holt, *The Rise and Fall of the American Whig Party: Jacksonian Politics and the Onset of the Civil War* (New York, 1999), 858–71.

8. Holt, *American Whig Party*, 869–71.

9. *Albany Evening Journal*, July 13, 1854, quoted in Gienapp, *Origins of the Republican Party*, 83. For Free Soilers' vexation with Seward and Weed, see Holt, *American Whig Party*, 830–35.

10. James W. Taylor to Hamilton Fish, November 11, 1854, Hamilton Fish Papers, Library of Congress; Edward L. Pierce to Salmon P. Chase, November 9, 1855, Salmon P. Chase Papers, Library of Congress.

11. By no means did all northern nativists abandon the Know-Nothings for

the Republicans in 1856. Millard Fillmore, the American party candidate, attracted almost 400,000 votes in the North that year.

12. William E. Gienapp, "Nativism and the Creation of a Republican Majority in the North Before the Civil War," *Journal of American History* 72 (December 1985): 529–59; Gienapp, "Who Voted for Lincoln?" in *Abraham Lincoln and the American Political Tradition*, ed. John L. Thomas (Amherst, Mass., 1986), 50–97; Gienapp, *Origins of the Republican Party*. For more on the Republicans' courtship of Know-Nothings in New York between the 1856 and 1860 elections, see Joel H. Silbey, *The Partisan Imperative: The Dynamics of American Politics Before the Civil War* (New York, 1985), 127–65. For the decisive contribution of former Know-Nothings to Republican gains in Pennsylvania's off-year elections between 1856 and 1860, see James L. Huston, *The Panic of 1857 and the Coming of the Civil War* (Baton Rouge, La., 1987), 155–60, 258. For the contrary view, that Know-Nothings contributed little to the Republican vote, at least in Massachusetts, see Dale Baum, "Know Nothingism and the Republican Majority in Massachusetts: The Realignment of the 1850s," *Journal of American History* 64 (March 1978): 959–86.

13. For examples of the warnings from Pennsylvania, see Francis Blackburn to Abraham Lincoln, Philadelphia, November 24, 1860, and James K. Moorhead to Lincoln, Pittsburgh, November 23, 1860, Abraham Lincoln Papers, Library of Congress, microfilm edition.

14. N. Field to George W. Julian, September 19, 1856, quoted in Eric Foner, *Free Soil, Free Labor, Free Men: The Ideology of the Republican Party Before the Civil War* (New York, 1970), 59.

15. Dwight L. Dumond is the leading representative of such historians.

16. For my interpretation, see Holt, *Political Crisis of the 1850s*, esp. 183–217; see also Gienapp, *Origins of the Republican Party*, 347–65.

17. Speech of John Jay at Bedford, Westchester County, New York, October 8, 1856. This speech was published as a Republican campaign pamphlet in 1856. I am indebted to Kate Pierce, a graduate student at the University of Virginia, for bringing it to my attention.

18. The "Irrepressible Conflict" speech is reprinted in Schlesinger, ed., *History of U.S. Political Parties*, 2: 1229–38.

19. Limits of space preclude an examination of the mechanics of the Republican campaign in 1856. They are skillfully treated in Gienapp, *Origins of the Republican Party*, 375–411. Briefly put, the Republican national committee managed to raise very little money in 1856 and then squandered most of its resources on Pennsylvania, where feuding local leaders totally mismanaged the campaign. As a result, Republicans in the critical states of Illinois and Indiana received very little help in terms of cash, campaign materials, or speakers from the national committee.

20. William E. Gienapp, "The Crime Against Sumner: The Caning of Charles Sumner and the Rise of the Republican Party," *Civil War History* 25 (September 1979): 218–45; Gienapp, *Origins of the Republican Party*, 348–65; Holt, *Political Crisis of the 1850s*, 194–97.

21. Nor did I until Kate Pierce brought the incident and Republicans'

politicization of it to my attention. I am indebted to her for the evidence cited in the following two notes.

22. John Jay, *America Free or America Slave* (New York, 1856).

23. Michigan Republican State Committee, *Important Facts Drawn from Authentic Sources, Proving Beyond a Doubt the Approaching Presidential Election Is to Decide the Question Between Freedom and Slavery* (Detroit, 1856).

24. Gienapp, *Origins of the Republican Party*, 545–46; Lex Renda, *Running on the Record: Civil War-Era Politics in New Hampshire* (Charlottesville, Va.,1997), 200; Michael Fitzgibbon Holt, *Forging a Majority: The Formation of the Republican Party in Pittsburgh, 1848–1860* (New Haven, Conn., 1969), 356.

25. Foner, *Free Soil, Free Labor, Free Men*, 149.

26. Gienapp, *Origins of the Republican Party*, 527–37; Renda, *Running on the Record*, 214.

27. One must not, however, minimize the contribution of partisan loyalty and ethnic and religious resentments among immigrants and Catholics in explaining Buchanan's vote or the popularity of Fillmore among diehard nativists and conservative Whigs.

28. Gienapp, "Who Voted for Lincoln?" 78–81. Gienapp's estimates also indicate that approximately one-twelfth of Buchanan's supporters in Maine and Connecticut and one-fifth in Massachusetts backed Lincoln in 1860, but those three states were already securely in the Republican column.

29. Don E. Fehrenbacher, *The Dred Scott Case: Its Significance in American Law and Politics* (New York, 1978), 563–67; see also the table on turnout rates in William E. Gienapp, "'Politics seem to Enter into Everything': Political Culture in the North," in *Essays on Antebellum Politics, 1840–1860*, ed. Stephen E. Maizlish and John J. Kushma (College Station, Tex., 1982), 18–19. The total turnout rates fell slightly in Illinois and New Jersey but sharply in Indiana and Pennsylvania between 1856 and 1858.

30. The best study of Republicans' economic policies during the Civil War is now Heather Cox Richardson, *The Greatest Nation of the Earth: Republican Economic Policies During the Civil War* (Cambridge, Mass., 1997).

31. Huston, *Panic of 1857*, 139–72. I have also relied heavily on Huston's meticulous analysis for my comments on Republicans' divided response on the banking and currency issues.

32. Holt, *Political Crisis of the 1850s*, 206–9.

33. At the risk of committing heresy, if not blasphemy, I believe that historians' neglect of this episode—that is, what was going on among non-Republican opponents of the Democrats—stems from their unwarranted focus on the Lincoln-Douglas debates of 1858 and their equally unwarranted insistence that Lincoln typified other Republicans.

34. Benjamin D. Pettengill to Edwin D. Morgan, May 16, 1859, Edwin D. Morgan Papers; James Ashley to Salmon P. Chase, November 28, 1858, Salmon P. Chase Papers.

35. Abraham Lincoln to Nathan Sargent, June 23, 1859, *Collected Works of*

Abraham Lincoln, ed. Roy P. Basler, Dolores Pratt, and Lloyd A. Dunlap, 9 vols. (New Brunswick, N.J., 1953), 8: 387–88. Sargent, a prominent conservative Whig, had supported Fillmore in 1856. For more on the divergent Republican responses in 1858–59, see Holt, *Political Crisis of the 1850s*, 209–13.

36. Gienapp, "Who Voted for Lincoln?" 83, 86.

37. The Republicans' national platform of 1860 is reprinted in Schlesinger, ed., *History of U.S. Political Parties*, 2: 1239–41. While some historians contend that there was no watering down of Republicans' antislavery and anti-southern commitments in the 1860 national platform, I agree with William Gienapp's analysis that it was in fact considerably more moderate than the 1856 platform. See Gienapp, "Who Voted for Lincoln?" 55–57; Huston, *Panic of 1857*, 259.

38. Lincoln carried Illinois with only 50.8 percent of the vote, his lowest proportion in any state he carried with a majority, although he won California and Oregon with much smaller pluralities of the popular vote.

39. Lincoln got a handful of votes in Virginia and did slightly better in the border slave states of Missouri, Kentucky, Maryland, and Delaware, where his proportionate share of the vote ranged from a high of 10 percent in Missouri to 1 percent in Kentucky.

40. The fullest analysis of the Upper South's effort to persuade Lincoln to disband the Republican party is Daniel W. Crofts, *Reluctant Confederates: Upper South Unionists in the Secession Crisis* (Chapel Hill, N.C., 1989), 195–332; see also Holt, "Abraham Lincoln and the Politics of Union."

41. George Fogg to Abraham Lincoln, February 5, 1861, quoted in Daniel W. Crofts, "The Union Party of 1861 and the Secession Crisis," *Perspectives in American History* 11 (1977–78): 368 n.48; W. G. Snethen to Abraham Lincoln, November 28, December 8, 13, 1860, Abraham Lincoln Papers.

Chapter 3. War Is the Health of the Party: Republicans in the American Civil War

1. Allen Guelzo, who dedicated his Lincoln biography to Jack Kemp, has asserted that a modern-day Lincoln would vote Republican. While this chapter is not a direct response to that assertion, there may be things in it that help us consider the merit of Guelzo's claim. Allen C. Guelzo, "Ten 'True Lies' About Abraham Lincoln, Part 1," *For the People: A Newsletter of the Abraham Lincoln Association* 2 (Summer 2000): 1–2, 6–8.

2. Bruce Tap, *Over Lincoln's Shoulder: The Committee on the Conduct of the War* (Lawrence, Kan., 2000); William B. Hesseltine, *Lincoln and the War Governors* (New York, 1948); William Zornow, *Lincoln and the Party Divided* (Norman, Okla., 1954); John C. Waugh, *Reelecting Lincoln: The Battle for the 1864 Presidency* (New York, 1997); T. Harry Williams, *Lincoln and the Radicals* (Madison, Wis., 1941).

3. See Phillip Shaw Paludan, "'The Better Angels of Our Nature': Lincoln, Propaganda and Public Opinion in the North During the Civil War Era," fifteenth Annual R. Gerald McMurtry Lecture, Fort Wayne, Indiana, 1992.

4. *Tribune Almanac and Political Register* for 1862–65 (New York, 1862, 1863, 1864, 1865); Michael Holt, "Abraham Lincoln and the Politics of Union," in *Abraham Lincoln and the American Political Tradition*, ed. John L. Thomas (Amherst, Mass., 1986), 115.

5. See the discussion in Phillip Shaw Paludan, *The Presidency of Abraham Lincoln* (Lawrence, Kan., 1994), 280–303 and sources cited there; William Harris, *With Charity for All: Lincoln and the Reconstruction of the Union* (Lexington, Ky., 1997), 186–90.

6. I have only found 20 state totals; of these, Republicans held 17 state legislatures and Democrats 3.

7. *Tribune Almanac and Political Register* for 1862–65. Adam I. P. Smith, "The Presidential Election of 1864" (PhD dissertation, Cambridge University, 2000), 54 and *Statistical History of the United States* (Stamford, Conn., 1965), 691, provide different figures for members of Congress from those in the almanac. I have followed the latter. On party-state, see Richard F. Bensel, *Yankee Leviathan: The Origins of Central State Authority in America, 1859–1877* (Cambridge, 1990).

8. Charles Jellison, *Fessenden of Maine: Civil War Senator* (Syracuse, N.Y., 1962), 116; Fawn Brodie, *Thaddeus Stevens: Scourge of the South* (New York, 1966), 180–85.

9. *Statistical History of the United States*, 682–91.

10. Jellison, *Fessenden of Maine*, 130–40; Harry Carmen and Richard Luthin, *Lincoln and the Patronage* (New York, 1943).

11. Eric Foner, *Free Soil, Free Labor, Free Men: The Ideology of the Republican Party Before the Civil War* (New York, 1995), 302–4; James M. McPherson, *Battle Cry of Freedom: The Civil War Era* (New York, 1988), 506.

12. Smith, "Election of 1864," 169 n.75.

13. The strategy of the Republicans in 1864 was described by a Simon Cameron correspondent: "We should flood the country with caricatures of the rebel convention at Chicago with McClellan in the centre and [Copperheads] Voorhees and Woods and Alex Long looking over his shoulders with their peculiar sentiments spread as streamers from their mouths." Quoted in Smith, "Election of 1864," 173; James G. Blaine, *Twenty Years in Congress from Lincoln to Garfield*, 2 vols. (Norwich, Conn., 1884), 2: 43.

14. Alexander Stephens as quoted in Frank Moore, ed., *The Rebellion Record: A Diary of American Events*, 12 vols. (New York, 1861–67), 1: 44–49.

15. Bensel, *Yankee Leviathan*, chap. 2.

16. In fact, one might argue that the Democratic party, by weakening national power in the prewar period, made necessary government action that would empower the capitalists of the Gilded Age. I am grateful to Jonathan Earle of the University of Kansas for this observation.

17. Heather Richardson, *The Greatest Nation of the Earth: Republican Economic Policies During the Civil War* (Cambridge, Mass., 1997), 57. My argument here relies on my *"A People's Contest": The Union and Civil War, 1861–1865* (New York, 1988), 141–42.

18. David Montgomery, *Beyond Equality: Labor and the Radical Republicans, 1862–1872* (New York, 1967), 112–13.

19. For the St. Louis strikes and Rosecrans's suppression, see Louis S. Gerteis, *Civil War St. Louis* (Lawrence, Kan., forthcoming 2002), 336–42 (manuscript pages, chap. 8).

20. See the discussion in Smith, "Campaign of 1864," 191–93.

21. Richardson, *Greatest Nation of the Earth*, 255; Gabor Boritt, *Lincoln and the Economics of the American Dream* (Memphis, Tenn., 1978); Daniel Walker Howe, *The Political Culture of the American Whigs* (Chicago, 1979).

22. Lawrence Costello, "The New York City Labor Movement, 1861–1873" (PhD dissertation, Columbia University, 1967); James C. Sylvis, *The Life, Speeches, Labors and Essays of William H. Sylvis* (Philadelphia, 1872), 97–115.

23. See *New York Times*, February 22, 1869, 2, for just one example of wage slave-chattel slave parallels. *Uncle Tom's Cabin* contained a long discussion of similarities and differences in the two forms of slavery. On child labor, see Edith Abbott, "Child Labor in America Before 1870," in Grace Abbott, *The Child and the State* (Chicago, 1938), 1: 275–76.

24. Paludan, *"A People's Contest"*, 180–85. See Boritt, *Lincoln and the Economics of the American Dream*, chap. 15, for Lincoln's sympathy to labor. Boritt also notes that the party as a whole did not share Lincoln's views.

25. Paludan, *"A People's Contest"*, 178 and chap. 7; Montgomery, *Beyond Equality*, chap. 3; Alan Dawley, *Class and Community: The Industrial Revolution in Lynn* (Cambridge, Mass., 1976).

26. Democrats had their own Society for the Diffusion of Political Knowledge, which was equally partisan if not as prolific in pushing pamphlets.

27. Frank L. Klement, *Dark Lanterns: Secret Political Societies, Conspiracies, and Treason Trials in the Civil War* (Baton Rouge, La., 1984).

28. Paludan, *"A People's Contest"*, 236, 244.

29. *Tribune Almanac and Political Register* for 1864, 55–67; for 1865, 56–63; Mark E. Neely, Jr., "The Civil War and the Two-Party System," in *"We Cannot Escape History": Lincoln and the Last Best Hope of Earth*, ed. James M. McPherson (Urbana, Ill., 1995), 86–104.

30. Montgomery, *Beyond Equality*, 109.

31. David E. Long, *The Jewel of Liberty: Abraham Lincoln's Re-Election and the End of Slavery* (Mechanicsburg, Pa., 1994), 265–71.

32. Michael Les Benedict, "The Politics of Reconstruction," in *American Political History: Essays on the State of the Discipline*, ed. John Marszalek and Wilson Miscamble (South Bend, Ind., 1977), 54–107.

33. Iver Bernstein, *The New York City Draft Riots: Their Significance for American Society and Politics in the Age of the Civil War* (New York, 1990); Grace Palladino, *Another Civil War: Labor, Capital, and the State in the Anthracite Regions of Pennsylvania, 1840–1868* (Urbana, Ill., 1990); Frank Klement, *Copperheads in the Middle West* (Chicago, 1960).

34. Fessenden, quoted in Jellison, *Fessenden of Maine*, 139.

Chapter 4. Politics Purified: Religion and the Growth of Antislavery Idealism in Republican Ideology During the Civil War

I want to thank my Penn State colleagues Anne C. Rose and William Blair for important criticism and advice about this essay. Phillip Shaw Paludan, a conference participant, also offered valuable advice on the organization and shape of the argument. The editors of this book, Robert Engs and Randall Miller, likewise gave me useful criticism—as well as the opportunity to present the paper.

1. *Congressional Globe*, 37th Cong., 1st sess., 222–23. The Senate version contained slight differences in wording (see pp. 257–65). Historians uniformly attribute the speedy and near-unanimous passage of the Crittenden Resolution to solicitude to the border slave states. See, for example, J. G. Randall and David Donald, *The Civil War and Reconstruction*, 2nd ed. (Boston, 1961), 280 and James M. McPherson, *Battle Cry of Freedom: The Civil War Era* (New York, 1988), 312.

2. "The Advantages of Defeat," *Atlantic Monthly* 8 (September 1861): 360–61.

3. Henry W. Bellows, *The State and the Nation—Sacred to Christian Citizens. A Sermon Preached in All Souls' Church, New York, April 21, 1861* (New York, 1861), 12.

4. Quoted by George M. Fredrickson from the *Christian Inquirer*, August 10, 1861, in *The Inner Civil War: Northern Intellectuals and the Crisis of the Union* (New York, 1965), 73.

5. Over a generation of historical writing, of course, certain parts of the book have undergone criticism. On its treatment of philanthropy, see Joan Waugh, *Unsentimental Reformer: The Life of Josephine Shaw Lowell* (Cambridge, Mass, 1997), 2–3. For criticism from the standpoint of the literary culture of the Civil War, see Alice Fahs, *The Imagined Civil War: Popular Literature of the North & South, 1861–1865* (Chapel Hill, N.C., 2001), 10–11. On religion, see Anne C. Rose, *Victorian America and the Civil War* (Cambridge, 1992), 2.

6. Fredrickson, *Inner Civil War*, 74–75. In emphasizing the call for discipline in the American volunteers in Norton's pamphlet *The Soldier of the Good Cause*, published in 1861, Fredrickson neglected to note that it appeared after the Bull Run rout when almost everyone in the North conceded that the northern armies needed more discipline. Compare Fredrickson, *Inner Civil War*, 69–70, and Charles Eliot Norton, *The Soldier of the Good Cause* (Boston, 1861), 12 ("Is the day of Bull Run to be the type of coming days of battle?"). Bellows is characterized on pp. 56, 70, 101, 109 of Fredrickson's book.

7. See, for example, T. Harry Williams, *Lincoln and the Radicals* (Madison, Wis., 1941). For a classic critique, see David Donald, "The Radicals and Lincoln," in his *Lincoln Reconsidered: Essays on the Civil War Era*, 2nd ed. (New York, 1956), 103–27.

8. Eric L. McKitrick identified the agenda of the radicals in his "Party Politics and the Union and Confederate War Efforts," in *The American Party Systems: Stages of Political Development*, ed. Walter Dean Burnham and William Nisbet Chambers (New York, 1967), 144–45. Note the centrality of the discussion of Republican

radicalism in Michael F. Holt's "An Elusive Synthesis: Northern Politics During the Civil War," in *Writing the Civil War: The Quest to Understand*, ed. James M. McPherson and William J. Cooper, Jr. (Columbia, S.C., 1998), 113, 119–22.

9. See Papers of Salmon P. Chase, ed. John Niven, microfilm edition, and Niven's *Salmon P. Chase: A Biography* (New York, 1995). Rehabilitation of Chase's reputation began with the chapter devoted to Chase in Eric Foner, *Free Soil, Free Labor, Free Men: The Ideology of the Republican Party Before the Civil War* (New York, 1970), 73–102.

10. See for example Phillip Shaw Paludan's statement that the "vital two-party system kept opposition within bounds by requiring platforms that spoke to the broad middle of the political spectrum, not to the extremes," in his book *"A People's Contest": The Union and Civil War, 1861–1865* (New York, 1988), 378.

11. For more on this point, see Mark E. Neely, Jr., *The Union Divided: Party Conflict in the Civil War North* (Cambridge, Mass., 2002).

12. "Advantages of Defeat," 361, 362, 364.

13. Fredrickson, *Inner Civil War*, 56.

14. Ibid., 70.

15. Bellows, *State and the Nation*, 8–9.

16. *New York Times*, October 23, 1864.

17. George H. Hepworth to Abraham Lincoln, October 24, 1864, Abraham Lincoln Papers, Library of Congress, reel 85. All manuscript sources cited in this article come from the Abraham Lincoln Papers, Library of Congress, microfilm edition, and hereafter I shall cite only the reel number after identifying the document.

18. James H. Moorhead, *American Apocalypse: Yankee Protestants and the Civil War, 1860–1869* (New Haven, Conn., 1978), 132n.

19. Ibid., 150.

20. See George M. Fredrickson, "The Coming of the Lord: The Northern Protestant Clergy and the Civil War Crisis," in *Religion and the American Civil War*, ed. Randall M. Miller, Harry S. Stout, and Charles Reagan Wilson (New York, 1998), 110–30.

21. Fredrickson, "Coming of the Lord," 108.

22. Ibid., 119.

23. Ibid., 20.

24. Ibid., 121.

25. On the Confederacy, see Harry S. Stout and Charles Grasso, "Civil War, Religion, and Communication: The Case of Richmond," in *Religion and the American Civil War*, ed. Miller, Stout, and Wilson, 318–19.

26. For Norton's criticism of Lincoln's order rescinding Frémont's proclamation, see Norton to G. W. Curtis, October 2, 1861, in *Letters of Charles Eliot Norton with Biographical Comment*, ed. Sara Norton and M. A. DeWolfe Howe, 2 vols. (Boston, 1913), 1: 243.

27. James H. Moorhead depicts the Protestant clergy as followers of antislavery reforms rather than leaders in antislavery reforms during the war. See *American Apocalypse*, esp. 126, 127.

28. Stockton, Ford Co., Illinois, Church of Christ, Resolutions, at September 2, 1861, reel 25.

29. For other resolutions sustaining Frémont, see Methodist Episcopal Church, Illinois Conference, Carlinville, Illinois, September 1861, reel 25; Free Regular Baptist Association of Branch County, Michigan, September 28, 1861, reel 26; Hamilton, Illinois, ministers and people, October 1, 1861, reel 26.

30. United Presbyterian Church Synod, August 28, 1861, reel 28.

31. New Jersey Central Baptist Association, Sandy Ridge, New Jersey, Resolutions, October 16, 1861 and Samuel Sproul to Abraham Lincoln, October 21, 1861, reel 28.

32. September 14, 1862, reel 41.

33. Indeed, the Reformed Presbyterians, who identified themselves as "an antislavery church of the most radical school," complained that the Constitution did not acknowledge God. Reformed Presbyterian Church Committee. Washington, D.C., Resolutions, September 21, 1862[?], reel 41.

34. Resolutions, New Hampshire General Association of Congregationalist and Presbyterian Ministers, Concord, New Hampshire, August 28, 1862, reel 40.

35. Resolutions, Chicago, Illinois, Christian citizens, September 8, 1862, reel 41. The Jefferson quotation was a standard in the repertoire of antislavery advocates. It came from answers prepared for questions posed by Jean Nicolas Demeunier, June 26, 1786. See *Thomas Jefferson: Writings . . .*, ed. Merrill D. Peterson (New York, 1984), 592. For its routine use (by Charles Eliot Norton) see "Immorality in Politics," *North American Review* 202 (January 1864): 116.

36. Resolutions, Baptist Church, Clarion [Pennsylvania], to Andrew Gregg Curtin, forwarded to Lincoln, August 23, 1862, reel 40.

37. Resolutions, Reformed Presbyterian Church, Chicago Presbytery, October 8, 1862, reel 42.

38. Myer S. Isaacs, editor of the *Jewish Messenger* in New York City, warned the president in the election autumn of 1864 that there was "no 'Jewish vote,'" that "Jews, as a body, have no politics," and that "the Israelites are not, as a body, distinctively Union or democratic in their politics." See Isaacs to Abraham Lincoln, October 26, 1864, reel 85.

39. Secretary of State William H. Seward kept open lines of communication with Archbishop John Hughes of New York. Hughes has more than a half dozen letters to Seward or Lincoln in the Abraham Lincoln Papers.

40. Board of Delegates of American Israelites, executive committee, New York, October 6, 1862, reel 42; Protestant Episcopal Church, bishops and clergy, November 20, 1862 (after the Sioux Indian uprising in Minnesota), reel 44.

41. See Protestant Episcopal Church, Diocese of Western New York, Annual Convention, Utica, Request for draft exemption of ministers, August 17, 1864, reel 79.

42. Damariscotta Mills, Maine, Baptist Association Resolutions, September 5, 1863, reel 58.

43. United Brethren, Sandusky Annual Conference Resolutions, October 10, 1863, reel 60; Baptist Church, New York State Missionary Convention Resolutions, October 15, 1863, reel 61.

44. Stephentown Baptist Association, Resolutions, September 15, 1863; H. A. Guild to Abraham Lincoln, September 15, 1863, reel 58.

45. Methodist Episcopal Church, Indiana Annual Conference, Washington, Indiana, Resolutions, September 24, 1863, reel 59.

46. United Brethren in Christ, Sandusky Annual Conference, Melmore, Ohio, Resolutions, October 10, 1863, reel 60.

47. Milwaukee, Wisconsin, Spring Street Congregational Church, Resolutions, September 5, 1862, reel 40.

48. Beaver Baptist Association, Resolutions, September 5, 1863, reel 58. The more radical resolution's acceptance was characterized as "general" but not "universal."

49. Methodist Episcopal Church, North Ohio Conference, Resolutions, September 7, 1863, reel 58.

50. Methodist Episcopal Church, California Conference, Resolutions, September 8, 1863, reel 58. The resolution referred to Lincoln's order of July 30, 1863, threatening retaliation if African American prisoners of war were not treated according to the laws and usages of war. See *The Collected Works of Abraham Lincoln*, ed. Roy P. Basler, Marion Dolores Pratt, and Lloyd A. Dunlap, 9 vols. (New Brunswick, N.J., 1953–55), 6: 357.

51. Universalists, General Convention Annual Session, Resolutions, September 15, 1863, reel 58. The Wisconsin State Baptist Convention likewise mentioned not the Book of Romans but Isaiah in their resolutions. See Baptist Church, Wisconsin State Convention, Resolutions, October 15, 1863, reel 61.

52. United Brethren in Christ, Auglaize (Ohio) Conference, Resolutions, October 5, 1863, reel 60.

53. Unitarian Church Convention, October 19, 1863, reel 61.

54. Baptist Church, New York State Missionary Convention, Resolutions, October 15, 1863, reel 61.

55. Methodist Episcopal Church, California Conference, Resolutions, September 8, 1863, reel 58.

56. Rhode Island and Massachusetts Christian Conference, Resolutions, September 11, 1863, reel 58.

57. United Brethren in Christ, Sandusky Annual Conference, Melmore, Ohio, Resolutions, October 10, 1863, reel 60.

58. United Brethren in Christ, Ohio Conference, Milton, Ohio, Resolutions, October 3, 1863, reel 59.

59. United Brethren in Christ, Western Reserve Annual Convention, Resolutions, October 10, 1863, reel 60.

60. The same is true of the highest-brow intellectual sources. Charles Eliot Norton by no means harkened back to "his Puritan clerical ancestors" or turned his back on "rationalistic" beliefs in constructing arguments for northern patriotism, as Fredrickson suggests. Instead, he too blended various intellectual and national traditions to come up with a doctrine of loyalty and to support Republican policies during the Civil War. In 1864 he affirmed as "a doctrine which lies not only at the foundation of the American system, but is essential to Christianity itself,—the doctrine of the brotherhood of men as the equal children of the common Father,

and of their unalienable rights as His children." See Fredrickson, *Inner Civil War*, 69–70 and Norton, "Immorality in Politics," 115. Rose noted the "coexistence of sacred and profane perspectives" in *Victorian America and the Civil War*, esp. 66.

61. Pennsylvania Baptist Convention, Annual Meeting, Resolutions (from October 26–27, 1863), December 27, 1863, reel 64. State elections in Pennsylvania were held in October.

62. George M. Wharton and other prominent Philadelphia Democrats asked to reprint the letter in April 1863. See John Henry Hopkins, *A Scriptural, Ecclesiastical, and Historical View of Slavery, . . . Addressed to the Right Rev. Alonzo Potter . . .* (New York, 1864). This book reprints the controversial pamphlet and adds more.

63. Hopkins, *Scriptural, Ecclesiastical, and Historical View of Slavery*, 19.

64. Ibid., 24. Norton denounced Hopkins's pamphlet in the version published by the Society for the Diffusion of Political Knowledge, a Democratic publishing auxiliary headed by Samuel F. B. Morse and aimed at answering Republican "fanaticism." See "Immorality in Politics," 105–27.

65. The literature on the Second Inaugural as a source for Lincoln's religious ideas is substantial. I have been influenced by Nicholas Parrillo, "Lincoln's Calvinist Transformation: Emancipation and War," *Civil War History* 46 (September 2000): 227–53; Ronald C. White, Jr., "Lincoln's Sermon on the Mount: The Second Inaugural," in *Religion and the American Civil War*, ed. Miller, Stout, and Wilson, 208–28; Stewart Winger, "Lincoln's Economics and the American Dream: A Reappraisal," *Journal of the Abraham Lincoln Association* 22 (2001), esp. 76–77 and *Lincoln's Religious Rhetoric and the Antislavery Impulse* (Dekalb, Ill., forthcoming); Allen C. Guelzo, *Abraham Lincoln: Redeemer President* (Grand Rapids, Mich, 1999). Although these works add to my confidence in emphasizing religious themes in Republican ideology, none used the religious resolutions in the Abraham Lincoln Papers, which I regard as essential grounding for such emphasis. For a different view of the Second Inaugural Address, see Eric Foner's paper presented in South Bend, Indiana, March 31, 2001, at the "Abraham Lincoln: Myth and Image" Symposium, Indiana University at South Bend. His paper terms parts of the address "frightening."

66. "Response to a Serenade," July 7, 1863, in *Collected Works of Abraham Lincoln*, 6: 319–20; annual message of December 3, 1861, ibid., 6: 48. See also the special message of July 4, 1861, ibid., 6: 438.

67. Parrillo, "Lincoln's Calvinist Transformation," 253.

68. *Collected Works of Abraham Lincoln*, 8: 356.

69. The conventional interpretation of the address emphasizes only its warning against revenge and against self-righteousness.

70. *Collected Works of Abraham Lincoln*, 8: 333.

71. United Brethren in Christ, Sandusky Annual Conference, Melmore, Ohio, Resolutions, October 10, 1863, reel 60.

72. This biographical sketch is based on the excellent one in William E. Gienapp, *The Origins of the Republican Party, 1852–1856* (New York, 1987), 135–36 and on the entry in Dumas Malone, ed., *Dictionary of American Biography*, 20 vols. (New York, 1936), 20: 322–24.

73. See William Safire, *Freedom* (Garden City, N.Y., 1987).

74. The letter appears in *Collected Works of Abraham Lincoln*, 6: 406–10. The political motives behind the letter are emphasized in Mark E. Neely, Jr., "The Civil War and the Two-Party System," in *"We Cannot Escape History": Lincoln and the Last Best Hope of Earth*, ed. James M. McPherson (Urbana, Ill., 1995), 93.

75. Henry Wilson to Abraham Lincoln, September 3, 1863, reel 58.

Chapter 5. Defining Postwar Republicanism: Congressional Republicans and the Boundaries of Citizenship

1. John Murrin's concept of settlement—a period such as that after the American Revolution when the terms of citizenship and relations of peoples to their government are periodically reordered—aptly fits the years of Reconstruction and the argument presented in this essay. See John Murrin, "The Great Inversion, or Court Versus Country: A Comparison of the Revolution Settlements in England (1688–1721) and America (1776–1816)" in *Three British Revolutions, 1641, 1688, 1776*, ed. J. G. A. Pocock (Princeton, N.J., 1980), 368–430. The concept of settlement is defined on 377–78.

2. *Philadelphia Press*, November 6, 1868.

3. Radical Republicans did consider the ban on restrictions on Asians. When Charles Sumner moved to strike the word "white" from naturalization requirements, westerners objected. As a result of a change in the naturalization laws that made native-born children of immigrants eligible for citizenship, Asian parents faced the anomalous situation that they could not become citizens—as European immigrants could—but their native-born children automatically became Americans. See Philip Foner and Daniel Rosenberg, eds., *Racism, Dissent, and Asian Americans* (Westport, Conn., 1993), 223–25; Luella Gettys, *The Law of Citizenship in the United States* (Chicago, 1914).

4. Quoted in William Gillette, *The Right to Vote: Politics and the Passage of the Fifteenth Amendment* (Baltimore, 1965), 43.

5. Heather Cox Richardson, *The Death of Reconstruction: Race, Labor, and Politics in the Post-Civil War North, 1865–1901* (Cambridge, Mass., 2001), 36; Howard Rabinowitz, ed., *Southern Black Leaders of the Reconstruction Era* (Urbana, Ill., 1982); for the expression of blacks' opinions in various conventions, Emma J. Thornbrough, *Black Reconstructionists* (Englewood Cliffs, N.J., 1972).

6. William Nelson, *The Fourteenth Amendment: From Political Principle to Judicial Doctrine* (Cambridge, Mass., 1988), 7; Robert Kaczorowski, *Judicial Interpretation: The Federal Courts, the Department of Justice and Civil Rights, 1866–1876* (New York, 1985). Kaczorowski is responsible for shifting historiographical interpretations from the view that Reconstruction was conservative to the view that Republicans during the period were responsible for a significant empowerment of the federal government.

7. Arthur Schlesinger, Jr., *The Disuniting of America: Reflections on a Multicultural Society* (New York, 1991), 58.

8. Douglas Dion, *Turning the Legislative Thumbscrew: Minority Rights and Procedural Change in Legislative Politics* (Ann Arbor, Mich., 1997).

9. See Michael Perman, *The Road to Redemption: Southern Politics, 1869–1879* (Chapel Hill, N.C., 1984), 21-56.

10. Nelson, *Fourteenth Amendment*, 110; Gillette, *Right to Vote*, 22.

11. Quoted in Herman Belz, *A New Birth of Freedom: The Republican Party and Freedmen's Rights, 1861–1866* (Westport, Conn., 1976), 133.

12. Richardson, *Death of Reconstruction*, 51.

13. Benjamin Kendrick, *The Journal of the Joint Committee of Fifteen on Reconstruction* (New York, 1914).

14. Joseph James, *The Framing of the Fourteenth Amendment* (Urbana, Ill., 1956) for the history of the Amendment's origins.

15. Alexander M. Bickel, "The Original Understanding and the Segregation Decision," *Harvard Law Review* 69 (November 1955): 1, 58.

16. *Congressional Globe*, 39th Cong., 1st sess., 1866, 1090, quoted in Robert Kaczorowski, "To Begin the Nation Anew: Congress, Citizenship, and Civil Rights After the Civil War," *American Historical Review* 92 (February 1987): 47 n.9.

17. *Congressional Globe*, 39th Cong., 1st sess., 1866, 385.

18. Kaczorowski, "To Begin the Nation Anew," 67.

19. *Congressional Globe*, 38th Cong., 2nd sess., 768.

20. Herman Belz, *Emancipation and Equal Rights: Politics and Constitutionalism in the Civil War Era* (New York, 1978), 116–17.

21. *Harper's Weekly*, October 12, 1867; September 7, 1867; *Philadelphia Inquirer*, August 13, 1867.

22. David Herbert Donald, Jean H. Baker, and Michael Holt, *The Civil War and Reconstruction* (New York, 2000), 536–72.

23. *Chicago Tribune*, February 4, 1870.

24. Elizabeth Cady Stanton, Susan B. Anthony, and Mathilda Joslyn Gage, eds., *History of Woman Suffrage*, 6 vols. (Rochester, N.Y., 1881), 2: 154.

25. Ibid., 2: 153, 174.

26. Ibid, 2: 317.

27. Wendell Phillips to Elizabeth Cady Stanton, May 10, 1866, Stanton-Anthony Papers, Scholarly Resources microfilm edition, reel 11; see also Patricia Holland and Ann D. Gordon, eds., *Papers of Elizabeth Cady Stanton and Susan B. Anthony* (Wilmington, Del., 1991).

28. Stanton et al., *History of Woman Suffrage*, 382, 383.

29. Nelson, *Fourteenth Amendment* , 45.

30. *Congressional Globe*, 39th Cong., 1st sess., 1866, 1090 quoted in Kaczorowski, "To Begin the Nation Anew," 67.

31. Stanton et al., *History of Woman Suffrage*, 1: 524.

Chapter 6. The Reforging of a Republican Majority

1. Ulysses S. Grant to Joseph R. Hawley, May 29, 1868, and Grant to William T. Sherman, June 21, 1868, *Papers of Ulysses S. Grant*, ed. John Y. Simon, 24 vols. to date (Carbondale, Ill., 1967–), 18: 263–64, 292–93.

2. Robert D. Sawrey, *Dubious Victory: The Reconstruction Debate in Ohio* (Lexington, Ky., 1992), 138.

3. Salmon P. Chase to James B. Craig, October 16, 1868, *The Papers of Salmon P. Chase*, ed. John Niven et al., 5 vols. (Kent, Ohio, 1998), 5: 82.

4. Chase to Hiram Barney, August 9, 1868, *Papers of Salmon P. Chase*, 5: 273.

5. Morton quoted in Salmon P. Chase to Murat Halstead, July 14, 1868, *Papers of Salmon P. Chase*, 5: 267.

6. Richard H. Abbott, *The Republican Party and the South, 1855–1877: The First Southern Strategy* (Chapel Hill, N.C., 1986), 204–5.

7. Washington, D.C., *National Republican*, March 4, 1870; *Nation*, April 28, 1870.

8. David J. Rothman, *Politics and Power: The United States Senate, 1869–1901* (New York, 1969); Michael Perman, *The Road to Redemption: Southern Politics, 1869–1879* (Chapel Hill, N.C., 1984), 17–18.

9. Rutherford B. Hayes to John Sherman, April 1, 1871, John Sherman Papers, Library of Congress; William Gillette, *Retreat from Reconstruction, 1869–1879* (Baton Rouge, La., 1979), 52–53.

10. Brooks D. Simpson, *The Reconstruction Presidents* (Lawrence, Kan., 1998), 156–57.

11. Leon B. Richardson, *William E. Chandler: Republican* (New York, 1940), 139.

12. Morton Keller, *Affairs of State: Public Life in Late Nineteenth Century America* (Cambridge, Mass., 1977), 278.

13. *The Diary of George Templeton Strong*, ed. Allan Nevins and Milton Halsey Thomas, 4 vols. (New York, 1952), 4: 485.

14. Ibid., 4: 523.

15. *New York Herald*, January 18, 1874; Simpson, *Reconstruction Presidents*, 168–69.

16. James A. Garfield to Burke Hinsdale, January 7, 1875, in Mary L. Hinsdale, ed., *Garfield-Hinsdale Letters: Correspondence Between James Abram Garfield and Burke Aaron Hinsdale* (Ann Arbor, Mich., 1949), 309; William B. Hesseltine, *Ulysses S. Grant, Politician* (New York, 1935), 358; Henry Dawes to Samuel Bowles, February 2, 1875, Samuel Bowles Papers, Yale University.

17. Simpson, *Reconstruction Presidents*, 186–87.

18. John Eaton, *Lincoln, Grant, and the Freedmen* (New York, 1907), 270–71.

19. Stanley P. Hirshson, *Farewell to the Bloody Shirt: Northern Republicans and the Southern Negro* (Bloomington, Ind., 1962), 27–28, 34.

20. Simpson, *Reconstruction Presidents*, 211–12, 216, 219.

21. *Hayes: Diary of a President, 1875–1881*, ed. T. Harry Williams (New York, 1964), 210; Hinsdale to Garfield, April 27, 1879, in Hinsdale, ed., *Garfield-Hinsdale Letters*, 409.

22. Garfield to Hinsdale, May 20, 1879, in Hinsdale, ed., *Garfield-Hinsdale Letters*, 417.

23. Simpson, *Reconstruction Presidents*, 223.

Select Bibliography

The literature on the Republican party, party realignment, and politics during the Civil War era is vast and growing. Much of the literature focuses on the causes and character of the sectional conflict and the ways sectionalism, the war, and its aftermath affected American political life and culture. Much of the work devoted to the Republican party properly situates the story within the context of the sectional struggles that gave birth to the party and the war and Reconstruction that remade it. Scholars have devoted much less attention to the life cycle of the first generation of the party and Republicanism—the principal concerns of this book. This select bibliography offers the essential works on the genesis and growth of the Republican party for consideration, with the emphasis on books and on recent work, which the dictates of space require. It does so with the understanding that many important works on particular figures, campaigns, state and local party development and politics, party management, and political process generally also invite review. In the absence of any comprehensive bibliography on the Republican party and politics in the mid-nineteenth century, this select bibliography then also serves as a guide, listing the critical recent works as a way to point to the issues already engaged and, by implication at least, to point to concerns needful of study.

Useful general histories of the party include Robert A. Rutland, *The Republicans: From Lincoln to Bush* (1996), which devotes five chapters to the party's first twenty-five years; and George H. Mayer, *The Republican Party, 1854–1964* (1964), which remains standard. For biographies of Republican leaders, see the listing of "Biographical and Related Works," in James M. McPherson, *Ordeal by Fire: The Civil War and Reconstruction* (rev. ed., 1992), a book that also offers an excellent history and analysis of the turbulent times.

For the long view on party formation and practices and the character of politics in the Civil War era, see Joel H. Silbey, *The American Political Nation, 1838–1893* (1991); Richard L. McCormick, *The Party Period and Public Policy from the Age of Jackson to the Progressive Era* (1986); the essays by Ronald P. Formisano, Michael F. Holt, and Joel H. Silbey especially in Byron E. Shafer and Anthony J. Badger, eds., *Contesting Democracy: Substance and Structure in American Political History, 1775–2000* (2001); and the essays in "Round Table: Alternatives to the Party System in the 'Party Period,'" *Journal of American History* 86 (1999), especially Ronald Formisano, "The 'Party Period' Revisited" (93–120),

Mark Voss-Hubbard, "The 'Third Party Tradition' Reconsidered: Third Parties and American Public Life, 1830–1900" (121–50), and Michael F. Holt, "The Primacy of Party Reasserted" (151–57). Useful in understanding the reconfiguration of the party system in the Civil War era are Paul Kleppner, *The Third Electoral System, 1853–1892: Parties, Voters, and Political Cultures* (1979); and the essays in Lloyd Ambrosius, ed., *A Crisis of Republicanism: American Politics During the Civil War Era* (1990).

On elections and party positions, see Arthur M. Schlesinger, Jr., and Fred L. Israel, eds., *The History of American Presidential Elections* (4 vols., 1971), vol. 1, for essays on particular elections; Donald B. Johnson, ed., *National Party Platforms*, vol. 1, *1840–1956* (rev. ed., 1978); Joel H. Silbey, ed., *The American Party Battle: Election Campaign Pamphlets, 1828–1876*, vol. 2, *1854–1876* (1999); W. Dean Burnham, *Presidential Ballots, 1836–1892* (1955). For voting patterns, see, for example, the essays in Frederick C. Luebke, ed., *Ethnic Voters and the Election of Lincoln* (1971), especially on the German vote in 1860; and Paul Kleppner, *The Cross of Culture: A Social Analysis of Midwestern Politics, 1850–1890* (rev. ed., 1970), on ethnoreligious loyalties superseding class interests in voting behavior. For the material culture and imagery of campaigning, see Roger A. Fischer, *Tippecanoe and Trinkets Too: The Material Culture of American Presidential Campaigns, 1828–1984* (1988); and Keith Melder, *Hail to the Candidate: Presidential Campaigns from Banners to Broadcasts* (1992).

Several recent works probe the civic life and political culture of the period, with attention to the place of the new Republican party in the changing world of politics, citizenship, and civic obligations. Pertinent among them are Glenn C. Altschuler and Stuart M. Blumin, *Rude Republic: Americans and Their Politics in the Nineteenth Century* (2000); Michael Schudson, *The Good Citizen: A History of American Civic Life* (1998); Mary P. Ryan, *Women in Public: Between Banners and Ballots, 1825–1880* (1990); Ellen Carol DuBois, *Feminism and Suffrage: The Emergence of an Independent Women's Movement in America, 1848–1869* (1978); Melanie S. Gustafson, *Women and the Republican Party, 1854–1924* (2001); Richard Carwardine, *Evangelicals and Politics in Antebellum America* (1993); Susan-Mary Grant, *North over South: Northern Nationalism and American Identity in the Antebellum Era* (2000).

For perceptive overviews of antebellum politics and party realignments, see especially Michael F. Holt, *The Political Crisis of the 1850s* (1978); Joel H. Silbey, *The Partisan Imperative: The Dynamics of American Politics Before the Civil War* (1985); the essays in George Harmon Knoles, ed., *The Crisis of the Union, 1860–1861* (1965); the essays in Stephen E. Maizlish and John J. Kushma, eds., *Essays on American Antebellum Politics, 1840–1860* (1982); and Michael F. Holt, *Political Parties and American Political Development from the Age of Jackson to the Age of Lincoln* (1992). On the political culture, see Mark W. Summers, *The Plundering Generation: Corruption and the Crisis of the Union, 1849–1861* (1987). Much wisdom generally, and prescience particularly, on political history can be found in David M. Potter, *The Impending Crisis, 1848–1861* (1976).

The political structures and dynamics of the 1850s—a time of party destruction, reformulation, and birth—is discussed in works on the other parties. Especially instructive are Michael F. Holt, *The Rise and Fall of the American Whig Party: Jacksonian Politics and the Onset of the Civil War* (1999); Daniel Walker Howe, *The Political Culture of the American Whigs* (1979); Jean H. Baker, *Affairs of Party: The Political Culture of Northern Democrats in the Mid-Nineteenth Century* (1983); Frederick J. Blue, *The Free Soilers: Third Party Politics, 1848–1854* (1973); Tyler Anbinder, *Nativism and Slavery: The Northern Know Nothings and the Politics of the 1850s* (1992); William E. Gienapp, "Nativism and the Creation of a Republican Majority in the North Before the Civil War," *Journal of American History* 72 (1985): 529–59; and the essays in Alan M. Kraut, ed., *Crusaders and Compromisers: Essays on the Relationship of the Antislavery Struggle to the Antebellum Party System* (1983).

Also useful in understanding the interests and ideas driving the politics of the period are Marc Egnal, "The Beards Were Right: Parties in the North, 1840–1860," *Civil War History* 47 (2001): 30–56; Richard H. Sewell, *Ballots for Freedom: Antislavery Politics in the United States, 1837–1860* (1976); Robert W. Johannsen, *Frontier Politics on the Eve of the Civil War* (1955 ed.); James L. Huston, *The Panic of 1857 and the Coming of the Civil War* (1987); Bruce C. Levine, *The Spirit of 1848: German Immigrants, Labor Conflict, and the Coming of the Civil War* (1992); the essays in Michael J. Birkner, ed., *James Buchanan and the Political Crisis of the 1850s* (1996); Kenneth M. Stampp, *The Imperfect Union: Essays on the Background of the Civil War* (1980); Kenneth M. Stampp, *America in 1857: A Nation on the Brink* (1990); William R. Brock, *Parties and Political Conscience: American Dilemmas, 1840–1850* (1979); William W. Freehling, *The Road to Disunion*, vol. 1, *The Secessionists at Bay, 1776–1854* (1990); Michael A. Morrison, *Slavery and the American West: The Eclipse of Manifest Destiny and the Coming of the Civil War* (1997); Gerald Wolff, *The Kansas-Nebraska Bill: Party, Section, and the Coming of the Civil War* (1980); and Leonard L. Richards, *The Slave Power: The Free North and Southern Domination, 1780–1860* (2000).

On the formation, values, and interest(s) of the Republican party particularly, Eric Foner, *Free Soil, Free Labor, Free Men: The Ideology of the Republican Party Before the Civil War* (1970), is the starting point, and now the touchstone for the literature. Also essential, if also contested, is William E. Gienapp, *The Origins of the Republican Party, 1852–1856* (1987). Among the state and local studies, the following warrant special attention: Hendrik Booraem V, *The Formation of the Republican Party in New York: Politics and Conscience in the Antebellum North* (1983) and Michael F. Holt, *Forging a Majority: The Formation of the Republican Party in Pittsburgh, 1848–1860* (1969).

Among the many studies of the party and politics at the state and local level, the following are especially relevant to understanding the ways and means of the Republicans, and other topics on the birth of new parties and the reordering or collapse of old ones: Dale Baum, *The Civil War Party System: The Case of Massachusetts, 1848–1876* (1984); Mark L. Berger, *The Revolution in the New York Party Systems, 1840–1860* (1973); John F. Coleman, *The Disruption of the Pennsylvania Democracy, 1848–1860* (1975). Ronald P. Formisano, *The Birth of Mass Political*

Parties: Michigan, 1827–1861 (1971); Jean H. Baker, *The Politics of Continuity: Maryland Political Parties from 1858 to 1870* (1973); Lex Renda, "The Polity and the Party System: Connecticut and New Hampshire, 1840–1876" (PhD dissertation, 1991); Stephen L. Hansen, *The Making of the Third Party System: Voters and Parties in Illinois, 1850–1876* (1980); Stephen E. Maizlish, *The Triumph of Sectionalism: The Transformation of Ohio Politics, 1844–1856* (1983); and Daniel W. Crofts, *Reluctant Confederates: Upper South Unionists in the Secession Crisis* (1989).

More than anyone else, Abraham Lincoln came to symbolize the aspirations and interests of the Republican party, in his day (though his stature was not so large while he was alive) and very much so after his death. Among the revealing works treating aspects of Lincoln and Republicanism are Don E. Fehrenbacher, *Prelude to Greatness: Lincoln in the 1850s* (1962 ed.); Robert W. Johannsen, *Lincoln, the South and Slavery: The Political Dimensions* (1991); James M. McPherson, *Abraham Lincoln and the Second American Revolution* (1991); Mark E. Neely, Jr., *The Last Best Hope of Earth: Abraham Lincoln and the Promise of America* (1993); David Herbert Donald, *Lincoln* (1995); Harry V. Jaffa, *A New Birth of Freedom: Abraham Lincoln and the Coming of the Civil War* (2000); John L. Thomas, ed., *Abraham Lincoln and the American Political Tradition* (1986); William E. Gienapp, *Abraham Lincoln and the Civil War: A Biography* (2002); and Merrill Peterson, *Lincoln in American Memory* (1994), for the mythology.

Wartime politics, Republican policies, and the changing character of the Republican party are variously discussed in Eric McKitrick, "Party Politics and the Union and Confederate War Efforts," in *The American Party Systems: Stages of Development*, ed. William Nisbet Chambers and Walter Dean Burnham (1967), 117–51; Mark E. Neely, Jr., "The Civil War and the Two-Party System," in *"We Cannot Escape History": Lincoln and the Last Best Hope of Earth*, ed. James M. McPherson (1995), 86–104, for a counterview; James A. Rawley, *The Politics of Union: Northern Politics During the Civil War* (1974); Allan Bogue, *The Earnest Men: The Republicans of the Civil War Senate* (1981); Hans L. Trefousse, *The Radical Republicans: Lincoln's Vanguard for Racial Justice* (1969); Leonard P. Curry, *Blueprint for Modern America: Nonmilitary Legislation of the First Civil War Congress* (1968); Richard F. Bensel, *Yankee Leviathan: The Origins of Central State Authority in America, 1859–1877* (1990); Heather Cox Richardson, *The Greatest Nation of the Earth: Republican Economic Policies During the Civil War* (1997); Robert P. Sharkey, *Money, Class, and Party: An Economic Study of the Civil War and Reconstruction* (1967); Allan G. Bogue, *The Congressman's Civil War* (1989); Bruce Tap, *Over Lincoln's Shoulder: The Committee on the Conduct of the War* (2000); Michael S. Green, "Freedom, Union, and Power: The Ideological Transformation of the Republican Party During the Civil War" (PhD dissertation, 2000); LaWanda Cox, *Lincoln and Black Freedom: A Study in Presidential Leadership* (1981); Herman Belz, *A New Birth of Freedom: The Republican Party and Freedmen's Rights, 1861–1866* (1976); William F. Zornow, *Lincoln & the Party Divided* (1964): John C. Waugh, *Reelecting Lincoln: The Battle for the 1864 Presidency* (1997); Adam I. P. Smith, "The Presidential Election of 1864" (PhD dissertation, 2000); David E. Long, *The Jewel of Liberty: Abraham Lincoln's Re-Election and the*

End of Slavery (1994); William Harris, *With Charity for All: Lincoln and the Reconstruction of the Union* (1997); David Herbert Donald, *The Politics of Reconstruction, 1863–1867* (1965); Phillip Shaw Paludan, *The Presidency of Abraham Lincoln* (1994); Phillip Shaw Paludan, *"A People's Contest": The Union and the Civil War, 1861–1865* (1988); and Mark E. Neely, Jr., *The Union Divided: Party Conflict in the Civil War North* (2002). For the Democrats, see Joel H. Silbey, *A Respectable Minority: The Democratic Party in the Civil War Era, 1860–1868* (1977). For an excellent analysis of the literature, see Michael F. Holt, "An Elusive Synthesis: Northern Politics During the Civil War," in *Writing the Civil War: The Quest to Understand*, ed. James M. McPherson and William J. Cooper, Jr. (1998), 112–34, 283–88 (notes).

Republican efforts to establish the party in the South, to win the peace, and to secure the party's ideological and political interests during Reconstruction are variously examined in Eric L. McKitrick, *Andrew Johnson and Reconstruction* (1960), which still informs much work on the Republicans and the president; Richard H. Abbott, *The Republican Party and the South, 1855–1877: The First Southern Strategy* (1986); Brooks D. Simpson, *Let Us Have Peace: Ulysses S. Grant and the Politics of War and Reconstruction, 1861–1868* (1991); Michael Perman, *Reunion Without Compromise: The South and Reconstruction, 1865–1868* (1973); LaWanda and John H. Cox, *Politics, Principle, and Prejudice, 1865–1866: Dilemma of Reconstruction America* (1961); W. R. Brock, *An American Crisis: Congress and Reconstruction, 1865–1867* (1963); Michael Les Benedict, *A Compromise of Principle: Congressional Republicans and Reconstruction, 1863–1869* (1974); Martin E. Mantell, *Johnson, Grant, and the Politics of Reconstruction* (1973); and Brooks D. Simpson, *The Reconstruction Presidents* (1998). On party realignments, see the essays in Richard O. Curry, ed., *Radicalism, Racism, and Party Realignment: The Border States During Reconstruction* (1969); and for the understudied North, see the essays in James C. Mohr, ed., *Radical Republicans in the North: State Politics During Reconstruction* (1976). On Johnson's impeachment as it related to politics and the law, see especially Michael Les Benedict, *The Impeachment and Trial of Andrew Johnson* (1973). On the politics of the Reconstruction Amendments, see William E. Nelson, *The Fourteenth Amendment: From Political Principle to Judicial Doctrine* (1988); and William Gillette, *The Right to Vote: Politics and the Passage of the Fifteenth Amendment* (1965). The now standard work on Reconstruction that puts black rights at the center of the Reconstruction issues is Eric Foner, *Reconstruction: America's Unfinished Revolution, 1863–1877* (1988).

Constitutional changes pushed by Republicans are best surveyed in Herman Belz, *Emancipation and Equal Rights: Politics and Constitutionalism in the Civil War Era* (1978); Harold M. Hyman and William M. Wiecek, *Equal Justice Under Law: Constitutional Development, 1835–1875* (1982); Harold M. Hyman, *A More Perfect Union: The Impact of the Civil War and Reconstruction on the Constitution* (1973); Michael Vorenberg, *Final Freedom: The Civil War, the Abolition of Slavery, and the Thirteenth Amendment* (2001); Robert Kaczorowski, *Judicial Interpretation: The Federal Courts, the Department of Justice and Civil Rights, 1866–1876* (1985); Bernard Schwartz, *From Confederation to Nation: The American Constitution,*

1835–1877 (1973); and the essays in Jennifer M. Lowe, ed., *The Supreme Court and the Civil War* (1996).

On the opposition to Republican Reconstruction and Republican withdrawal, see especially William Gillette, *Retreat from Reconstruction, 1869–1879* (1979); and Michael Perman, *The Road to Redemption: Southern Politics, 1869–1879* (1984). For the intraparty differences between northern and southern Republicans that undermined Republican Reconstruction, see Terry L. Seip, *The South Returns to Congress: Men, Economic Measures, and Intersectional Relationships, 1868–1879* (1983). For the Democratic party, see Lawrence Grossman, *The Democratic Party and the Negro: Northern and National Politics, 1868–92* (1976).

On the formation of Republican parties, political leadership, and Republican policies in the South, see Thomas Holt, *Black over White: Negro Political Leadership in South Carolina during Reconstruction* (1977); William McKee Evans, *Ballots and Fence Rails: Reconstruction on the Lower Cape Fear* (1967); Richard G. Lowe, *Republicans and Reconstruction in Virginia, 1856–1870* (1991); Edmund Lee Drago, *Black Politicians and Reconstruction in Georgia: A Splendid Failure* (1982); Elizabeth Nathans, *Losing the Peace: Georgia Republicans and Reconstruction, 1865–1871* (1968); Carl H. Moneyhon, *Republicanism in Reconstruction Texas* (1980); Joe Gray Taylor, *Louisiana Reconstructed, 1863–1877* (1974); Ted Tunnell, *Crucible of Reconstruction: War, Radicalism, and Race in Louisiana, 1862–1877* (1984); Charles Vincent, *Black Legislators in Louisiana During Reconstruction* (1976); Richard N. Current, *Those Terrible Carpetbaggers* (1988); Howard N. Rabinowitz, ed., *Southern Black Leaders of the Reconstruction Era* (1982); Eric Foner, *Freedom's Lawmakers: A Directory of Black Officeholders During Reconstruction* (rev. ed., 1996); Laura F. Edwards, *Gendered Strife and Confusion: The Political Culture of Reconstruction* (1997); and Mark W. Summers, *Railroads, Reconstruction, and the Gospel of Prosperity: Aid Under the Radical Republicans, 1865–1877* (1984). For additional works on Republicans and Reconstruction and related topics at all levels of government, consult David A. Lincove's masterful *Reconstruction: An Annotated Bibliography* (2000).

On postwar political alignments, issues, and interests, see Mark W. Summers, *The Press Gang: Newspapers and Politics, 1865–1878* (1994); Michael McGerr, *The Decline of Popular Politics: The American North, 1865–1928* (1986); Heather Cox Richardson, *The Death of Reconstruction: Race, Labor, and Politics in the Post-Civil War North, 1865–1901* (2001); David Montgomery, *Beyond Equality: Labor and the Radical Republicans, 1862–1872* (1967), on the limits of Republicanism as regards labor; Stanley P. Hirshson, *Farewell to the Bloody Shirt: Northern Republicans and the Southern Negro* (1962); Xi Wang, *The Trial of Democracy: Black Suffrage and Northern Republicans, 1860–1910* (1997); and Rebecca Edwards, *Angels in the Machinery: Gender in American Party Politics from the Civil War to the Progressive Era* (1997), on a surprisingly understudied topic.

Contributors

Jean H. Baker is Professor of History at Goucher College. Among her books are *The Politics of Continuity: Maryland Political Parties During the Civil War, Ambivalent Americans: A Study of the Know Nothing Party,* and *Affairs of Party: The Political Culture of Northern Democrats.* She also has written *Mary Todd Lincoln: A Biography* and *The Stevensons of Illinois: A Family Biography.* Her most recent book (with David Herbert Donald and Michael Holt) is *Civil War and Reconstruction.*

Robert F. Engs is Professor of History at the University of Pennsylvania. His books include *Freedom's First Generation: Black Hampton, Virginia, 1861–1890* and *Educating the Disenfranchised and Disinherited: Samuel Chapman Armstrong and Hampton Institute, 1839–1893.*

Eric Foner is DeWitt Clinton Professor of History at Columbia University. Among his books are *Free Soil, Free Labor, Free Men: The Ideology of the Republican Party Before the Civil War, Tom Paine and Revolutionary America; Politics and Ideology in the Age of the Civil War;* and *Nothing but Freedom: Emancipation and Its Legacy.* His 1989 book, *Reconstruction: America's Unfinished Revolution, 1863–1877,* was the winner of the Bancroft Prize.

Michael F. Holt is Langbourne M. Williams Professor of American History at the University of Virginia. He is the author of several essays and four books on antebellum political history, includeing *Forging a Majority: The Formation of the Republican Party in Pittsburgh, 1848–1860; The Political Crisis of the 1850s; Political Parties and American Political Development from the Age of Jackson to the Age of Lincoln;* and *The Rise and Fall of the American Whig Party: Jacksonian Politics and the Onset of the Civil War.* With Jean Baker and David Donald, he wrote *Civil War and Reconstruction.*

James M. McPherson is George Henry Davis '86 Professor of History at Princeton University. He has published widely on Civil War era topics. Among his many books are *The Battle Cry of Freedom: The Civil War Era,* for which he won the Pulitzer Prize, and *For Cause and Comrades: Why Men Fought in the Civil War,* for which he won the Lincoln Prize.

Randall M. Miller is William Dirks Warren '50 Sesquicentennial Chair and Professor of History at Saint Joseph's University. His most recent books relating to the Civil War era are (with Paul Cimbala) *The Freedmen's Bureau and Reconstruction: Reconsiderations*; (with Paul Cimbala) *Union Soldiers and the Northern Home Front*; and (with Harry S. Stout and Charles Reagan Wilson) *Religion and the American Civil War*.

Mark E. Neely, Jr. is McCabe-Greer Professor in the American Civil War Era at the Pennsylvania State University. He has published several books, including *The Abraham Lincoln Encyclopedia*; *The Last Best Hope of Earth: Abraham Lincoln and the Promise of America*; and *Southern Rights: Political Prisoners and the Myth of Confederate Constitutionalism*. *The Fate of Liberty: Abraham Lincoln and Civil Liberties* was awarded the Pulitzer Prize in History. He has just completed a book entitled *The Union Divided: Party Conflict in the Civil War North*.

Phillip Shaw Paludan is Naomi Lynn Professor of Lincoln Studies at the University of Illinois at Springfield. Among his books are *A Covenant with Death: The Constitution, Law, and Equality in the Civil War Era*; *Victims: A True Story of the Civil War*; *"A People's Contest": The Union and the Civil War, 1861–1865*; and *The Presidency of Abraham Lincoln*, which won the Lincoln Prize.

Brooks D. Simpson is Professor of History and Humanities at Arizona State University. His books include *America's Civil War*; *The Political Education of Henry Adams*; *The Reconstruction Presidents*; and *Ulysses S. Grant: Triumph over Adversity, 1822–1865*. He is currently writing a short history of Reconstruction and the second volume of his three-part Grant biography, to be entitled *Ulysses Grant: The Fruits of Victory, 1865–1885*.

Index

DATE DUE
